MARKET LEADER

Course Book

UPPER INTERMEDIATE
BUSINESS ENGLISH

David Cotton David Falvey Simon Kent

PEARSON
Longman

Map of the book

	Discussion	Texts	Language work	Skills	Case study
Unit 1 Communication page 6	What makes a good communicator	Reading: Communication problems Listening: An interview with a communications expert	Words to describe good and bad communicators Idioms	Problem-solving on the phone	Creating a sense of identity: Improve communications in a global company Writing: memo
Unit 2 International marketing page 14	Discussion of international brands	Reading: International marketing mix – *Financial Times* Listening: Authentic brainstorming meeting	Marketing collocations Noun compounds and noun phrases	Brainstorming	Zumo – creating a global brand: Reposition a sports drink for the global market Writing: memo
Unit 3 Building relationships page 22	Discuss business relationships and do a quiz	Reading: Relationship marketing Listening: Interviews with people promoting business relations	Words to describe relations Multi-word verbs	Networking	Getting to know you: Discuss ways to promote customer loyalty Writing: sales letter
Unit 4 Success page 30	Defining success Learning from mistakes	Reading: Mobile phones – *Financial Times* Listening: An interview with a management development expert	Prefixes Present and past tenses	Negotiating	Camden FC: Negotiate a sponsorship deal for a football team Writing: press release or letter
Unit 5 Job satisfaction page 38	Discuss motivation and do a quiz on stress Discuss how job titles affect motivation	Reading: Fringe benefits – *Financial Times* Listening: An interview with an expert on job satisfaction	Words for describing motivating factors Passives	Handling difficult situations	Office attraction: Devise a policy on close relationships at work Writing: guidelines
Unit 6 Risk page 46	Discuss everyday risk and risk in business	Reading: Risks from globalisation – *PR newswire* Listening: An interview with an expert in risk management	Words for describing risk Intensifying adverbs	Reaching agreement	A risky business: Consider options to improve a clothing company's profit Writing: report
Unit 7 e-commerce page 54	Discuss the use of the Internet	Reading: Using the Net – *Business Week* Listening: An interview with an e-commerce entrepreneur	Internet terms Conditionals	Presentations	KGV Europe: Decide whether a music retailer should trade on the Internet Writing: memo
Revision unit A page 62					

Grammar reference: page 130   **Quiz**: page 137   **Writing file**: page 138

	Discussion	Texts	Language work	Skills	Case study
Unit 8 Team building page 68	Do a quiz about thinking styles	Reading: Successful teamworking – *Accountancy* magazine Listening: An interview with a team-building expert	Prefixes Modal perfect	Resolving conflict	The new boss: Look at ways of improving the performance of a sales team Writing: letter
Unit 9 Raising finance page 76	Ways of raising money	Reading: Financing start-up businesses – *Financial Times* Listening: Interview with the founder of an Internet business consultancy	Financial terms Dependent prepositions	Negotiating	Vision Film Company: Negotiate a finance package to make a feature film Writing: e-mail
Unit 10 Customer service page 84	What people complain about Customer complaints	Reading: Customer delight – *Financial Times* Listening: New ideas in customer care	Handling complaints Gerunds	Active listening	Hermes Communications: Prioritise and deal with complaints Writing: memo
Unit 11 Crisis management page 92	When is a problem a crisis?	Reading: Airline crashes – *Financial Times* Listening: An interview with a crisis management expert	Noun phrases with / without *of* Similarities and differences	Asking and answering difficult questions	Game over: Manage a crisis over pirated software Writing: report
Unit 12 Management styles page 100	Do's and don'ts for managers	Reading: Who would you rather work for? – *Guardian* Listening: An interview with a business author	Management qualities Text reference	Putting people at ease	Zenova: Assess feedback from employees to improve management styles Writing: action minutes
Unit 13 Takeovers and mergers page 108	Pros and cons of takeovers and mergers	Reading: Why mergers fail – *Financial Times* Listening: An interview with an executive who has recently made a large acquisition	Words to describe takeovers and mergers Headlines	Summarising in presentations	Group Bon Appetit PLC: Discuss the risk of takeover and consider making new acquisitions Writing: report
Unit 14 The future of business page 116	Personal predictions	Reading: Products and services of the future – *Financial Times* Listening: An interview with a trend watcher	Describing the future The language of prediction	Getting the right information	Yedo Department Stores: Look at trends and increase profitability of a department store Writing: report
Revision unit B page 124					

Introduction

What is Market Leader and who is it for?

The authors are grateful for the many useful ideas and suggestions from teachers and students (for example, the addition of revision units) which have helped to shape their new course and build on the successful approach of Market Leader Intermediate. Developed once again in association with the Financial Times, one of the world's leading sources of business information, Market Leader Upper Intermediate comprises 14 units based on topics of great interest to everyone involved in international business.

If you are in business, the course will greatly improve your ability to communicate in English in a wide range of business situations. If you are a student of business, the course will develop the communication skills you need to succeed in business and will enlarge your knowledge of the business world. Everybody studying this course will become more fluent and confident in using the language of business and should increase their career prospects.

The authors

Simon Kent *(left)* has 12 years' teaching experience including three years as an in-company trainer in Berlin at the time of German reunification. He is currently a lecturer in business and general English, as well as having special responsibility for designing new courses at London Guildhall University.

David Cotton *(centre)* has 30 years' experience teaching and training in EFL, ESP and English for Business, and is the author of numerous business English titles, including *Agenda*, *World of Business*, *International Business Topics*, and *Keys to Management*. He is also one of the authors of the best-selling *Business Class*. He is currently a Senior Lecturer at London Guildhall University.

David Falvey *(right)* has 20 years' teaching experience in the UK, Japan and Hong Kong. He has also worked as a teacher trainer at the British Council in Tokyo, and is now Head of the English Language Centre and Principal Lecturer at London Guildhall University.

What is in the units?

Starting up

You are offered a variety of interesting activities in which you discuss the topic of the unit and exchange ideas about it.

Vocabulary

You will learn important new words and phrases which you can use when you carry out the tasks in the unit. A good business dictionary, such as the *Longman Business English Dictionary,* will also help you to increase your business vocabulary.

Discussion

You will build up your confidence in using English and will improve your fluency through interesting discussion activities.

Reading

You will read authentic articles on a variety of topics from the *Financial Times* and other newspapers and books on business. You will develop your reading skills and learn essential business vocabulary. You will also be able to discuss the ideas and issues in the articles.

Listening

You will hear authentic interviews with business people. You will develop listening skills such as listening for information and note-taking.

Language review

This section focusses on common problem areas at upper intermediate level. You will become more accurate in your use of language. Each unit contains a Language review box which provides a review of key grammar items.

Skills

You will develop essential business communication skills such as making presentations, taking part in meetings, negotiating, telephoning, and using English in social situations. Each Skills section contains a Useful language box which provides you with the language you need to carry out the realistic business tasks in the book.

Case study

The Case studies are linked to the business topics of each unit. They are based on realistic business problems or situations and allow you to use the language and communication skills you have developed while working through the unit. They give you the opportunities to practise your speaking skills in realistic business situations. Each Case study ends with a writing task. A full writing syllabus is provided in the Market Leader Practice File.

Revision units

Market Leader Upper Intermediate also contains two revision units, based on material covered in the preceding seven Course Book units. Each revision unit is designed so that it can be done in one go or on a unit by unit basis.

Communication

> *Everything that can be said can be said clearly.*
>
> Ludwig Wittgenstein (1889–1951),
> Austrian philosopher

OVERVIEW ▼

☐ **Vocabulary**
Good communicators

☐ **Listening**
Improving communications

☐ **Reading**
Communication problems

☐ **Language review**
Idioms

☐ **Skills**
Problem-solving on the phone

☐ **Case study**
Creating a sense of identity

Starting up

A **What makes a good communicator? Choose the three most important factors.**

- fluency in the language
- an extensive vocabulary
- being a good listener
- physical appearance
- a sense of humour
- grammatical accuracy
- not being afraid of making mistakes
- an awareness of body language

B **What other factors are important for communication?**

C **Discuss these questions.**

1 Which of the forms of written and spoken communication below do you use most:
   a) in your own language?   **b)** in English?

Written	Spoken
e-mails	conversations
faxes	interviews
letters	meetings
memos	negotiations
minutes	phone calls
reports	presentations

2 Which do you feel you do best? Which do you like least?

3 Do you use any other forms of communication?

4 What kinds of problem can occur with some of the forms of communication above? Think about:
   - formality / informality
   - jargon
   - standard ways of doing things
   - technology
   - tone of voice
   - visual gestures

Vocabulary
Good communicators

A Which words below apply to good communicators and which apply to bad communicators? Add two adjectives of your own to the list.

> articulate   coherent   eloquent   fluent   focussed
> hesitant   inhibited   lucid   persuasive   rambling
> responsive   sensitive   succinct   tongue-tied

B Which of the words above have the following meanings?

1 concise
2 unable to speak
3 talking in a confused way
4 able to express ideas well
5 clear and easy to understand
6 good at influencing people

C Use a prefix to form the opposites of these words from Exercise A.

- articulate
- coherent
- focussed
- inhibited

D Think of a good communicator you know. Explain why they are good at communicating.

Listening
Improving communications

▲ Penny Logier

A 🎧 1.1 Listen to the interview with Penny Logier, Retail Director at the London-based communications agency MediaComTMB, and answer these questions.

1 What two factors have improved communication between companies and their customers?
2 What does she say about e-mail?
3 What is an intranet? How has an intranet helped her company to communicate with the Volkswagen group?
4 What can happen to client relations if communication is unclear?

B 🎧 1.1 Penny says it is not possible to be a good manager but a poor communicator. Complete this extract of what Penny then goes on to say.

> Communication is key. People have to ....¹ what you're trying
> to tell them to do. They have to have a long-term ....² in terms
> of their career ....³. You must make it clear, as a manager,
> what those ....⁴ are. ....⁵ is more important
> than written. People can talk to you on a ....⁶ basis. You
> actually encourage ....⁷ then and you actually get a
> ....⁸ and a ....⁹ with the individual.

A Recent trends in business have been towards larger and larger organisations. This has many advantages but can also present challenges for effective communication within an organisation.

For what reasons can communication sometimes break down in larger organisations?

B Read the text and complete the chart that follows it.

Hard Sell around the Photocopier

Sociologists have long recognised that businesses of less than 200 individuals can operate through the free flow of information among the members. Once their size exceeds this figure, however, 5 some kind of hierarchical structure or line management system is necessary to prevent total chaos resulting from failures of communication. Imposing structures of this kind has its costs: information can only flow along certain channels because only 10 certain individuals contact each other regularly; moreover, the lack of personalised contacts means that individuals lack that sense of personal commitment that makes the world of small groups go round. Favours will only be done when there is a 15 clear *quid pro quo*, an immediate return to the giver, rather than being a matter of communal obligation. Large organisations are less flexible.

One solution to this problem would, of course, be to structure large organisations into smaller units 20 of a size that can act as a cohesive group. By allowing these groups to build reciprocal alliances with each other, larger organisations can be built up. However, merely having groups of, say, 150 will never of itself be a panacea to the problems of the 25 organisation. Something else is needed: the people involved must be able to build direct personal relationships. To allow free flow of information, they have to be able to interact in a casual way. Maintaining too formal a structure of relationships 30 inevitably inhibits the way a system works.

The importance of this was drawn to my attention a couple of years ago by a TV producer. The production unit for which she worked produced all the educational output for a particular TV station. 35 Whether by chance or by design, it so happened that there were almost exactly 150 people in the unit. The whole process worked very smoothly as an organisation for many years until they were moved into purpose-built accommodation. Then, 40 for no apparent reason, everything started to fall apart. The work seemed to be more difficult to do, not to say less satisfying.

It was some time before they worked out what the problem was. It turned out that, when the 45 architects were designing the new building, they decided that the coffee room where everyone ate their sandwiches at lunch times was an unnecessary luxury and so dispensed with it. The logic seemed to be that if people were encouraged to 50 eat their sandwiches at their desks, then they were more likely to get on with their work and less likely to idle time away. And with that, they inadvertently destroyed the intimate social networks that empowered the whole organisation. 55 What had apparently been happening was that, as people gathered informally over their sandwiches in the coffee room, useful snippets of information were casually being exchanged. Someone had a problem they could not solve, and began to discuss 60 it over lunch with a friend from another section. The friend knew just the person to ask. Or someone overhearing the conversation would have a suggestion, or would go away and happen to bump into someone who knew the answer a day 65 or so later; a quick phone call and the problem was resolved. Or a casual comment sparked an idea for a new programme.

It was these kinds of chance encounter in the coffee room, idle chatter around the photocopier, 70 that made the difference between a successful organisation and a less successful one.

From *Grooming, Gossip and the Evolution of Language*,
by Robin Dunbar

Communication

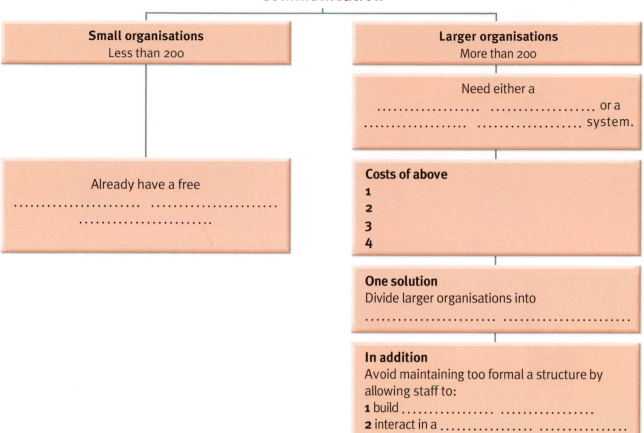

Small organisations
Less than 200

Larger organisations
More than 200

Need either a
.... or a
.... system.

Already have a free
....
....

Costs of above
1
2
3
4

One solution
Divide larger organisations into
....

In addition
Avoid maintaining too formal a structure by allowing staff to:
1 build ....
2 interact in a ....

C Answer these questions about words and phrases from the article.

1 Look at this key sentence from paragraph 4: *And with that, they inadvertently destroyed the intimate social networks that empowered the whole organisation.*
   a) What does *that* refer to?
   b) Who does *they* refer to?

2 In the same sentence, what do these words and phrases mean?
   a) inadvertently destroyed
   b) intimate social networks
   c) empowered

3 Choose the correct answer. In line 15, *quid pro quo* means:
   a) something that you give or do in exchange for something else
   b) a situation that exists at a particular time without changes being made to it
   c) money in pounds sterling that you give in return for a favour

4 In line 24, *panacea* means something that people think will:
   a) make everything better
   b) make everything worse
   c) not change the situation

5 Explain the meaning of *purpose-built* in line 39.

D In your own words describe what happened to the effectiveness of the TV production unit.

E The article mentions informal communication over lunch and around the photocopier. Can you give other examples of this kind of informal communication? What are the benefits of this?

F What changes can you suggest to improve communication within your own organisation or an organisation you know well?

Language review
Idioms

'It's like talking to a brick wall.'

- An idiom is an expression with a meaning that can be difficult to guess from the meanings of its separate words:
  talk to a brick wall means *talk to an unresponsive person*;
  hear something from the horse's mouth means *get the information directly from the person concerned.*

  For example:
  I've asked my boss for a pay rise several times, but no luck. It's like talking to a brick wall.
  I know he's leaving. I heard it from the horse's mouth.
- Common areas for idioms in business are war (*hit your targets*), gambling (*there's a lot of money at stake*) and shipping (*don't rock the boat*).

 page 130

A Complete these sentences with idioms from the box below.

a) put you in the picture	**e)** get a word in edgeways
b) talking at cross purposes	**f)** beating about the bush
c) get straight to the point	**g)** heard it on the grapevine
d) have a quick word	**h)** on the same wavelength

'Let me put you in the picture.'

1 OK, I'll . . . . I'm afraid we're going to have to let you go.

2 'You and your boss seem to agree on most things.'
'Yes, we are . . . .'

3 Susan, I know you are busy, but can I . . . . with you?

4 Some important decisions were taken at yesterday's meeting. Let me . . . .

5 I think we have been . . . . I meant next month, not this month.

6 Anja dominates all our meetings. Once she starts you can't . . . .

7 He never gives you a straight answer. He's always . . . .

8 I . . . . that he's been fired. Is it true?

B Choose the correct word to complete each sentence.

1 They were at a social event but they talked *kiosk / shop / store* all evening.

2 It's on the *edge / end / tip* of my tongue. I'm sure I'll remember her name soon.

3 She's our best sales rep. She's really got the *gift / skill / talent* of the gab.

4 When they told me I was fired I was at a *lack / loss / shortage* for words.

5 She lost the notes for her talk so she had to speak off the *collar / cuff / sleeve*.

6 He wanted a 30% discount and 90 days' credit! We weren't even talking the same *language / meaning / words*.

7 I haven't got the information to hand but, off the top of my *brain / head / mind*, I'd say about 2.5 million.

8 I've studied their accounts carefully but I can't make head or *foot / hand / tail* of them.

Skills
Problem-solving on the phone

A What kinds of problem can arise between companies and their suppliers? For example, in delivery, payment, quality control?

B 🎧 1.2 Listen to a telephone conversation between a customer and her supplier. What is the customer's problem? What solution does the supplier offer?

C 🎧 1.2 Listen again and decide who says the following. Is it the supplier or customer?

a) We've got a problem with those air conditioners.
b) There's so much going on at the moment. It slipped my mind.
c) I'm sorry, I can't promise anything.
d) Surely you can give our order priority?
e) Well it just isn't good enough.
f) Hold on, there is a solution.
g) Can you give me a few details?
h) Shall I call you back in a few minutes time?

D 🎧 1.3 Now listen to a telephone conversation between a manager and her PA. What is the problem? How is it resolved?

E 🎧 1.3 Listen again, then discuss how well the participants handled the problem. Support your opinions with examples from the dialogue.

F Study the Useful language box. Then role play the situations below.

> **1** A sales manager from Euro Financial Services (EFS) plans to leave for a sales trip to Poland tomorrow. However the tickets for the flight have only just arrived and the dates on the tickets are incorrect. He/she phones the representative of the travel agency, Sunset Travel, to complain.

> **2** The Sands department store in Riyadh, Saudi Arabia, has ordered a consignment of glasses from Hedvika Crystal, a supplier in the Czech Republic. The goods are required by an important businessman who, in a week's time, is hosting a dinner to celebrate the 50th anniversary of his company. Unfortunately, because of stormy weather, most of the consignment was broken in transit. The Chief Buyer of the department store phones the supplier to discuss the problem and work out a solution.

Useful language

Stating the problem
I wonder if you can help me. I've got a problem ...
There seems to be a problem. We haven't received ...

Offering to help
How can I help?
I'll look into it right now and get back to you.

Apologising / showing understanding
I'm really sorry about that. I do apologise ...
I understand how you feel.

Making suggestions
Perhaps we could ...
Would it be possible to ... ?

Requesting action
Could you look into the matter?
Please can you check with ...

CASE STUDY

Creating a sense of identity

Background

The international construction and engineering group KMB is based in Munich, Germany and has manufacturing subsidiaries and associated companies throughout the world. Its company magazine is published five times a year and is distributed by post to staff worldwide. The following letter, sent by a member of staff in its Brazilian sales office, appeared in the magazine's latest issue.

Dear editor,

I know I'm not the only one who feels uninformed about what's going on in KMB worldwide.

When I was at our recent sales conference in Munich several other people from overseas subsidiaries said they felt a lack of involvement and wanted more information from head office about new developments within the group. For example, why has KMB bought a major civil engineering company in Australia? How does this acquisition fit into our overall strategy? Unfortunately we could only guess at the reasons.

We also think it's essential to share best practice among our subsidiaries. We must know about ideas for improving efficiency as soon as possible. For example, if a marketing technique has been successful in one market, other areas of our business should be told.

We all agreed that the new Global Communications Director should overhaul KMB's communication system so that *all* members of staff are kept fully informed – both about overall strategy, and about news from overseas subsidiaries. What's the use of a worldwide network if no one knows what's going on?

Aldo Renato
SÃO PAULO, BRAZIL

The new Global Communications Director, Dominique Lapierre, sent the following e-mail to the Chief Executive of KMB after Aldo Renato's letter had been discussed at a board meeting.

	New Message - 1

Send | Address | Attach | Reply | Reply All | Forward | Draft | Print | Delete

☒ Log ☐ Receipt
Normal ▼

From Dominique Lapierre
Sent Monday, 11 September, 9.53am
To Franz Zimmermann
Subject Poor group communication

1 Item 0 Bytes

Message Text 1

It seems this complaint is quite common. Overseas staff don't think they get enough information about developments within the group, or about our latest acquisitions, etc. Ideas about best practice aren't shared either.

We urgently need to improve our communication system to show that we value staff, and to strengthen their sense of common purpose within the organisation globally.

Task

You are members of the working group which will discuss suggestions for improving KMB's communication system.

1 Brainstorm ideas of your own which you could add to the draft agenda.
2 Choose the three best ideas and add them to the agenda.
3 Then, hold an informal meeting. Discuss the advantages and disadvantages of the suggestions. Also consider the cost implications of each proposal. Finally, work out an action plan for improving communications within the company.

AGENDA (DRAFT)

Suggestions for improving communications:

i) Introduce an 'employee of the month' scheme.

ii) ....
....

iii) ....
....

iv) ....
....

Writing

As a member of the working group, write a memo to the heads of all of KMB's subsidiaries. This should inform them that the meeting took place and should outline the plan of action agreed. Finally, the memo should ask for their co-operation in implementing the suggestions.

➡ *Writing file* page 140

International marketing

OVERVIEW ▼

☐ **Vocabulary**
Marketing collocations

☐ **Reading**
International marketing mix

☐ **Language review**
Noun compounds and noun phrases

☐ **Skills**
Brainstorming

☐ **Case study**
Zumo – creating a global brand

❝*The last stage of fitting the product to the market is fitting the market to the product.*❞

Clive James, Australian writer and broadcaster

Starting up

A What products do you know that are marketed internationally?

B Discuss these questions.

1 What are the advantages for a company of expanding beyond its domestic market?

2 What kinds of problem do companies face when they go international?

3 What methods can companies use to enter overseas markets?

C Coca-Cola have had several successful slogans. For example, *I'd like to buy the world a Coke*; *Can't beat the feeling*; *Coke adds life*. What slogans for products have impressed you? Explain why.

D Choose three products and discuss ideas for slogans which could be used throughout the world.

Vocabulary
Marketing collocations

A Complete the statements with suitable marketing expressions from the box.

> buying habits   economic situation
> government bureaucracy   income distribution
> monetary regulations   political stability

1 Because of tight .... company profits could not be taken out of the country.

2 Red tape and other examples of .... hinder a company's entry into a market.

3 The country is attractive to exporters because it has enjoyed .... for the last 50 years.

4 The purchasing behaviour of consumers can be described as their ....

5 The .... is improving leading to a rise in employment.

6 .... is a term used by economists to describe how wealth is shared in a country.

B Discuss these questions.

1 What are some of the main benefits of political stability?

2 How would you describe the present economic situation of your country compared to 20 years ago?

3 Would you like to see a more equal income distribution in your country? Explain why or why not.

C Look at the words and phrases below. Underline the odd one out.

1 a) growing market   c) expanding market
   b) developing market   d) declining market

2 a) swamp a market   c) flood a market
   b) corner a market   d) saturate a market

3 a) opinion poll   c) spot check
   b) focus group   d) survey

4 a) market sector   c) market segment
   b) market potential   d) market niche

5 a) international market   c) domestic market
   b) overseas market   d) worldwide market

6 a) launch a product   c) bring out a product
   b) introduce a product   d) exhibit a product

7 a) sluggish market   c) stable market
   b) flat market   d) volatile market

8 a) point of sale   c) end user
   b) retail outlet   d) sales network

9 a) special offer   c) discount
   b) free sample   d) slogan

10 a) intermediary   c) wholesaler
    b) distributor   d) exporter

A Think of some global brands – for example in the car, fast food or soft drink industries. How are they tailored to meet local needs?

B What are the advantages and disadvantages of adapting a product to different overseas markets?

C Read the article. Then complete the table that follows it.

Finding the right international mix

In these days of increasing global integration, the task many international marketers face is not so much market entry as managing the marketing mix in different national markets. Is it better to standardise or to adapt it across different markets?

Consumer tastes in cars are very different in North America, the UK, Germany, Italy, Japan and India. A 'global' car that does not have country-specific differentiating features will fail. The manufacturer, therefore, has to find the balance between designing a separate car for each market – which would be exorbitantly costly – and designing one car for all markets. Nissan was a pioneer in this area. It reduced the number of different chassis designs from 40 to 8 for cars meant for 75 different national markets.

Some companies, however, do develop the same product for all markets regardless of existing local preferences. Companies such as Kellogg have succeeded in changing consumption patterns. Breakfast cereal was unknown in France 20 years ago. Today it is common. Kellogg ignored the research that said cereal would not sell in France. In contrast, Coca-Cola changes the flavour of its soft drink to conform to local tastes. Coke in the US tastes different from Coke in the UK, which in turn tastes different from Coke in India.

Thus there is a spectrum of new product development strategies. Firms sometimes customise a product to every market; at other times they offer one standardised product everywhere; and sometimes they compromise and settle in the middle.

New product development that co-ordinates efforts across national markets leads to better products and services. Such opportunities are not normally available to a company that operates only in one country or is only just entering a new country.

The advent of the Internet and Intranets has the potential to accelerate the process of mining all markets for relevant information and for features that can be included in new products. Unilever has four global research laboratories that develop products for their different national markets while providing inputs for global products. The laboratories co-ordinate their efforts by looking at the possibilities of melding product ideas arising from different countries. Motorola's software development establishments co-ordinate their efforts in working on different modules of the same project.

Companies also develop products in different countries in markedly different ways. Japanese companies, for example, tend to believe much more in getting new products to market and then gauging the reaction to them. The product itself may have been developed with reference to observations of present and potential customers rather than conventional market research. US companies, on the other hand, tend to use more formal market research methods. And for German companies, product development schedules tend to be more important.

Clearly, companies decide on different launch strategies for different categories of products. Toshiba launched the Digital Video Disk (DVD) in Japan in November 1996, in the US in March 1997 and in Europe in autumn 1997. However, Intel launches its latest PC chips practically simultaneously in all countries. The launch decision also includes marketing mix decisions. When Citibank introduced its credit card in the Asia-Pacific region, it launched it sequentially and tailored the product features for each country while maintaining its premium positioning. The promotional, pricing and distribution strategies also differed from country to country.

As a contrast, consider Rolex. The genuine Rolex watch is the same certified chronometer anywhere in the world; its positioning – as the timepiece for the elegant high achiever – is the same around the world, as is the advertising message. One will always find a Rolex in an upmarket distribution outlet and at a premium price. Or consider Unilever's Lifebuoy soap, which has different ingredients in India compared to East Africa. However, Unilever positions the soap in the same way in both markets – as an inexpensive everyday soap that has antibacterial properties and protects health.

From the *Financial Times*

FINANCIAL TIMES
World business newspaper.

Company logo	Product	Marketing approach
NISSAN	cars	reduced number of chassis designs
Kellogg's		
Enjoy Coca-Cola REGISTERED TRADE MARK		
CITIBANK®		
Unilever		

D What other companies does the article mention? What does it say about their marketing approaches?

E Discuss the following questions.

1 How has new technology contributed to the development of new products, according to the article?

2 How do Japanese, US and German companies differ in their approaches to product development?

F Choose the best definition of the words below.

1 exorbitantly (line 23)
   a) much higher than usual
   b) much lower than usual
   c) the same as usual

2 spectrum (line 52)
   a) range   b) choice   c) potential

3 customise (line 55)
   a) design specially
   b) order specially
   c) test specially

4 compromise (line 59)
   a) choose a middle way   b) make a promise   c) achieve your aim

5 gauging (line 100)
   a) assessing   b) guessing   c) predicting

Language review
Noun compounds and noun phrases

1 Noun compounds are common in business because they are shorter and more convenient than noun phrases. For example:
an export licence rather than *a licence to export*
a consumer protection law rather than *a law for the protection of consumers*

2 New compounds are formed all the time. There are no absolute rules about spelling. Sometimes they are two words (with or without a hyphen) and sometimes, when widely established, they become one. For example:
data protection   data-mining   database

3 Longer noun phrases are also common. They may consist of adverbs, adjectives and compound nouns. The following patterns are typical:

Adverb	Adjective / *-ing* participle	Noun / Gerund	Head noun
increasingly	difficult	market	conditions
	long-term	marketing	strategy
	expanding	overseas	sales

 page 130

A Find noun phrases in the article on page 16 which have similar meanings to the phrases below.
  1 things that make a product different for a particular country (paragraph 2)
  2 general trends in the way people buy and use goods (paragraph 3)
  3 ways of developing a new product (paragraph 4)
  4 places where worldwide markets are investigated (paragraph 6)
  5 places where software is produced (paragraph 6)
  6 methods of investigating markets (paragraph 7)
  7 programmes for developing goods (paragraph 7)
  8 choices about price, product, promotion, place (paragraph 8)
  9 a place where expensive goods are sold (paragraph 9)
  10 a high price for something special or unusual (paragraph 9)

B Copy the table from the Language review box. Choose five of the noun phrases that you found in the article and write them in your table.

C The words in each of the noun phrases below are in the wrong order. Write the phrases in your table in their correct form.
  1 impressive figures sales really
  2 department new public relations
  3 highly research market ambitious programme
  4 overseas expanding operations
  5 rapidly sheet balance improving
  6 extremely rate exchange volatile
  7 highly marketing report confidential
  8 successful incredibly fair trade

Skills
Brainstorming

A **Brainstorming is a useful way of generating creative ideas in meetings. Decide which tips below are good advice and which ones you disagree with. Then compare your answers with a partner.**

1 Explain the purpose of the meeting clearly.
2 Ask each person to speak in turn, starting with the most senior.
3 Announce the time limit for the meeting.
4 Avoid criticising or judging ideas during the session.
5 Encourage ideas, however unusual they may be.
6 Don't interrupt when people are offering suggestions.
7 Make sure everyone keeps to the point.
8 Don't spend time on details.

B 2.1 **Listen to the first part of an authentic brainstorming meeting between three members of the Marketing Department at Business Solutions Limited. Then answer these questions.**

1 What is the purpose of the meeting?
2 What types of promotion are mentioned by participants?

C 2.2 **Now listen to the rest of the meeting and answer these questions.**

1 What other ideas for promoting the website are mentioned by participants?
2 When is the next meeting? What information will the participants get then?

D **Match the comments made by the participants to the headings in the Useful language box below. You can use the Audio scripts on pages 156 and 157 to check the context of the comments. (Some comments can be put under more than one heading.)**

1 Fire away.
2 Excellent!
3 I think we'd reach a wide audience ...
4 We should definitely do some of that.
5 Absolutely!
6 What about press advertising?
7 That might be one way ...
8 Would it be worth sponsoring some kind of event?
9 It would be great to do a presentation ...
10 What about that?

Useful language

Stating objectives	Making suggestions	Expressing enthusiasm
The purpose of the meeting this morning is ...	I think we could send out glossy brochures ...	That's great!

Encouraging contributions	Agreeing	
Anything goes ...	Yes, that's a good idea.	

E **Choose one of the situations below and hold a brainstorming meeting.**

1 Your company has developed a new fabric which is exceptionally strong, light and waterproof. Brainstorm ideas for new products using the fabric.
2 Your company will shortly be receiving a visit from some important Chinese business people who wish to set up a joint venture with your firm. Brainstorm ideas for suitable gifts for the three Chinese visitors.

CASE STUDY

Zumo – creating a global brand

Background

The best-selling sports drink, Zumo, is produced by Zumospa, a food and drinks company based in Valencia, Spain. In the last financial year, Zumo contributed €30 million to Zumospa's annual sales revenue, accounting for 20% of the company's total turnover, and €4.5 million in profits. It is, in fact, Zumospa's cash cow, generating more revenue than any other of its products.

At present, Zumo is sold only in Europe. However, the sports drink market is the most rapidly growing segment of the world beverage market. Zumospa would like to make Zumo a global brand, even though the market is very competitive, with major companies such as Coca-Cola, Pepsi Cola and Heinz fighting for market share.

Key features of Zumo

- Contains caffeine, vitamins and glucose.
- Has a secret ingredient, 'herbora', made from roots of rare African plants.
- Scientific studies show that the body absorbs Zumo faster than water or other soft drinks.
- The unique formula contributes to Zumo's taste and thirst-quenching properties.

Marketing

- Launched in the mid 1980s. Positioned as an energy product for fitness-conscious people, especially sportsmen and women between the ages of 20 and 45.

- Distributed mainly through grocery stores, convenience stores and supermarkets. Also through sports clubs. Also, sales generated through contracts with professional leagues, such as football, golf and tennis associations.

- Press, TV and radio advertising is backed up by endorsement contracts with famous European footballers and tennis stars.

- Zumo is offered in four flavours and its price is in the medium range.

Developing a global brand

Zumospa needs to reposition Zumo for the global market. Initial research suggests that Zumo is perceived as a Spanish drink, and its close identification with Spain may not be suitable when developing a global brand.

Zumospa would like to launch a global campaign focussing first on South America, Mexico, the Southern states of the US and Japan, where they have regional offices. A decision has been taken to use a standardised advertising theme in these markets, although the copy of the advertisements and language of the TV and radio commercials will be adapted to local needs.

Before setting up focus groups in these areas and commissioning market surveys, the Marketing Department of Zumospa have organised an informal departmental meeting to brainstorm ideas for their global marketing strategy.

Brainstorming Session

1. Does Zumo need a new name? If so, what?
2. Introduce new Zumo varieties for different market segments eg. Diet Zumo? Other versions?
3. Re-design Zumo bottle/can? If so, how?
4. Create a new slogan? Suggestions?
5. Ideas for TV or radio advertisement? Also, newspapers and magazines?
6. Price - Medium range?
7. How to compete against similar products from Coke, Pepsi, Heinz, etc?
8. New market opportunities for Zumo?
9. Create a special division to market Zumo worldwide?
10. Apply to be official sponsor at next Olympic Games?

Writing

As Marketing Manager for Zumospa, write a memo to the directors of the company informing them of the key ideas which came out of the brainstorming session you attended. You should indicate which ideas you favour and why.

➡ *Writing file* page 140

Task

You are members of the Marketing Department of Zumospa. Work in groups and brainstorm the points listed in the rough notes. Then meet as one group and select some of the best suggestions for further study.

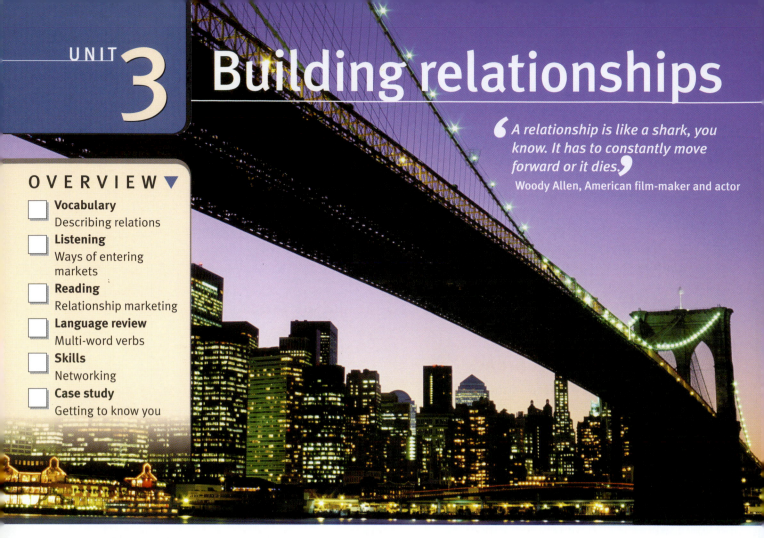

UNIT
3 Building relationships

OVERVIEW ▼

Vocabulary
Describing relations

Listening
Ways of entering markets

Reading
Relationship marketing

Language review
Multi-word verbs

Skills
Networking

Case study
Getting to know you

‘ *A relationship is like a shark, you know. It has to constantly move forward or it dies.* ’
Woody Allen, American film-maker and actor

Starting up

A **Discuss these questions.**

1 What are the most important relationships for you? Why? Choose from your relationships with the following:

- your company
- your division or team
- your boss
- your clients / customers
- your suppliers
- other

2 What benefits do you get from each relationship above?

B **Ward Lincoln, Business Relations Manager with an international training organisation, is talking about areas for companies to consider in order to build strong business relationships. What factors do you think he will mention?**

C 🎧 3.1 **Listen to the interview and check the predictions you made in Exercise B.**

D **Answer the questions in the quiz. Then turn to page 152 to find out how good you are at building relationships.**

1 In a large group, do you more often
   a) introduce others
   b) get introduced?

2 When you meet strangers, do you find it
   a) pleasant, or at least easy
   b) something that takes a good deal of effort?

3 When you are introduced to people, do you remember
   a) their name b) their face?

4 In your business, do you
   a) focus on building relationships with one or a few people
   b) try to make as many relationships as possible?

5 Your normally reliable supplier lets you down on an important order. Do you
  a) change suppliers
  b) ask for an explanation and give them another chance?

6 Can you keep a conversation going
  a) only with people who share some interest of yours
  b) with almost anyone?

7 Do you socialise with colleagues from work because
  a) you like to
  b) you think that you ought to?

8 Your best customer is making an unjustified complaint. Do you
  a) point out their error
  b) agree with them because they're important?

Vocabulary

Describing relations

A The verbs below are often used with the word *relations*. Use them to complete the table.

> break off   build up   cement   cloud   cut off   develop   disrupt
> encourage   establish   impair   improve   jeopardise   maintain
> promote   restore   resume   sever   sour   spoil   strengthen

Positive meaning	Negative meaning
build up relations	break off relations

B The adjectives in the box below are often used with the word *relations*. Place them on the line below according to their meaning.

> amicable   close   cool   excellent   friendly   stormy   strained

Very bad	Very good
	excellent

C Match the halves of sentences below. Then make five more sentences with the verbs and adjectives above.

1 Widespread rumours of a hostile take-over bid are certain

2 The Accounts Department's very slow payment of invoices

3 The long-term contracts, which will run for the next five years,

4 The excellent relations the company enjoys with the local community

5 As a result of the government's imposition of currency controls,

a) are a credit to its highly effective PR Department.

b) have cemented relations between the two companies.

c) its close relations with several major foreign investors have been jeopardised.

d) is causing stormy relations with some of the company's suppliers.

e) to strain relations between the two leading French software companies.

Listening

Ways of entering markets

▲ Miguel Adao

▲ Tong Yan

A 🎧 **3.2** Miguel Adao works for the health insurance company CIGNA. Tong Yan is involved in promoting closer relations between the UK and his home province in China.

Before you listen, decide which points below you think Miguel will make about Latin America and which ones Tong will make about China. Tick the appropriate column on the right. Then listen and check your predictions.

	Latin America	China
1 It is important to find an intermediary.	◯	◯
2 These people tend to work with friends and relatives.	◯	◯
3 You may need to shake hands and even hug.	◯	◯
4 Long lunches or dinner meetings may be important.	◯	◯
5 These people trust those who are loyal to them and show respect.	◯	◯
6 The best way to build a business relationship is through networking.	◯	◯

B What are the similarities between the two cultures described in Exercise A? What about the differences?

C 🎧 **3.3** Listen to the rest of the interview. Summarise how business decisions are made in China, according to Tong.

Reading

Relationship marketing

A Discuss these questions. Then read the first two paragraphs of the article on page 25 and check your answers.

1 Do you think companies spend most of the time:
   a) attracting new customers?   **b)** keeping existing customers?

2 What percentage of its customers does an average company lose each year, do you think?
   a) 2–5   **b)** 5–10   **c)** 10–30   **d)** 30–50

B Now read the rest of the article and answer these questions.

1 What do these numbers refer to in paragraphs three and four?
   a) Five   **b)** 25   **c)** 85   **d)** 5,000

2 What are the six main advantages of keeping customers that the article mentions?

3 What kinds of customer are identified in the article? Use the five different customer types to complete the *ladder of customer loyalty*.

C What do the following words from the article mean? Use a good dictionary to help you.

humdrum (line 11)	**a)** exciting	**b)** boring	**c)** technical
defecting (line 30)	**a)** leaving	**b)** joining	**c)** complaining
nurturing (line 43)	**a)** taking advantage of	**b)** taking care of	
	c) taking part in		
correlation (line 51)	**a)** connection	**b)** difference	**c)** similarity
customer retention (line 51)	**a)** exploiting customers	**b)** keeping customers	
	c) losing customers		

....

....

....

....

....Prospect....

▲ Ladder of customer loyalty

D Match words from each column to make word partnerships. Then check your answers in the article.

1 lost   a) sensitive
2 price   b) implications
3 financial   c) opportunities
4 customer   d) advertising
5 word-of-mouth   e) loyalty

E Think of a company that you buy products from regularly. What does it do to keep you as a customer? What could it do to strengthen your customer loyalty in the future?

RELATIONSHIP MARKETING

Everyone in business has been told that success is all about attracting and retaining customers. It sounds reassuringly simple and achievable. But, in reality, words of wisdom are
5 soon forgotten. Once companies have attracted customers they often overlook the second half of the equation. In the excitement of beating off the competition, negotiating prices, securing orders, and delivering the product,
10 managers tend to become carried away. They forget what they regard as the humdrum side of business – ensuring that the customer remains a customer.

Failing to concentrate on retaining as well as
15 attracting customers costs businesses huge amounts of money annually. It has been estimated that the average company loses between 10 and 30 per cent of its customers every year. In constantly changing markets this
20 is not surprising. What is surprising is the fact that few companies have any idea how many customers they have lost.

Only now are organisations beginning to wake up to these lost opportunities and
25 calculate the financial implications. Cutting down the number of customers a company loses can make a radical difference in its performance. Research in the US found that a five per cent decrease in the number of
30 defecting customers led to profit increases of between 25 and 85 per cent.

Rank Xerox takes the question of retaining customers so seriously that it forms a key part of the company's bonus scheme. In the US,
35 Domino's Pizzas estimates that a regular customer is worth more than $5,000 over ten years. A customer who receives a poor quality product or service on their first visit and as a result never returns, is losing the company
40 thousands of dollars in potential revenue (more if you consider how many people they are liable to tell about their bad experience).

The logic behind nurturing customer loyalty is impossible to refute. 'In practice most

LOST PROPERTY

HAVE ANY OF MY CUSTOMERS BEEN HANDED IN..?

45 companies' marketing effort is focussed on getting customers, with little attention paid to keeping them', says Adrian Payne of Cornfield University's School of Management and author of *The Essence of Services Marketing*. 'Research
50 suggests that there is a high degree of correlation between customer retention and profitability. Established customers tend to buy more, are predictable and usually cost less to service than new customers. Furthermore, they
55 tend to be less price sensitive, and may provide free word-of-mouth advertising and referrals. Retaining customers also makes it difficult for competitors to enter a market or increase their share of a market.'

60 Payne points to a ladder of customer loyalty. On the first rung, there is a prospect. They are then turned into a customer, then a client, then a supporter and finally, if the relationship is successful, into an advocate persuading others
65 to become customers. Developing customers so they travel up the ladder demands thought, long-term commitment and investment.

From *Key Management Ideas*, Stuart Crainer

Language review
Multi-word verbs

Multi-word verbs are very common in English. They are made with a verb and particles such as *at, away, down* and *off*. Four types are:

1 Without an object
   *I'm going to be **tied up** in meetings all day.*

2 With an object – separable
   *In the excitement of **beating off** the competition, managers become carried away.*
   *In the excitement of **beating** the competition **off**, managers become carried away.*

3 With an object — inseparable
   *I'll **look into** the matter immediately.*

4 With two particles
   *Organisations are beginning to **wake up to** these lost opportunities.*

 page 131

A 🎧 3.4 **Two managers are talking about building relationships with agents. Put the conversation in the correct order. Then listen and check your answers.**

☐ **a)** Well, I hope you get a result. I must be going. I've got to draw up an agency agreement myself, I've put it off far too long already.

☐ **b)** What exactly was the problem?

☐ **c)** Yes, my job was on the line. Our results were terrible. We tried to build up market share but it just didn't happen. We just managed to hold on to what we had.

☐ **d)** Unfortunately, our agent let us down. We thought we could count on him to boost sales but he had no commitment, no motivation.

☐ **e)** He should be. He's got a very good track record. We'd set up a meeting on Friday, but he had to call it off – something came up.

1 **f)** How's it going in France, Gina? We didn't do too well there last year.

☐ **g)** Well, I suppose you terminated his contract then.

☐ **h)** Good. Let's hope he'll be better than the last one.

☐ **i)** All the best. Speak to you soon.

☐ **j)** Yes, there was no way we could renew it. We sounded out a few possible replacements and found someone else. We get on really well.

B **Underline all the multi-word verbs in the conversation in Exercise A. Then match each one to a verb with a similar meaning below.**

1 have a friendly relationship
2 depend on / rely on
3 make bigger / stronger
4 keep / maintain
5 postpone / delay
6 find out opinions / intentions
7 disappoint
8 arrange
9 compile / write down
10 cancel

C **Rephrase these comments using the multi-word verbs from Exercise A.**

1 We can't hold the meeting tomorrow.
   *We'll have to **call** the meeting **off** tomorrow.*

2 Let's have the presentation next week – we're too busy at the moment.

3 We always know our suppliers will meet their deadlines.

4 We have now established a first class distribution network in Europe.

5 Could you please prepare a contract as soon as possible.

6 Could you fix a meeting with them for next week.

7 We've kept the same market share as we had last year.

8 The new sales manager is very popular with his team.

Skills
Networking

A 🎧 **3.5** Networking is a vital part of establishing good business relationships. Listen to four conversations at business conferences. For each one decide whether the statements are true or false.

1 a) The first speaker introduces herself straightaway.
  b) The second speaker doesn't remember her until she introduces herself.

2 a) The second speaker knows that Henry Willis is in New York.
  b) The second speaker offers to contact the New York office.

3 a) Both speakers know Jon Stuart.
  b) The second speaker isn't able to offer any help.

4 a) Both speakers have been doing business in Asia for some time.
  b) In the end they establish an area of common interest.

B 🎧 **3.6** Listen to the telephone conversation, then answer the questions.

1 What is the purpose of the call?

2 Does it have a successful outcome? Why? Why not?

C 🎧 **3.6** Now listen again and complete the extracts from the conversation.

1 I .... you don't .... me .... Silvana said it would probably be OK.

2 Is it a .... time to ring or could I call you .... at a better time?

3 Silvana .... that you might be able to .... me on franchising contracts.

4 Mmm, I don't know. I could maybe give you a little help, but I know someone .... in that area.

5 You haven't got her phone number .... ?

6 Can I .... when I call her?

D Work in pairs and role play these situations.

1 The owner of a department store visits Moscow to find a supplier of amber jewellery. He/she phones a Russian contact recommended by a colleague. The owner wants to find out if the Russian is interested in doing business with his/her company.

2 You are networking at a conference about sports goods. You are either
a sales manager, turn to page 147
or a sports goods wholesaler, turn to page 154.

Useful language

Mentioning people you know
Harry Kaufman suggested I gave you a call.
I was given your name by Jon Stuart.

Giving advice
I suggest you give her a call.
You could try to track him down through our New York office.

Referring to previous meetings
Haven't we met somewhere before?
We both went to that presentation …

Asking for help / contacts
Can I mention your name when I call him?
He mentioned that you might be able to help me.
You haven't got his phone number by any chance?
Is this a convenient time or shall I call back later?

Establishing common interests
Maybe we could help you out there.
Are you in sales or product development?

Getting to know you

Background

Kimsoong, a Korean car manufacturer, has its European headquarters near Paris. It has retail sales franchises in most European countries which not only sell cars and motor accessories but also have servicing facilities. The larger outlets also offer fast-fitting of tyres and exhausts, and deal in used cars.

Over the last ten years Kimsoong, with its reputation for reliability at low prices, has built up market share at the lower end of the market. Their basic models include many 'extras' which other manufacturers charge for. Kimsoong also makes large donations to environmental groups and is seen as an organisation with a social conscience. Furthermore, its R&D Department is developing an 'eco-car' which uses an alternative power source.

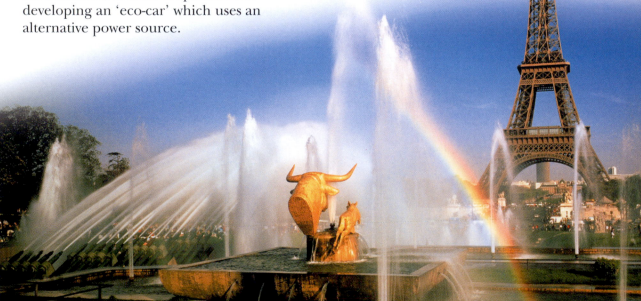

Problems

Intense competition is forcing Kimsoong to consider new ways of generating business. Management believe that if the company looks after existing customers well, they may buy three or four Kimsoong vehicles over a ten-year period. Therefore, Kimsoong's new strategy is to hold on to existing customers and increase customer loyalty. They also hope to develop a more accurate buyer profile. (At present, data is from questionnaires sent to customers following sales but only 40% are returned.) However, because of pressure on profits, they need to achieve these objectives at a low cost.

Solutions

A customer loyalty programme will be developed by the Customer Services Department at head office. It will be available to all European franchises and costs will be shared 50/50 with head office. Its aims are:

- to build up long-term customer relationships, thereby increasing profits
- to increase customer loyalty
- to draw up an accurate buyer profile
- to encourage staff to be more active in building up good customer relations.

Kimsoong customer profile

Age		Sex		Occupation	
Under 30	48%	Male	52%	Student	8%
31–40	27%	Female	48%	Self-employed	15%
41–50	15%			Employed	75%
Over 51	10%			Retired	2%

Interests (in order of importance)		Percentage of repeat buyers	Income group	
1 Eating / drinking	5 Health / fitness	15%	Higher income	2%
2 Sport	6 Reading		Middle income	82%
3 Travel	7 The arts		Lower income	16%
4 Environment	8 Politics			

Reason for not repeating purchase		After-sales care (customer rating)		Customers' priorities (in order of importance)
Bought a competitor's model	52%	Excellent	4%	1 Economy
Dissatisfied with service	26%	Very good	12%	2 Price
Relocated	8%	Good	17%	3 Reliability
No longer drive	5%	Fair	61%	4 After-sales service
Don't know	9%	Poor	6%	5 Length of warranty
				6 Performance
				7 Comfort

Task

Work in small groups. You work in Customer Services at head office.

1 Prepare a presentation of your plans for the customer loyalty programme. In addition to your own ideas, you may want to include some of the following:
   - discounts to existing customers who buy a new Kimsoong car
   - a monthly company magazine sent free to all customers
   - free servicing for the first three years of ownership
   - generous terms when customers trade in old models.
2 Present your ideas to your colleagues.
3 Working as one group, devise a customer loyalty programme using the best ideas from each group.

Writing

Choose a company you are familiar with. Write a sales letter to Roger Eastwood, one of a group of priority customers. Outline a special offer which you are making to this priority customer group. Make your letter appear as personalised as possible.

 Writing file page 138

UNIT 4 Success

OVERVIEW ▼

☐ **Listening**
Successful people and companies

☐ **Discussion**
Epic failures

☐ **Reading**
Mobile phones

☐ **Language review**
Present and past tenses

☐ **Vocabulary**
Prefixes

☐ **Skills**
Negotiating

☐ **Case study**
Camden FC

❝ *The only place where success comes before work is in the dictionary.* ❞
Vidal Sassoon, hairstylist

Starting up

A What makes people successful? Add more words to the list below. Then choose the five most important.

charm	drive	looks	nepotism
dedication	imagination	luck	ruthlessness
discipline	intuition	money	stamina

B Give examples of people who owe their success to some of the items on your list. Explain your choices.

C What are the best indicators of an individual's level of success? How important are the following in your culture?

> chauffeur(s)   cosmetic surgery   designer clothes   domestic help
> exotic holidays   expensive jewellery   flash car(s)   influential friends
> leisure activities   pedigree pets   respect   smart house(s)

D How do you judge the success of a business? Discuss the statements below.
You can tell that a business is a success because ...

1 ... it's always increasing its profit.
2 ... it has a big share of the market.
3 ... it's always in the news.
4 ... people like working for it.
5 ... its customers are loyal.
6 ... its brand can sell anything.
7 ... its shares are worth millions.
8 ... it has a prestigious head office.
9 ... it has branches all over the world.
10 ... it puts people first.

Listening
Successful people and companies

▲ Sally Muggeridge

A 🎧 **4.1** Sally Muggeridge is Management Development Director at Pearson plc. Listen to the first part of the interview and take notes about what makes a successful business person.

B 🎧 **4.2** Listen to the rest of the interview and make notes about what makes a successful company.

Successful business people	Successful companies
Know their job very thoroughly	*Often have well-known brand names*

C Use your notes, and any other ideas of your own, to write a short article for a business magazine entitled either a) *Successful business people* or b) *Successful companies*.

Discussion
Epic failures

A Work in pairs. One of you reads *New Coke for Old* on page 151; the other reads *Ford Edsel: Remember My Name* below. When you have finished, tell your partner about what mistakes were made and why.

Ford Edsel: Remember My Name

In the late 1940s Ford decided it needed a medium-price model to compete with General Motors – 'a car for every purse and purpose' – which would appeal both to the young executive and the professional family on the way up. Named after Henry Ford's son, Ford spent 10 years and $250m on the Edsel's planning and development. With $50m being spent on advertising, the launch in September 1957 was the most expensive for any commercial product to date.

Problems began when, due to an increase in road deaths, the US Automobile Manufacturers' Association agreed not to advertise a car's power and performance – two of the Edsel's main features. Also motoring journalists said the car was not the great innovation which Ford claimed. What's more, it had a conflicting image of speed against suitability for young families more interested in safety and comfort. Finally, many Edsels were faulty. Word spread and sales fell. Despite this, Ford spent $400,000 on a TV broadcast with Frank Sinatra and Bing Crosby. Next they sent a mailshot to 1.5m car owners offering a test drive. An economic recession in the US contributed further to disappointing sales.

On 19 November 1959 production was stopped. In total only 109,466 Edsels were sold (although only one was ever reported stolen) making a total loss of $350m. As *Time* magazine said, 'It was a classic case of the wrong car for the wrong market at the wrong time'.

B What would you have done in the situations described in the articles? What lessons can be learned?

Reading
Mobile phones

A Before you read the article, discuss these questions.

1 Do you own a mobile phone? Why? Why not?

2 What do you think is important when choosing a mobile phone?

3 What are the advantages of mobile phones? What about the disadvantages? Think about both users and non-users.

B Read the article. Then make notes under the headings below.

PROFILE – NOKIA

1 Country of origin
2 Chief Executive
3 Chief Executive's main objectives
4 Industry position
5 Market share
6 Market capitalisation
7 Main competitors
8 Reasons for success (at least seven)
9 Potential threats

C Use your notes to write a brief profile of Nokia.

At the forefront of innovation

By Christopher Brown-Humes

It is the biggest company in one of the world's fastest-growing industries. Not only is Nokia selling three out of every ten mobile handsets being made – it overtook Motorola last year to become the world's biggest mobile phone maker – but its market share is rising fast.

The dramatic success gives the Finnish group, led by Chief Executive Jorma Ollila, an obvious claim to membership of any league ranking the world's most respected companies. According to one of the respondents to the FT/PwC survey, the company has quite simply 'changed the future'.

Success has happened in less than a decade. Moreover, it has happened in a country, on Europe's outer fringes, which has a population of just 5m and where the traditional industry – pulp and paper – is anything but high tech. Luck has played a part too: nobody quite realised a decade ago that the mobile phone would move so quickly from being an expensive status symbol to a popular mass-market product. The group's decision to concentrate on the

Jorma Ollila, CEO Nokia

GSM segment was also a fortuitous one, because GSM has become the *de facto* world standard.

Back in 1992, shortly after Mr Ollila took over as Chief Executive, he wrote down the four phrases which he saw as the key to the group's future. They were 'telecom-orientated', 'global', 'focus' and 'value-added'.

Nobody can say he did not stick to his own brief. Focus meant turning Nokia from a sprawling conglomerate, with a promising mobile business, into a dedicated mobile phone company. Out went much of 'the baggage' – chemicals, tyres, cables and television-set manufacturing were among the businesses offloaded during the early 1990s.

On the telecommunication side, the company has succeeded in establishing a strong brand that is recognised throughout the world. There may even have been an initial benefit from some customers thinking it was a Japanese company. In fact, the name comes from a town in southern Finland.

The group has outstripped its rivals, Motorola and Ericsson, because it has allied engineering excellence with great marketing flair. Analysts say it has usually produced more fashionable, reliable, and user-friendly handsets than its competitors.

Moreover, it has kept at the forefront of innovation, shortening product cycles, and launching new models just when the margins on old ones are starting to dive. It has a consistent record of increasing volumes by more than enough to offset falling prices. Also, the company has been able to manage its growth – staff numbers have grown from 25,000 in 1993 to 44,000 today – and bureaucracy has not been allowed to stifle the culture of innovation.

If success is measured by market capitalisation, Nokia can have few equals.

In January 1994, it was worth just €3.5bn. In mid-November 1999, the figure had risen to €142bn. The company is Europe's fifth largest and singlehandedly accounts for more than 50 per cent of the Helsinki stock exchange and a substantial chunk of Finnish GDP growth.

Analysts, not surprisingly, are fulsome in their praise. 'Nokia has a 30 per cent and growing share of the handsets market and more than 60 per cent of the profit in the sector. It is incredibly efficient, with the best products, the best brand and the best logistics,' says Lauri Rosendahl, analyst at Aros Securities in Helsinki.

So far, the company has defied predictions that its rivals will catch up. So far it has managed growth. And so far, the US Internet giants have stayed out of the mobile arena. But even more advanced technologies are on their way, rivals are snapping at its heels, and living up to the market's high-placed expectations will be an ever more daunting challenge.

From the *Financial Times*

FINANCIAL TIMES
World business newspaper.

D What is the most successful company in your country? Explain your answer.

Language review
Present and past tenses

Complete the rules with the words *present simple, present continuous, present perfect* or *past simple*.

1 We use the .... to describe actions and situations which are generally true: *We sell our products into many markets.*

2 We use the .... to describe completed actions or events which took place at a particular time or over a period of time in the past: *She telephoned me yesterday; He became Chief Executive in 1999.*

3 We use the .... to describe current or temporary situations: *Petrol is getting more expensive by the week; She's working in Poland on a fixed-term contract.*

4 We use the .... to describe life experiences, present results of past actions or announce news: *The company has done well recently.*

 page 131

A **Discuss these questions about the article on page 32.**

1 In paragraph four, which tense is used and why?

2 In paragraph seven, which tense is used and why?

3 In the final paragraph, find an example of the present continuous. Why is this tense used?

4 In paragraph three, identify the tense of each verb and explain its use.

B **Write an article on Chupa Chups, the Spanish confectionery manufacturer, for a business magazine. Use the notes below, putting the verbs in brackets into appropriate tenses.**

The company and its markets

Chupa Chups – Barcelona-based sweetmaker
Number 25 worldwide
Market share 0.9%
Lollipops market share 34%
Manufacturing sites – five countries
Familiar to many children in the world

How the company started

1954 Enric Bernat (try) revive sweet manufacturer Granja Asturias
He (succeed) in turning company around
1985 (buy) all shares / (drop) entire product range / (concentrate) on new Chups lollipop

What it is doing now

Now (build) adult customer base
(Attract) older customers with new flavours

Recent Events

(Launch) highly-coloured 'tongue-painter' lollipops
Also (diversify) into sugar-free mints with Smint range
Resulting sales surge (be) spectacular
Revenues (grow)
Last year (sell) 4 bn lollipops

Vocabulary
Prefixes

A Match the prefixes *over-* and *out-* to the verbs below.

> bid   book   charge   manoeuvre   number
> run   strip   subscribe   take   vote

B Do any of the verbs above take both prefixes?

C Complete these sentences using the prefixes *over-* or *out-*, and the correct form of the verbs above. Use each prefix and verb combination only once.

1 Nokia ..*overtook*.. Motorola last year to become the world's biggest mobile phone maker.

2 The group has *outstripped* its rivals Motorola and Ericsson.

3 AT&T .... two of Mexico's largest suppliers to win the right to build 60% of the network.

4 The CEO and three other board members combined to .... the three non-executive directors.

5 We were completely .... in the negotiation and ended up paying too high a price.

6 In our company, females .... males four to one.

7 The airline offers cash as compensation for passengers when flights are ....

8 They refused to commit themselves in case the project's costs .... its budget.

9 He is alleged to have .... them for production and repair work.

10 The share issue was a success and was hugely ....

D What is the basic meaning of the prefixes *over-* and *out-*?

E Choose the best definition of the verbs in italics in these extracts.

1 Nokia has a consistent record of increasing volumes by more than enough to *offset* falling prices.
   a) to make one thing less than another resulting in a great difference
   b) to cause something to happen
   c) to balance one amount against another so that there is no great difference as a result

2 Chemicals, tyres, cables and television-set manufacturing were among the businesses *offloaded* during the early 1990s.
   a) to sell a company at a higher price than expected
   b) to get rid of something you do not want by giving or selling it to someone
   c) to sell a company at a lower price than expected

3 You can use your frequent flyer mileage to *upgrade* to business class.
   a) to get something earlier than you expected
   b) to get something better than you paid for
   c) to pay less money than you expected

Skills
Negotiating

(A) **Three key skills in negotiating are**

1 signalling (drawing attention to what you're about to say)
2 checking understanding
3 summarising.

Study the examples of each in the Useful language box.

Useful language

Signalling
I'd like to make a suggestion. I think we should leave this point and come back to it later.
I want to ask a question. How are we going to pay for this?

Checking understanding
Sorry, could you repeat that?
Are you saying you don't have that quantity in stock?
So what you're saying is you will ...

Summarising
Can we just summarise the points we've agreed so far?
OK, so we're agreed. You'll pay for delivery and get everything to us by the end of June.

(B) **Now read the negotiation between the Commercial Director of a car manufacturer and the General Manager of a business equipment firm. Underline any examples of *signalling*, *checking understanding* or *summarising*.**

Director   We're willing to give you a 12% discount on our list price if you buy over 30 vehicles – that's OK. It'll mean you'll be paying just under £14,400 for each vehicle. But that's providing you don't have any special requirements which cost us more money.

Manager   Special requirements? What do you mean exactly?

Director   Oh, I don't know, if you want the interior of the car to be changed, for example. The price we've agreed is for our standard model. Or if you wanted a modification which costs money, more storage compartments, for example.

Manager   Right. It's true, some of our top sales staff can be fussy. I don't know though, we'd still like a 12% discount, given the size of our order.

Director   Mmm, OK, let me make a suggestion. We give you 12% but if someone wants extras or a modification, we'll offer you a 10% discount on that car. That's fair enough, isn't it?

Manager   OK, so you're saying you will modify the car if we ask you to?

Director   Exactly.

Manager   Right then, let's see what we've got. The price will be £14,400, providing there are no extras or modifications to the interior. You'll make small changes if we ask you to, but reduce the discount by 2%.

Director   That's it. OK, Let's talk about delivery now.

(C) 🎧 **4.3 Listen to these expressions, which were used later in the same negotiation. Which ones are *not* examples of *signalling*, *checking understanding* or *summarising*?**

(D) **Role play the following situation.**
An Italian shoe manufacturer has produced a new range of women's leather boots. A German retailer is considering placing an order for 250 pairs of each design. The Sales Manager and Chief Buyer negotiate the contract.

Sales Manager turn to page 153. Chief Buyer turn to page 149.

CASE STUDY

Background

Camden Football Club is one of the great success stories in English football. Today, it is third in the Premier Division (the top division) and has reached the quarter finals of the European Champions League competition, which is held every year. They get huge crowds at their ground and their Polish manager, Cristos Sroda, is idolised by their fans. Camden is also a great commercial success and is very profitable.

What has brought about their success? Firstly, their manager Cristos had a clear strategy for the team from the start. He developed young players who had come through the club's youth training scheme. The team was also strengthened by one or two carefully chosen foreign players.

The extraordinary commercial success of Camden is due to their Commercial Director, Sophie Legrange. She greatly increased profits from the club's main business areas: corporate hospitality, advertising, sponsorship and conferences and banqueting.

At the same time, she skilfully exploited the Camden brand and diversified into other areas: a travel agency for fans and also for companies using the club's hospitality facilities; a joint venture with an insurance agency to provide financial products for the club's corporate clients; and finally, training courses in the club's conference rooms run by local companies. Turnover increased by over 400% to £70m and profits leapt to £15m. TV rights, soon to be renegotiated, will provide another very lucrative source of income.

Current situation

Camden's current four-year sponsorship deal with an insurance company is about to finish. Sophie Legrange is considering a new and better deal with United Media plc, the powerful publishing, TV production and mobile phone group. It is not only the increased money from sponsorship which appeals to Camden, however. United Media's broad range of business activities would offer many other opportunities to increase revenue.

United Media are interested in Camden because the club's success has brought it over 4m fans in the UK and 40m in the Far East. Camden played a friendly match recently in China which was watched live by a Chinese audience of over 250m.

Representatives of Camden and United Media are meeting shortly to discuss a possible sponsorship deal. The following factors will influence the negotiation:

1 Because of their recent successes, Camden feel they are in a strong position to negotiate a valuable four-year contract.

2 Some experts say Camden were lucky to win their last European Cup match, and that they rely too much on their star South American player, Paolo Rosetti. Now aged 30, he has a poor discipline record and is rumoured to have marital and drink problems.

3 Sophie Legrange has full negotiating rights over sponsorship. She will only choose United Media as a sponsor if she can negotiate a good deal for the club.

Task

You are members of the negotiating team of either: Camden FC (turn to page 147) or United Media plc (turn to page 154).
Read your role card and prepare for the negotiation. Work out your objectives, priorities, strategy and tactics. Think carefully about what concessions you are willing to make. An agenda has been prepared in advance of the meeting.

AGENDA

Date: 10 May
Time: 10am
Venue: Conference room, Camden Football Ground

1 Total value of the contract
2 Timing of payments
3 Advertising
4 Control of players and club activities
5 Paolo Rosetti
6 Official supplier of Camden football boots
7 Other commercial opportunities
8 Fringe benefits for players
9 Other points

Writing

1 If the negotiation was successful, write a press release from the point of view of either Camden FC or United Media outlining the main points of the agreement and the benefits to the organisation you represent. The tone and style of the message should express pleasure and optimism.
or

2 If the negotiation was unsuccessful, write a letter to your opposite number in the negotiation expressing your regret that you were unable to make a deal. However, you should indicate that you might be willing to reopen negotiations in the future as clearly there could be areas of mutual benefit.

➡ *Writing file* pages 138 and 141

Job satisfaction

'It is not real work unless you would rather be doing something else.'

Sir James Barrie (1860–1937),
Scottish dramatist and novelist

OVERVIEW ▼

☐ **Reading**
Fringe benefits

☐ **Vocabulary**
Synonyms and
word building

☐ **Listening**
Motivating factors

☐ **Discussion**
What's in a title?

☐ **Language review**
Passives

☐ **Skills**
Handling difficult
situations

☐ **Case study**
Office attraction

Starting up

A Which of the following would motivate you to work harder? Choose your top five and rank them in order of priority. Which ones have you experienced?

bonus	more responsibility	working for a successful company
bigger salary	threat of redundancy	a better working environment
commission	hard-working boss	promotion opportunities
praise	good colleagues	perks or fringe benefits

B Discuss these questions.

1 A recent US survey showed children preferred parents to go out and earn money rather than spend more time with them. What does this show, in your opinion?

2 Would you prefer a male or female boss? Why?

3 For what reasons might you change jobs? How often would you expect to do so in your lifetime?

- *Turn to page 137 for the quiz 'Are you in danger of burning out?'*

Reading
Fringe benefits

A What fringe benefits do you think companies should provide for their workers? Have you heard of any unusual ones?

B The article on page 39 describes a number of benefits provided by companies. Which of the following do you think it will mention?

childcare	company holidays	cosmetic surgery
counselling	dance classes	guitar lessons
haircuts	masseurs sushi	tennis lessons

C Skim the article to check your answers.

Is there a place for time in corporate Utopia?

Employees of SAS Institute live in a workers' Utopia. On the company's wooded campus in North Carolina is everything a person could need: doctors, dentists, on-site childcare, masseurs ...

SAS has just been chosen by *Fortune* magazine as one of the best companies to work for in the US. Like the other 99 companies singled out, SAS is not content to reward employees with a mere pay cheque. Instead, the company is dead set on making their lives easier.

Indeed, there is little these good employers will not do to take the load off their workers' shoulders. Some provide subsidised housekeepers. Some deliver ready-cooked gourmet meals to employees' doors in the evening. Others offer haircuts, free Viagra, cut-price sushi, free ergonomic chairs. One company even provides $10,000 (£6,070) towards the cost of adopting a child.

Not content with the above, some employers are helping their staff fill their leisure hours too. Many offer swimming pools and fitness centres, some arrange guitar lessons or provide garden allotments. Some even lay on company holidays, whisking workers and their partners off to luxury island locations.

And that is not all: some companies also set the standard for employees to follow in their private lives. At First Tennessee, employees get a $130 cash bonus if they are seen to be practising 10 specified healthy behaviour patterns.

For these forward-looking employers the vexed problem of work / life balance – assumed to be one of the greatest workplace issues facing us – is magically eliminated. These companies are mounting a take-over bid for their employees' lives with the result that the issue of balance no longer arises.

And at these companies hardly anyone ever leaves. Which might mean everyone is gloriously happy. Or it might mean the prospect of severing one's entire life from an employer is so daunting that it seems easier to stay put.

Amid all this bounty there is just one thing that none of these companies offer. And that is time. If employers really want to show that they are helping employees balance their lives, the answer is not to do their shopping, fix their teeth and issue them with laptops so that they can work 'flexibly' right through the night. It is to ensure that people do not work too hard. To write it into the company's culture that no one will be expected to work more than, say, 40 hours a week on average. And for the Chief Executive to show the way.

Certainly this would not be easy, and probably not cheap either. But an employer that tackled the long-hours culture would be reaching the parts that all the free hair-dos, Viagra and guitar lessons in the world will never reach.

From the *Financial Times*

FINANCIAL TIMES
World business newspaper.

D **Answer these questions about the article.**

1 How can employees at First Tennessee earn $130? What do you think they have to do to earn this money?

2 What is the problem of *work / life balance*? How are companies in the article trying to solve the problem? Have they been successful?

3 What two reasons does the writer give for employees remaining with one of these companies? Which do you think is the more likely one? Why?

4 'SAS is not content to reward employees with a mere pay cheque.'
Does this mean SAS thinks workers should:
a) have more than a salary?   **b)** be happy with a salary?

5 Which benefits in the article are *partly* paid for by the companies? What expressions are used to describe them?

E **Discuss these questions.**

1 How much should companies be involved in the lives of their employees?

2 How can businesses help to improve the balance between employees' working and leisure hours?

Vocabulary
Synonyms and word building

A Match the terms with similar meanings.

1	appraisal	**a)**	assessment
2	autonomy	**b)**	breakdown
3	burnout	**c)**	fringe benefits
4	bureaucracy	**d)**	human resources
5	homeworking	**e)**	independence
6	pay	**f)**	red tape
7	perks	**g)**	remuneration
8	personnel	**h)**	telecommuting

B Complete each sentence with the correct form of the word in bold. Sometimes you will need to use a negative form using a prefix (*un-, dis-, de-*).

1 satisfy
  a) Women are more .... with their jobs than men in many countries.
  b) Low pay and poor working conditions create .... workers.
  c) Small European countries are at the top of job .... league tables.

2 motivate
  a) What are the strongest .... factors in people's lives?
  b) Workers become .... if they work long hours for low pay.
  c) What was your .... for becoming a salesperson?

3 fulfil
  a) Becoming Department Head was the .... of a lifelong ambition.
  b) He .... his role as manager very effectively.
  c) I feel .... in my job because I am not given enough responsibility.

4 inspire
  a) Jack Welch was an .... business leader who motivated employees.
  b) He has been an .... to the new members of staff.
  c) After an .... launch, the new model quickly failed.

5 frustrate
  a) You could see the .... building up in the workforce.
  b) I find talking to him .... because he never listens to anything I say.
  c) I felt so .... with their attitude that I decided to resign.

Listening
Motivating factors

▲ Andrew Oswald

A Andrew Oswald is Professor of Economics at Warwick University, UK, and specialises in research into job satisfaction. Which groups of workers below do you think he will say are most satisfied and which are least satisfied?

women	those without job security
the highly paid	those who commute long distances
those with promotion opportunities	the Swiss
the self-employed	Americans
those who work long hours	Eastern Europeans
those in large workplaces	the Japanese

B 🎧 5.1 Listen to the interview and check the predictions you made in Exercise A.

C 🎧 5.1 Which three factors does he say are the most motivating at work?

D 🎧 5.1 Which of the statements are true and which are false, according to Andrew?

1 Job insecurity is rising.

2 The average length of a job is similar to what it was a decade or two ago.

3 Commuting time has a significant impact on job satisfaction.

Discussion
What's in a title?

A Discuss these questions.

1 To what extent do you judge someone by their job title?

2 Which would motivate you more: a pay rise or a better job title? Why?

3 Why might job titles cause problems among staff?

4 What do you think people with the following job titles do at work?
a) Digital Data Executive c) Reprographic Engineer
b) Data Storage Specialist d) Office Logistics Co-ordinator

B Read the article. Compare your answers to Exercise A with what the writer says. Does any of the article surprise you?

Job satisfaction is all in a name

By Tim Reid

Bosses who are cash-strapped but want decent typists without having to give them a pay rise would do well to call them 'Digital Data Executives'.

A report published yesterday revealed that office workers have become so 'snobby' about job titles that they would be willing to forgo an increase in salary for a more 'professional'-sounding position.

According to the study by Office Angels, the secretarial recruitment consultancy, job-title snobbery creates such envy that 90 per cent of employers and 70 per cent of employees said that it caused staff division.

Filing clerks long to be known as 'Data Storage Specialists', photocopying clerks as 'Reprographics Engineers', secretaries as 'Executaries' and post-room workers as 'Office Logistics Co-ordinators'.

The report found that 70 per cent of office workers questioned replied that they might give up a bigger pay cheque for a more 'motivational or professional' job title to make their job role seem more dynamic and inspirational. It also found that 70 per cent of staff believed the people they meet outside work instantly judged them by their job title.

From *The Times*

C Discuss these questions about words from the article.

1 If you are *cash-strapped* (lines 1–2)
a) you are short of money. b) you have a lot of money.

2 If you are *snobby* (line 11) you are very concerned
a) with possessions. b) with social status.

3 If you *forgo* something (line 13)
a) you give it up. b) you give it back.

4 If you *long to be* something (line 26)
a) you want it very much. b) you regret it very much.

D In the final part of the same article the writer mentions other job titles. Match the jobs on the left with their more professional-sounding job titles on the right. Then try to make up some job titles of your own.

1 Cleaner   a) Chief Imagination Officer
2 Telephonist   b) Voice Data Executive
3 Tea Lady   c) Environment Technician
4 Creative Assistant d) Catering Assistant

Language review
Passives

- We use the passive when we are not interested in who performs an action or it is not necessary to know: *The product has been withdrawn.*
- We often use it to describe processes and procedures because we are more interested in the process itself than who carries it out: *In the final stage of manufacture, the pills are packaged and wrapped.*
- We use the passive to write in a more formal style because it is less personal than the active. It is often used in reports, minutes and business correspondence: *It was agreed that the budget would be reviewed at the next board meeting.*

➡ page 132

A Match the news extracts a)–h) to the tenses 1–8.

1 Present simple
2 Past simple
3 Present perfect
4 Past perfect
5 Present continuous
6 Future simple
7 Modal verbs with passives
8 Passive infinitives

a) The report says supervisors *should be trained* to manage telecommuters and should define the hours and tasks expected of them.
b) Those least happy with their work / life balance were the ones who felt they *had been forced* to choose between work and home.
c) Campaigners for paternity leave say it *is* particularly *needed* in the UK where men work the longest hours in the EU.
d) Half-term *is being seen* as an increasingly attractive break by working parents in their late 30s and early 40s.
e) A survey of workers in 13 industrialised countries found the desire for a decent work / life balance *was rated* more highly than a good salary.
f) It *used to be argued* that women had not achieved pay equality because discrimination kept them in more junior jobs.
g) Efforts to encourage more women to return to work after having children *will be hampered* if employers force staff to stick to rigid hours and limit their time off.
h) Some smaller businesses *have been founded* on the principle that work / life balance makes for commercial success.

B Complete the extract below with passive forms of the verbs in brackets.

Several surveys ....[1] (conduct) recently concerning the relationship between work and play. According to psychologists, activities are more likely to ....[2] (perceive) as play – and therefore attractive – rather than work – and therefore unattractive – if they ....[3] (enter) into voluntarily. In one experiment, for example, volunteers ....[4] (give) a problem-solving game to perform: some ....[5] (pay) to perform the game and some were not. Those who ....[6] (pay) spent less free time performing than those for whom the only motivation was the pleasure of the game. Thus, motivation to play springs from within and the readiness to perform activities ....[7] (reduce) by external rewards.

C Read the notes on page 43 for two sections of a report on a proposed Employee Incentive Scheme. Then write sentences, using the passive, to include in the report. For example, *Questionnaires were distributed to all departments.*

PROCEDURE:
• Distribute questionnaires: all depts
• Interview managers
• Canvass sample of workers
• Consult data on similar schemes

RECOMMENDATIONS:
• Introduce new scheme from 1 Jan
• Adopt system of team bonuses
• Investigate other incentives besides financial
• Carry out further research into share option scheme
• Maintain existing range of fringe benefits

Skills
Handling difficult situations

A For each of the situations 1–8 choose an appropriate response a)–h).

1 Someone asks about a colleague who's been fired.
2 You are invited out to dinner when you don't really want to go.
3 A colleague tells you some very bad news about themselves.
4 You arrive late for a meeting.
5 You recognise someone but you can't recall their name.
6 You want to end a conversation at a business reception.
7 You want someone to stop smoking in a no-smoking area.
8 You spill coffee over a client's desk at a meeting.

a) 'Excuse me. I'm afraid smoking isn't allowed here.'
b) 'I'm sorry but there's someone over there that I have to talk to.'
c) 'How clumsy of me. I'm really sorry.'
d) 'I'm terribly sorry to hear that.'
e) 'I'm so sorry. The traffic was a nightmare.'
f) 'I know we've met before but I'm afraid I can't remember the name.'
g) 'That's really kind of you but I'm exhausted after the flight.'
h) 'I'm afraid he left the company last month.'

B 🎧 5.2 Listen to these four conversations. In each case, match what the second speaker says to one of these headings.

- Saying 'no' politely
- Apologising
- Showing sympathy
- Ending a conversation

C 🎧 5.2 Listen again. Add one expression from each conversation under an appropriate heading in the Useful language box.

D Discuss what you would do and say in these difficult situations.

1 Your colleague applied for a promotion but didn't get it.
2 You borrowed a colleague's mobile phone but now it's stopped working.
3 You invite a client for a meal and they ask if they can bring a friend. You see this as a business rather than a social occasion.
4 You're staying at a hotel that your host is paying for. It is uncomfortable and you want to move. Your host asks, 'How do you like the hotel?'

Useful language

Saying 'no' politely
It's very kind / nice of you, but …
I'm very sorry, but …

Apologising
I must apologise …
I'm terribly sorry, but …

Showing sympathy
I quite understand …
I know how you feel …

Ending a conversation
Sorry, I really must be off …
Please excuse me, I really have to leave …

Office attraction

Background

Karl Jansen, Managing Director at London-based Crawford PLC, has always believed that employees perform better in a relaxed working atmosphere. The staff rule book is slim and he'd like to keep it that way. However, recent events have made him wonder whether the company culture has become a little too casual. It could be because staff are working later at night and at weekends, or because fierce competition is causing more stress. Whatever the reason, close relationships between colleagues are definitely becoming more common.

Memo	**URGENT AND CONFIDENTIAL**
From	Karl Jansen, Managing Director
To	Jenny Cunningham, Human Resources Director
Date	30 June

Policy on office relationships

I'm extremely concerned about the growing number of close relationships between members of staff. This is having a very bad effect on both performance and morale.

As you know, there have been three cases recently where employees have developed personal relationships which seriously affected both their own performance and their colleagues'. Furthermore, I've heard this morning that one of the individuals concerned is threatening the company with legal action.

As a result, I'd like the Human Resources Department to review in detail each of the three cases and advise how to proceed. These are:

1 The appointment of Tania Jordan
2 The re-assignment of John Goodman
3 Complaints against Derek Hartman

The details

1 Appointment of Tania Jordan

A few months ago, Karl and two other directors, Marcus Ball and Julia Kovacs, appointed a new manager. There were three excellent candidates. Finally Tania Jordan was selected – mainly because Marcus had argued strongly in her favour. Karl discovered later that she and Marcus had started living together. When Karl told him he should have withdrawn from the selection process, Marcus said angrily, 'Listen, I didn't know her so well at the time. In any case, it's my private life. I supported Tania because she was the best person for the job.'

Karl discussed the matter with Jenny. They decided to take no further action.

2 Re-assignment of John Goodman

A few weeks later, a problem arose in the Finance Department. The Financial Director and her ambitious deputy, John Goodman, had formed a very close relationship. Unfortunately, the relationship went sour and they had bitter rows in public. Because of these problems, serious mistakes were made in the annual report and the morale of the whole department was affected.

Karl and the other directors decided to move John to another department. However, John's new position is less challenging with little opportunity for promotion. He believes he's been very badly treated by the management and is threatening to take his case to an industrial tribunal.

3 Complaints against Derek Hartman

A week ago, a part-time employee in the General Office, Claudia Northcott, e-mailed Karl asking for a private meeting with him. When they met, he found out that she was representing all the part-time staff in the department. According to her, the Office Manager, Derek Hartman, is showing favouritism towards one of his staff, Petra Palmer, and this is upsetting everyone in the office. Karl asked for more details.

🎧 **5.3** Listen to an extract from their conversation.

Specific questions

Later on in his memo, Karl asked Jenny and her team to consider the following questions.

1 Did we make the right decisions concerning Marcus Ball and John Goodman? What further action, if any, should we take in each case?

2 If the accusation against Derek Hartman is true, what action should we take?

3 Should the company have a written policy on close relationships at work? If so, what should be the main guidelines for staff? What sanctions should there be for staff who don't follow the guidelines?

4 How can we avoid someone gaining an unfair advantage from having a close relationship with another member of staff? Are there any specific examples of bad practice that could be written into the policy document?

Task

You are members of the Human Resources Department at Crawford PLC. Discuss the questions in Karl's memo and agree what action to take. One of you should take the role of Jenny and chair the meeting.

Writing

As a member of the Human Resources Department, write a set of guidelines which could be used as a discussion document at the next board meeting.

➡ *Writing file* page 142

OVERVIEW ▼

☐ **Vocabulary**
Describing risk

☐ **Listening**
Managing risk

☐ **Reading**
Risks from globalisation

☐ **Language Review**
Intensifying adverbs

☐ **Skills**
Reaching agreement

☐ **Case study**
A risky business

❝ *The policy of being too cautious is the greatest risk of all.* ❞
Jarwaharlal Nehru (1899–1964), India's first Prime Minister

Starting up

A Are you a risk-taker? What risks have you taken?

B Which item in each of the categories below carries the most risk? Explain why.

Travel	Lifestyle	Investment
car	drinking alcohol	foreign currency
plane	poor diet	property
train	smoking	stocks and shares

C What risks do businesses face? Note down three types.

D 🎧 6.1 Allan Smith is an expert in risk management. He is talking about the types of risks faced by businesses. Listen to the first part of the interview and note down the risks he mentions. Compare them with the list you made in Exercise C.

Vocabulary
Describing risk

A Put the verbs in the box under the most appropriate headings.

calculate	eliminate	encounter	estimate	face
foresee	minimise	prioritise	reduce	spread

Predict	Meet	Assess	Manage
		calculate	

B Match these halves of sentences from newspaper extracts.

1	Internet businesses ...	a)	risks involved when sending staff to work in dangerous locations.
2	We can reduce risk ...	b)	in order to advise insurance companies.
3	Trying to minimise risk ...	c)	involved in setting up a new business.
4	It is impossible to ...	d)	eliminate all risk when entering a new market.
5	It is difficult to foresee the risks ...	e)	face increasing risks of running out of money.
6	Actuaries calculate risk ...	f)	by spreading our lending to more businesses.
7	It's important to consider the ...	g)	is an important part of business strategy.

C The following adjectives can be used with the word *risk*. Which describe a high level of risk? Which describe a low level?

faint	great	huge	low
negligible	remote	serious	significant
slight	substantial	terrible	tremendous

D In pairs, talk about the risks facing one of the following:
a) your company / institution
b) your city / town
c) your country.

▲ Allan Smith

Listening
Managing risk

A 🎧 6.2 Listen to the second part of the interview with Allan Smith and answer these questions.

1 Are the statements below true or false?
   a) In its traditional sense, risk means the threat of harm, injury or loss.
   b) Change can present risks, but also opportunities for growth and profit-making.
   c) Businesses should avoid taking risks at the end of the day.

2 Allan mentions four types of risk. What does he say about each type?

B 🎧 6.3 Listen to the next part of the interview. What does Allan say about the following points?

1 the information that companies have about risk
2 the management of risk
3 communication lines

C 🎧 6.4 Listen to the final part of the interview. What mistakes were made? What were the results?

Reading

Risks from globalisation

A **Discuss these questions.**

1 Which areas of the world are considered to be the riskiest to do business in, do you think? Why?

2 Predict whether business people, according to the article on page 49, think risk is increasing in
   a) Russia   **b)** The Middle East   **c)** North Africa   **d)** Latin America

B **Match these words from the article with their meanings.**

1	volatile	**a)**	force someone to give you money by threatening them
2	fraud	**b)**	not moving, changing, or developing
3	unprecedented	**c)**	working hard to achieve changes in the way companies operate
4	sanctions	**d)**	never having happened before
5	extortion	**e)**	changing quickly and suddenly
6	activism	**f)**	laws stopping trade with another country as a way of forcing political changes
7	static	**g)**	illegally getting money from a person or organisation

C **Now scan the article quickly to check your predictions in Exercise A.**

D **What two factors have contributed significantly to the increased risk for international business, according to the article?**

E **Find all the risks that the article mentions. List them under the appropriate headings in the table below.**

a) personal security risk	c) political risk
b) reputational risk	**d) financial risk**

F **Choose three successful companies. Discuss what risks they face. How can they deal with them?**

Globalisation generates risks for business

INTERNATIONAL businesses believe they are not fully prepared to handle a growing number of threats in an increasingly volatile global marketplace, according to a report published by leading business risk consultancy Control Risks Group.

According to the company's annual assessment of risks facing international business, globalisation and the development of communications technologies have precipitated significant concerns among executives concerning risks, including organised crime, terrorism, internal fraud, corruption and direct action by pressure groups. Globalisation has also exacerbated many pre-existing, low-probability, high-impact risks, such as kidnappings.

These concerns were revealed through a business survey, conducted by the Industrial Research Bureau, of US and European companies about attitudes to risk and risk management among international business development directors.

'Although executives see globalisation as a driving force behind unprecedented opportunities internationally, there is real apprehension about a plethora of risks that may stand in their way,' according to Richard Fenning, Director of Control Risks New York, who released the report at a press conference today in

Washington DC. 'Anything from international sanctions, terrorism and currency devaluation, to extortion and kidnapping.'

According to the survey, a significant majority (68%) of those US executives polled believe that globalisation generates more risk for investors. Additionally, the survey indicated that businesses expect to be increasingly forced to address the challenge of reputational risks. Business development executives are firmly placing consumer activism, corruption, and human rights on their agendas.

The survey revealed shareholder action as the most critical reputational risk; kidnap as the most significant security risk; and international sanctions as the foremost political risk. Most respondents of the survey considered risks to be increasing in Russia and the former Soviet Union, with sophisticated fraud, corruption and organised crime as the driving factors. Interestingly, 76% of those polled considered the risks to be static or decreasing in the Middle East; 59% of respondents had the same feeling about North Africa; and 67% held a similar view about Latin America (excluding Brazil) where – with some clear exceptions – political and economic issues have replaced security as the prime source of risk over the past decade.

'Although traditional risks, such as political and extremist terrorism, are decreasing in incidence – yet not impact – problems such as organised and petty crime are likely to present a specific and harder range of risks than previously,' said Martin Stone, Head of Research for Control Risks.

From *PR Newswire*

Language review
Intensifying adverbs

Complete the rules.
- We can use adverbs to intensify the meaning of adjectives:
  *International businesses believe they are not **fully prepared** to handle a growing number of threats in an **increasingly volatile** global marketplace.*
- Most adverbs are formed by adding .... to the adjective.
- For adjectives ending in *-ic,* for example *dramatic* or *economic,* add ....

 page 132

A Complete the table below with adverbs from the box.

> a bit   entirely   exceptionally   extremely   fairly
> highly   increasingly   moderately   quite   rather
> reasonably   slightly   somewhat   totally   very

Intensifying adverbs		
weak	moderate	strong
a bit		

B Complete these dialogues with a suitable adverb.

1 'What were your results like last year?'
  '............. good. We increased profits by over 40%.'

2 'How was the launch of your new product?'
  '............. successful. We've been flooded with orders ever since.'

3 'Do you really think we should try to enter that new market?'
  'It's .... risky but on balance I think we should go ahead.'

4 'What did you think of the presentation?'
  'It was .... useless. Most of the audience lost interest after five minutes.'

5 'Are you confident about those sales projections?'
  '............. confident, although it's going to be tough.'

C Think of situations where you could use the phrases below.
Make six sentences.

incredibly well-prepared	deeply disappointed
absolutely awful	totally unrealistic
particularly liked	brilliantly executed
severely criticised	superbly presented
badly misjudged	thoroughly enjoyed

Skills
Reaching agreement

A 🎧 **6.5 Following the brainstorming meeting in Unit 2 International marketing (page 19), the team meets again to finalise their plans for the launch of the website. Listen to the authentic meeting and complete the table.**

Ideas	Approved Yes/No	Comments
On-line promotion		
TV advertising		
Sponsorship		
Advertisements in journals		
Using established contacts		
Newspapers / magazines		

B **Match the expressions below from the meeting to the appropriate heading in the Useful language box. (Some can be put under more than one heading.) Use the Audio script on pages 160 and 161 to check the context of each expression.**

1 ... I'm not sure if I agree with that.
2 I don't think we can ...
3 ... I would say it's really risky ...
4 OK.
5 Yes, I would agree with that.
6 Yeah. I think that's important ...
7 ... it's very important that we use the contacts ...
8 Could we combine the two maybe?
9 I just think ...
10 ... I think we've all agreed ...

C **Work in groups of three. Read the information below. Then role play the meeting.**

You are managers in a mobile phone company, Speakeasy Ltd. based in San Diego, California. The company wishes to send two executives to set up a branch office overseas. However, the location chosen is politically very unstable and there has been some terrorist activity in the area recently. Hold a meeting to decide:

a) whether to send the two executives to the area

b) if so, how to reduce the risks to which they will be exposed.

Manager A turn to page 146.
Manager B turn to page 148.
Manager C turn to page 152.

Useful language

Asking for opinions
Does anybody have any strong feelings about ...?

Giving opinions
Well, unfortunately, I think we'll probably have to ...

Disagreeing
Well hold on ...

Agreeing
I think I'd agree with you there ...

Making suggestions
What about if we ...?

Emphasising
I keep going on about this, but ...

Summarising
Can I just clarify that ...

A risky business

CASE STUDY

Background

Hi-Style, a family-owned company based in Manchester, makes fashionwear for 18- to 30-year-olds. Its branded merchandise, ETC, is sold throughout Western Europe. The company's image is of fashionable clothing at competitive prices. However, its core products – jeans and trainers – are losing appeal and the company is struggling in a very competitive market.

Zelal Sulen, the daughter of Hi-Style's founder, took over as Managing Director when her father retired last year. Zelal realises that Hi-Style is out of touch with its target consumers and is losing direction. Three months ago she appointed the management consultants, City Associates, to advise her on how to improve profits.

Hi-Style: Financial information

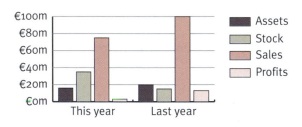

Task

You work for City Associates. Your firm has identified four options with different risks. Zelal can afford to choose one option. She has asked you to give your preferred choice and recommend a second choice. For each option, discuss these questions in small groups.

1 What are the option's strengths and weaknesses?
2 What opportunities does it offer Hi-Style?
3 How about the risks – for example, financial, legal, operational?
4 What will be the likely effect on Hi-Style's current business?
5 How much will the option cost?

Writing

You are the head of City Associates. Write a report to Zelal Sulen briefly analysing the four options. Make recommendations and give the reasons for your first and second choices.

⮕ *Writing file pages 144 and 145*

Option 1: Organic growth
Hi-Style could allocate up to €10m to new investment in the business. For example, it could:

• improve distribution and sales through an exclusive agreement with a major retailer

• launch new product ranges with major advertising campaigns

• improve its image by employing brand development consultants

• hire a top retailing executive to run the business

• commission City Associates to do a thorough review of all Hi-Style's activities.

Option 2: Acquisition of Smartwear Ltd

Based in Birmingham, Smartwear makes work clothes such as uniforms for bank staff and flight attendants. It has good sales agents in Europe and Asia, and strong connections with Indian manufacturers. It has a very creative design department with exciting new ideas.

Smartwear made deliveries worth €2m last month to two new customers in the Far East. Unfortunately, both have just gone into liquidation and the stock has disappeared. There has also been bad press about working conditions in overseas factories.

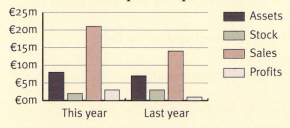

Smartwear Ltd. Acquisition price: € 10m

Option 3: Acquisition of Tan Clothing Company

Tan Clothing Company is a successful family-owned business based in the Far East. Because of connections with its country's military rulers, it has regular orders of uniforms and footwear for the armed forces. It owns a large factory which is working 30% below capacity. Recently there has been political unrest but, at present, the situation is under control. However, the three Tan family members disagree as to who owns the company and who should run it, and have threatened each other with legal action.

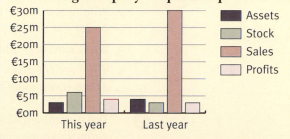

Tan Clothing Company. Acquisition price: € 10m

Option 4: Research and Development

A recent graduate in Textile Design, Hi-Style's Director of Research and Development wants to greatly increase its debt to finance work on materials technology. Options include:

- 'take anywhere' crushproof material you can wear straight out of a suitcase
- clothes which can alter their colour
- exceptionally warm clothing for cold climates.

She has identified five areas of research which could transform the company and give it a 'cutting edge' image. The research would cost € 10m– € 12m.

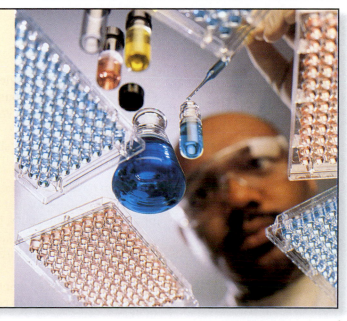

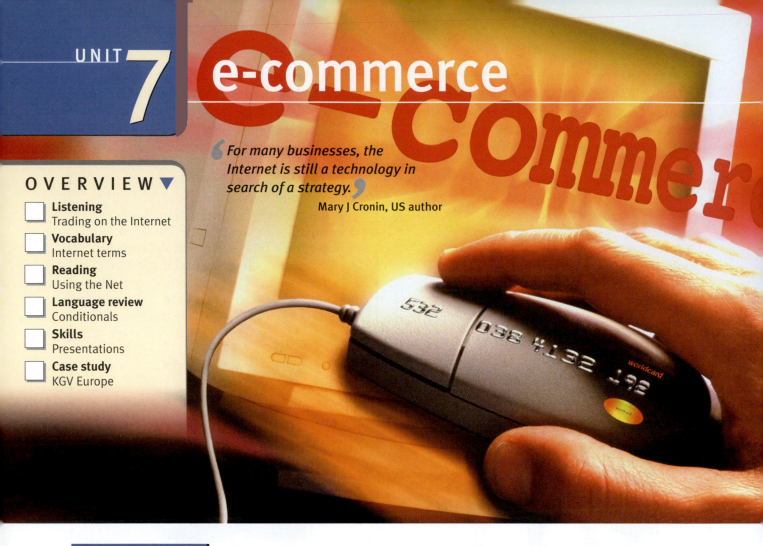

UNIT 7 e-commerce

OVERVIEW ▼

Listening
Trading on the Internet

Vocabulary
Internet terms

Reading
Using the Net

Language review
Conditionals

Skills
Presentations

Case study
KGV Europe

For many businesses, the Internet is still a technology in search of a strategy.
Mary J Cronin, US author

Starting up

A **Discuss these questions.**

1 Do you use the Internet? If so, what do you use it for?

2 What goods or services have you bought over the Net? What would you prefer not to buy over the Net?

3 What kind of products or services are best sold on the Net?

4 What are the risks of e-commerce for
   a) the companies involved?   **b)** their customers?

B 'The e-commerce revolution will be as significant as the industrial revolution or perhaps even more so ...'

Adam Rhodes, e-commerce entrepreneur

Do you agree?

Listening
Trading on the Internet

A 7.1 **Listen to an interview with Adam Rhodes, Managing Director of EFDEX, an e-commerce business in Reading, UK. He begins by explaining what his company does. What is EFDEX and what service does it provide?**

B 7.1 **Complete Adam's summary of the three key success factors for an e-commerce business.**

'But if you have those three things: a ....[1] – not just a ....[2] that is looking for a business home, but a business idea that uses technology – a ....[3] and the ....[4] – then those will be the three most important ingredients.'

C 7.1 **Adam is asked whether there are any 'downsides' to e-commerce. What is the one possible concern that he mentions?**

Vocabulary
Internet terms

A We often use the words below to talk about e-commerce. Check that you understand their meaning. Use a good dictionary to help you.

browse	directories	hits	key word	locate	Net
on-line	search	search engines	site	surfers	traffic

B *Topsite* is a service that helps companies improve their e-commerce business. Use the words above to complete this promotional page from its website.

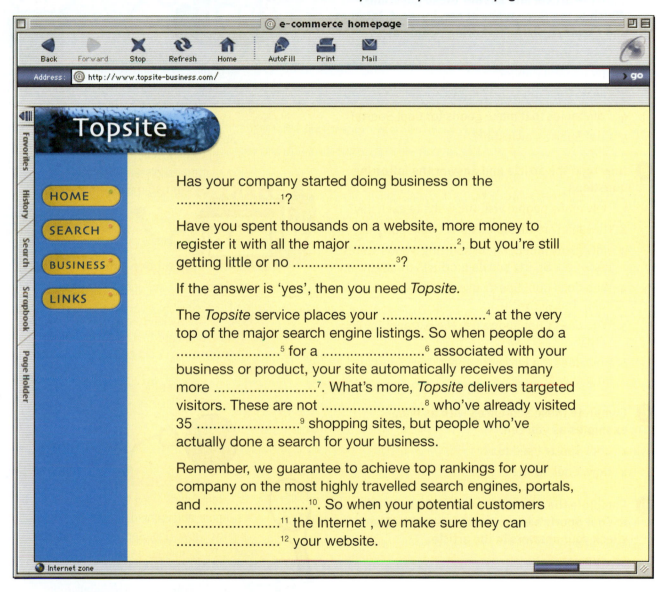

Has your company started doing business on the ....[1]?

Have you spent thousands on a website, more money to register it with all the major ....[2], but you're still getting little or no ....[3]?

If the answer is 'yes', then you need *Topsite*.

The *Topsite* service places your ....[4] at the very top of the major search engine listings. So when people do a ....[5] for a ....[6] associated with your business or product, your site automatically receives many more ....[7]. What's more, *Topsite* delivers targeted visitors. These are not ....[8] who've already visited 35 ....[9] shopping sites, but people who've actually done a search for your business.

Remember, we guarantee to achieve top rankings for your company on the most highly travelled search engines, portals, and ....[10]. So when your potential customers ....[11] the Internet , we make sure they can ....[12] your website.

C Complete the beginnings of sentences below with the appropriate endings.

1 An intranet operates

2 The Internet operates

3 An extranet operates

a) outside a company or organisation and is open to the public.

b) inside a company or organisation.

c) outside a company or organisation, but is not open to the public.

Reading
Using the Net

A Cool Sportz is a sporting goods retailer. It makes its own brand products as well as buying in products from others manufacturers. It sells both types of goods through its own chain of stores and through a network of independent outlets.

Scan the article and answer these questions. Which of the three types of net, intranet, Internet and extranet, do the following people use?

1 Cool Sportz's lawyers?

2 The general public?

3 Owners of Cool Sportz stores?

4 Companies that make goods for Cool Sportz?

5 Cool Sportz's own staff?

B Now read the article and answer the following questions.

1 How many people visit the website each day?

2 How many retail stores does Cool Sportz have?

3 How many independent sporting-goods stores does Cool Sportz sell its products through?

4 Who does Cool Sportz use the intranet to communicate with?

5 Who does Cool Sportz use the extranet for links with?

6 How does the intranet benefit Cool Sportz employees?

C Complete these sentences with as many examples as you can.

1 Cool Sportz used to ...

2 Now, Cool Sportz ...

D Complete the words below to make key players in Cool Sportz's e-commerce operation. Then check your answers in the article.

1 sup _ _ _ _ _

2 manu _ _ _ _ _ _ _ _

3 ret _ _ _ _ _

4 part _ _ _

5 cons _ _ _ _

6 merch _ _ _

7 emp _ _ _ _ _

8 buy _ _

9 dist _ _ _ _ _ _ _

10 desi _ _ _ _

E What are the advantages and disadvantages of Cool Sportz's e-commerce strategy for some of the groups you identified in Exercise D above?

RETAIL STORE

DISTRIBUTORS

Cool Sportz sells its CoolWear products through 2,500 independent sporting-goods stores around the country. Distributors who supply these shops use Cool Sportz's extranet to check on their commissions and read up on new merchandise-marketing programmes.

MART

MANUFACTURING

For years, Cool Sportz has placed orders with contract manufacturers using Electronic Data Interchange, or EDI, an old software standard that is neither cheap nor flexible. Now, Cool Sportz saves money by moving some of these orders over the Internet.

PURCHASING

Cool Sportz used to order shoes, ski gear and camping goods by phone and fax. Now, Cool Sportz saves time and money by sending orders electronically over the Internet. Some suppliers let Cool Sportz enter their private networks to place orders.

12

LIQUIDATION

When products don't sell, Cool Sportz auctions them through an on-line brokerage. The company posts info about the goods and a minimum price. Potential buyers enter bids, and Cool Sportz ships the goods to the winning bidder.

HOW A MYTHICAL MERCHANT USES THREE AVENUES OF THE NET FOR E-COMMERCE

OFFICE SUPPLIES

To centralise purchasing of office supplies, Cool Sportz lets managers in retail stores requisition everything from diskettes to display racks via their PCs. The orders are sent over the extranet from Cool Sportz to suppliers, who deliver directly to the stores.

Cool Sportz sits at the centre of a web of partners, all connected over the Internet using open software standards. Cool Sportz has a private company intranet to communicate with branch stores and employees in remote offices. A secure extranet links Cool Sportz to its contract manufacturers, suppliers, independent retailers, distributors and partners such as its law firm and ad agency.

PRODUCT DESIGN

Cool Sportz enlists freelance designers to create CoolWear products. The designers exchange drawings with Cool Sportz over the extranet. Then Cool Sportz's staff and designers can mark them up while talking together live over the Net.

INTRANET

RETAIL STORES

Cool Sportz collects sales data from its 1,200 retail stores around the country and fills hundreds of product reorders electronically. All stores are on the Cool Sportz intranet, a secure link that traverses the Internet. Cool Sportz also 'pushes' info on promotions and discounts to its stores.

PARTNERS

To help efficiency, Cool Sportz requires its law firm, accounting firm and ad agency to belong to the corporate extranet. This ensures privacy and security for e-mail and electronic files. Cool Sportz's marketers brainstorm over the Net with the ad agency.

EMPLOYEES

Instead of phoning the Human Resources department, Cool Sportz staff refer to an electronic version of the employee handbook on the company intranet. And they use a Java-based application to change their investment and health-care options and calculate their retirement benefits. Expense reports filed via the intranet are paid within 48 hours.

BANKING

While awaiting standards for Net-based electronic banking, Cool Sportz sends invoices by secure e-mail, which reduces paperwork and speeds up payment. The CFO likes collecting bills faster, but is less eager to see accounts payable go electronic.

C O O L S P O R T Z

www.coolsportz.com

EXTRANET

INTERNET

RETAIL STORE

CONSUMERS

Cool Sportz's website is promoted in TV ads, and gets thousands of hits a day. From surveys on its site, Cool Sportz collects demographic data. And it advises registered surfers on sales and new products.

RETAIL STORE

From *Business Week*

Language review
Conditionals

There are many different types of conditional sentence:

- First conditional: *If we get that designer, we'll have a winning team.*
- Second conditional: *If we relaunched our website, we'd get better results.*
- Third conditional: *If we'd prepared properly, we wouldn't have lost the contract.*
- Zero conditional: *When markets crash, everyone suffers.*

The following are also examples of conditional sentences:

- *Lose that password and we'll never be able to access that file again.*
- *Tell us what you need to get the job done and you'll have it.*
- *Should you need any further information, please contact our helpline.*
- *Had the market conditions been better, the share offer would have been a success.*
- *Given time, our factory can meet all those orders.*

 page 133

A Match sentences 1–12 to the six headings below.

| promise | invitation / request | speculating about the future |
| bargaining | reflecting on the past | advice / warning / threat |

1 They would've gone bust if they'd taken his advice.
2 If I were you, I'd redesign your website.
3 We'll deliver within 24 hours if you order on-line.
4 We'll be able to expand if they come up with the finance.
5 If you reduced your price by 8%, we'd increase our order substantially.
6 Your money back if not 100% satisfied.
7 If we go on-line our overheads will fall.
8 If you would like to apply, call Human Resources on 020 7753 3420.
9 If you order by the end of the month we can give you a discount.
10 I wouldn't do that if I were you.
11 If we'd had a better website, we'd have attracted more customers.
12 I would be grateful if you would advise your staff as soon as possible.

B Decide whether each of the situations below is a) *likely* or b) *unlikely* to happen to you. Then, tell your partner what you will or would do.

1 You win the lottery.
2 Your computer gets a virus.
3 Somebody offers you a bribe.
4 You have to give a presentation in English.
5 You have to entertain someone important.
6 Your firm is taken over by a competitor.

C Discuss what went wrong in the following situation. Use the notes in the box. For example, *If they'd set up the site properly, they wouldn't have had so many complaints.*

ClickShop.com is in the Internet shopping business. In order to save money when it redesigned its website six months ago, it decided not to employ a specialist design company. Instead, the work was done by some of its own employees who had limited experience. Technical problems have now led to customer complaints, which have impacted on sales.

- set up site properly
- use an expert
- allocate a bigger budget
- listen to customer feedback
- plan carefully
- not try to cut corners
- recognise problems earlier
- do more research

Skills
Presentations

▲ Roger Marris

A 🎧 **7.2** Roger Marris, Head of Business Development at Smarterwork – a London-based Internet company – is giving a presentation to some potential customers. In these two extracts he describes the company and the services it offers. Listen to the first extract and answer these questions.

1 What service does Smarterwork offer?
2 What do these figures refer to? **a)** 14 **b)** 60,000 **c)** 90
3 Who are its two types of users?

B 🎧 **7.3** Listen to the second extract and complete the stages in the process.

- The client posts a project.
- Suppliers visit the site and make bids.
- ....
- ....
- The client transfers the fee to a holding account.
- ....
- The task gets completed and the client signs off the work.
- ....
- Smarterwork takes a commission.

C 🎧 **7.2** Listen again to the first extract.

1 Which of the following does Roger do at the start of his presentation?
   a) introduce himself   **c)** tell a story
   b) greet the audience   **d)** ask a question
2 Complete what Roger says at the start of his presentation.

   This morning, ...¹ talk to you about
   Smarterwork. I'm going to ....² an overview of
   Smarterwork, then ....³ you about our two
   types of users and finally ....⁴ how it all works.
   Feel free to ask any questions you like as we go along.

D 🎧 **7.3** Listen again to the second extract. Note down the language Roger uses to introduce the stages in the process. For example, *Firstly* ...

E Match these expressions from the presentation to headings in the Useful language box.

1 Can you just raise your hands?
2 The great thing about the Internet is ...
3 What that means is ...
4 Right. The next thing I'd like to do is ...
5 As you can see, it outlines the steps involved.

Useful language

Commenting
I think that's interesting because ...

Emphasising
I'd just like to highlight ...

Changing subject
OK, I'll now move on to ...

Referring to visuals
Let's look at the chart.

Involving the audience
OK, what is Smarterwork?

F Prepare a three-minute presentation on a subject of your choice. For example, a product or service, your organisation or institution, or a city you know well.

CASE STUDY

KGV Europe

Background

KGV is a traditional high-street music retailer. Based in Amsterdam, it has 12 stores in the Netherlands, three of which are megastores. Some years ago, it expanded into the rest of Europe and now owns 65 stores – eight of these are megastores.

The company is at present going through a difficult period. Over the last three years, profits have steadily fallen, from €450m to €290m. The megastores' sales have risen by 8%, accounting for 55% of the company's turnover, but the increased revenue has been achieved only by heavy expenditure on advertising and promotion. Fierce competition, a narrow product range and a lack of innovation are some of the reasons for KGV's poor performance. The management are concerned, especially, that they are not exploiting the opportunities offered by selling through the Internet.

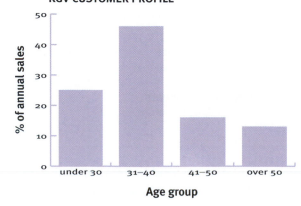

KGV CUSTOMER PROFILE

% of annual sales vs Age group (under 30, 31–40, 41–50, over 50)

Market study

A study by KGV's Marketing Department was recently carried out and it produced the following findings:

1 It is estimated that, in five years' time, 50% of all music products will be bought through the Internet.

2 65% of consumers under the age of 30 prefer to do their shopping on the Internet.

3 KGV's customers would like stores to provide a wider product range (see chart 1).

4 Average spending per month in KGV's medium-sized stores is highest among the 41–60 age group (see chart 2).

5 Spending on music products by the over 60 age group will increase significantly in the next ten years in Europe.

6 The various age groups have clear preferences as to the type of music they enjoy and purchase (see chart 3).

7.4 Listen to a conversation between Michael Johnson, a director of KGV, and Hanna Driessen, the recently appointed Financial Director of the company. They are discussing the company's strategy before a forthcoming management meeting about KGV's future. Make short notes on the opinions they express.

CHART 1: Preferences for additional products / services (% of respondents for each category)

	Age 18–40	Age 41 +
spoken word (talking books)	4	44
computer games	62	15
holiday information	35	48
computer software	58	32
banking services	25	12
concert tickets	70	75

CHART 2: Average spending per month in a medium-sized store

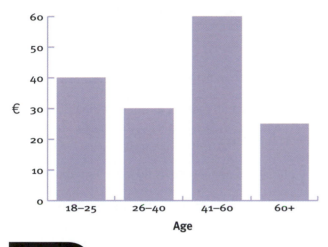

CHART 3: Preferences of consumers for music products

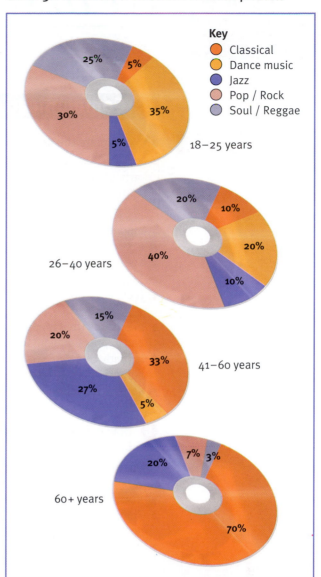

Key
- Classical
- Dance music
- Jazz
- Pop / Rock
- Soul / Reggae

18–25 years

26–40 years

41–60 years

60+ years

Task

You are a member of KGV's management. Hold a meeting with other managers and discuss these agenda items. Decide what action KGV should take concerning their future strategy.

1 Should KGV keep some of their stores but sell at least 50% of their goods through the Internet?
2 Should they close all their stores and offer a total on-line service? If so:
   a) what risks would be involved?
   b) how would the costs of the business change?
   c) what organisational changes would the company have to make?
3 Should KGV stay as it is, but follow Hanna's advice:
   a) outsource advertising and promotion
   b) hire a consultant to look at the product mix
   c) consider targeting new segments of the market.
4 What are the consequences of the chosen strategy? How can the problems be minimised?

Writing

You are the Managing Director of KGV. Write a memo to a director of the company who was unable to attend the management meeting. In the memo, summarise the discussion and decisions of the meeting and ask the director for his/her comments.

 Writing file page 140

Revision

1 Communication

Adjectives

A Complete the definitions with adjectives from the box.

articulate	coherent	eloquent	fluent	hesitant
inhibited	lucid	persuasive	responsive	succinct

Someone who
1 is good at persuading others is ....
2 speaks in a way that is logical and without contradictions is ...., ... and ....
3 feels shy about speaking and is worried about the effect of what they might say is .... and ....
4 expresses their ideas briefly and to the point is ....
5 can express difficult ideas clearly is ....
6 is ready to act in a useful or helpful way and openly shows their feelings about something is ....
7 speaks without hesitating, or speaks a foreign language without difficulty, is ....

B Now use some of these adjectives to complete the sentences below. Choose the best alternative from the words in brackets.

1 Customers can ring freephone numbers from any of the nine European countries in which Gateway trades. They are answered in Dublin by a native or (*articulate / fluent / persuasive*) speaker.
2 They are the literate, (*articulate / coherent / succinct*), middle-class professionals such as lawyers, academics, politicians and senior civil servants.
3 If you remember the 1960s, they say, you weren't there. Anita Pallenberg famously was there, but her recollections are amazingly detailed and (*hesitant / lucid / responsive*).
4 If you feel (*coherent / eloquent / inhibited*) in the way you move and express yourself, going to a workshop with a trained dance therapist may provide the help you need.
5 Many chapters conclude with useful sources of further information, and there is even a (*eloquent / lucid / succinct*) but comprehensive glossary.
6 The government should be more (*articulate / fluent / responsive*) to people and less preoccupied with special interest groups.

Problem solving

Two weeks ago, you ordered some books over the Internet from books-to-you.com. They were supposed to be delivered within 48 hours.
Your credit card has been debited, but the books have not arrived.
You have phoned books-to-you three times, but no one answered the phone.

1 Write an e-mail to books-to-you.com to complain and ask what they are going to do about the problem.
2 You are the Customer Services Manager at books-to-you.com. Reply to the e-mail, apologising and saying what you are going to do.

2 International marketing

Reading

Karen Hughes is Marketing Director at a multinational consumer electronics firm. Choose the correct word from the list below to complete what she says.

We are one of the world's ....[1] in consumer electronics, introducing new types of product that did not exist previously. However, where we are not first to the market with a new product-type, we look at the market ....[2]. If it looks good, we develop our own versions of the product. We usually test our offerings in focus ....[3] before ....[4] them on to the market, or, if there's not much time, we may just launch them, monitor market reaction and then modify them accordingly. We try to identify the different market ....[5]: groups of end-users with particular characteristics. We look at the marketing ....[6]. This includes the best way of distributing the product, deciding which ....[7] and retail ....[8] we are going to use. In the early stages, when the market is growing fast, it can be quite ....[9]: there are a lot of competitors, and the 'rules of the game' are not yet established. Later, when everyone who is going to buy the product has bought it, and the market is essentially one of replacement, there are usually fewer competitors and conditions are more ....[10]. Of course, we try to be among these surviving companies, preferably number one or number two in the market.

	a)	b)	c)	d)
1	beginners	pioneers	premiers	starters
2	possible	potency	potential	power
3	circles	classes	gatherings	groups
4	casting	lancing	releasing	throwing
5	sects	segments	selections	sets
6	combination	miscellany	mixture	mix
7	immediacies	intermediaries	intermediates	intermezzos
8	outcomes	outflows	outlets	outpourings
9	variety	various	vicarious	volatile
10	stability	stable	static	stationary

Writing

You work for the public relations agency that is launching the Lynx, a new upmarket saloon car for the global market. You have been asked to write a report of 150–200 words that will be used as the basis for a discussion with the client about the launch.

Your report should include:
- how the car will be positioned in relation to other luxury saloon cars
- the location for launching the car
- the location for the film shoot for the television advertising campaign
- film stars, sporting personalities or other celebrities to be present at the launch and used in advertising
- unusual ways of impressing tired journalists from the national press and the motoring press: new types of gifts, information packs, etc.
- other promotional activities.

3 Building relationships

Reading

Read the cultural advice. To which culture does each sentence 1–7 refer?

a) Here, a brief handshake is the usual greeting. People find hugging and kissing very embarrassing and they never occur. Small talk is brief. Don't expect to spend a long time over meals – you may be invited for a quick lunch, but clients are never invited out in the evening, either to restaurants or people's houses. Business discussions take place in the office and, if they go on late in the evening, takeaway food such as pizza is often ordered in from outside. Decisions are usually reached quite quickly.

b) In this culture, the normal form of greeting is to lean forward slightly towards the other person – people do not usually touch each other in business contexts. Expect no small talk – people feel uncomfortable if they talk about anything except business. Discussions will be broken off at 6.00 pm and continue the next day at 8.00 am, and decisions can come quite quickly. There are no invitations to restaurants or people's homes.

c) In this culture, physical contact is very important. Handshakes are long and firm, sometimes with a hug. Don't be offended if someone puts their arm round your shoulders in order to be friendly. Be ready to show photographs of your family: small talk revolves around the family. Here the idea of eating in the office is unheard of, and you may be invited out for long evenings of dining and drinking in restaurants, or sometimes people's homes. It may take several visits and evenings like this to reach a decision.

d) Don't be surprised if the other side seems unprepared and disorganised. Here, it's more important to have a good sense of humour and some amusing stories to tell. Shake hands when you meet someone for the first time, or if you haven't seen them for some time, but not every day. There is no physical contact otherwise. Long evenings out are unusual but do happen. Lunch with business contacts is quite common. You may be invited to sports events, especially in the summer. Decisions can sometimes be made quite quickly.

1 Be ready to talk about your children.
2 In business, people do not usually touch each other.
3 There is a lot of physical contact.
4 It's important to appreciate jokes.
5 Several visits may be necessary before a decision is made.
6 You may be invited to someone's house in the evening.
7 Eating in the office while discussing business is acceptable.

Multi-word verbs

Read this short article about customer relations. In most of the lines 1–5 there is one extra word that does not fit. One or two of the lines, however, are correct. If a line is correct, put a tick in the space next to that line. If there is an extra word in the line, write that word in the space.

In the excitement of getting new business, managers can often get carried away and forget
1 about their existing customers. Organisations are now beginning to wake off up to ....
2 the importance of the clients they already have. Cutting down about the number of ....
3 lost customers can make a big difference. Companies are increasingly looking into ....
4 ways of building for up loyalty. For example, many supermarkets have introduced ....
5 loyalty card schemes, and airlines have brought on in frequent flier programmes. ....
However, many supermarket customers and frequent fliers belong to more than one scheme, so all these schemes may just cancel each other out.

Writing a memo

You are the Managing Director of a small company. You are worried that you are losing customers because of the way your receptionists answer the phone. Write a memo of 75–100 words to the receptionists.

Your memo should cover the following points:
• you have had a number of complaints from customers about how they have been dealt with on the phone
• pick up the phone within three rings
• answer with the company name and an appropriate greeting
• the importance of courtesy and a pleasant tone of voice and end suitably.

4 Success

Verb tenses

You are a business journalist. You have been asked to write an article of 200–250 words about Texas Cake and Cookie Kings (TCCK), the US cake and biscuit manufacturer. Use the notes below and the correct form of the words in brackets as a basis for your article.

The company and its markets
San Antonio-based cakemaker
US cookie market share: 14%
Three manufacturing sites: San Antonio; Buffalo, NY; and Sacramento, California
Familiar to Americans, 64% (recognise) the brand; less familiar in rest of world

How the company started
1934 Betty Brandon (found) the company, (use) her grandmother's recipes
She (succeed) in (expand) company over next 20 years; (introduce) many new products
1955 Multilever, a large food and consumer product manufacturer, (offer) (buy) the company. Betty (refuse)
1960 Betty (retire). Company (head) by 'Wild' Bill Brandon, her son
1975 Multilever (buy) TCCK. Bill Brandon (remain) head of company

Recent events

(Develop) mail-order business, especially for Thanksgiving and Christmas
Bill Brandon (retire) two years ago. Now (manage) by Multilever executive, Laura Antonelli

What it is doing now

(Expand) ranges
(Establish) international presence. (Build) brand in Europe and Asia.
(Develop) further the mail-order business and also sales in fine foods section of department stores.
Sales last year: $550 million, of which 27% outside US.

Prefixes

Use one of the prefixes, *out-*, *over-* or *under-*, with the correct form of the verb in brackets to complete each of the sentences below.

1 Vickers has a good reputation for buying companies that are ....
   (perform), turning them round, and bringing them back to profitability.
2 The Dome's operators .... (estimate) the number of visitors: they forecast 10 million, but fewer than 7 million showed up.
3 Metro tried to buy Wertkauf, but was .... (bid) by Wal-Mart.
4 Under the agreement, NCR will .... (source) the manufacture of its computers to Solectron for at least five years.
5 We opened a chain of private nursery schools. We miscalculated our costs and .... (charge) parents by maybe 25 per cent, which is one reason we became popular and successful.
6 There are some companies with big problems because they .... (extend) themselves in real estate.
7 He is a skilful politician who has .... (manoeuvre) his rivals.
8 The government has .... (run) its spending commitments by € 1 billion.

5 Job satisfaction

Passives

A top manager feels lonely and is not satisfied with his job. He writes to an expert for advice. In each of lines 1–8 there is one wrong word. Write the correct word in the space provided. If all the words in the line are correct put a tick in the space provided.

Last summer I was appointed chairman of the board of the global company where I have spent most of my career. But now I feel very isolated and often lonely. Do other corporate presidents report such feelings?

It's lonely and tough at the top

Your earliest feelings of managerial loneliness probably occurred in your 20s or early 30s

1 when you were first promotion. Of necessity, moving up meant leaving close friends   ....
2 behind. You began to feel that you were isolating as you left them behind. Maybe your   ....
3 style as a manager were commented on, or perhaps there was an unspoken agreement by   ....
4 other managers not to talk about it, and it was not even discussion. Many managers want   ....
5 to be love and have their friends around them. Some even ask if they can return as a team   ....
6 player. For those who are motivating by close relationships at work, the decision to   ....
7 return to the team, to avoid be considered different, can be rewarding. As a top manager   ....
8 you are endlessly assess on your leadership style, your strategy and your charisma (or   ....
   lack of it). And one day, there is the realisation that your days of being chairman are numbered. Be warned: introverted, ex-chairmen can be very lonely indeed.

Tactful and less tactful responses

You are at a party at a professional conference. For each situation 1–5, there are two possible responses, a)–j). Match the situations to these responses, and underline the more appropriate response in each case.

1 You spill a lot of wine on someone's jacket.
2 You ask an old friend from another company about a colleague of hers that you know, and she says that he has lost his job.
3 You see someone you want to talk to but they are talking to someone else.
4 You are by yourself and someone you don't know comes up to you and starts talking, but you find them boring.
5 Someone comes up to you and says that they remember meeting you, but can't remember where.

a) Did he do something stupid?
b) May I join you?
c) I do apologise. Please send me the dry cleaning bill. Here's my address.
d) I'm sorry to hear that.
e) I'm going to have to go. I have to get back to my hotel to meet someone.
f) I'm not at all interested in football.
g) Does it matter where we met?
h) Can I butt in?
i) It must have been at this same conference last year.
j) Don't worry. It'll rub off.

6 Risk

Intensifying adverbs

Match the beginnings of the sentences to their endings a)–g).

1 This mining area was incredibly
2 Bank deposits are disappearing as nervous investors send their money abroad. 'The situation is absolutely
3 The organisation's systems have been severely
4 The finance minister said the budget was totally
5 The new management techniques were found to be highly
6 Making films in Britain is unbelievably
7 The country's international position is now exceptionally

a) disastrous', said one bank manager. 'It couldn't be worse.'
b) badly hit by the closure of the mines, which cost 10,000 jobs.
c) stable, secure and hopeful.
d) difficult, but much easier than it was before.
e) criticised by auditors, who found corruption and mismanagement.
f) unrealistic, and a new budget will have to be presented to parliament next week.
g) successful in 30% of companies and moderately successful in 45% of cases.

Writing

You work for a company that wants to expand in another country. You have been asked to write a memo to your Chief Executive about the best place for a regional office there. You have scored each place out of 10. (10 = very attractive, 1 = very unattractive. In the case of office rents, 10 = very low and 1 = very high.) Study these scores and write your report (120–140 words). Make your recommendation for the best place for the office, giving your reasons.

	Political stability	Business climate	Communications with rest of region	Office rents
Monroe	8	9	7	2
Newtown	2	1	0	10
Osborne	7	8	7	5

7 e-commerce

Conditionals

Complete these conditional sentences with the correct alternative.

1 If we don't get out there and get our stuff on-line, somebody else ....
   a) would   b) will   c) did
2 If you want to compete on a global scale, you .... to be where the largest market is, and that's the US.
   a) had   b) having   c) have
3 Use of the Internet for commercial transactions is possible only if you ....
   what you want to buy.
   a) knew   b) know   c) known

4 All the company's engineers have access to the Internet, even if they .... thousands of kilometres from the office.
   a) are   **b)** be   **c)** were

5 Supermarkets will only stay ahead if they .... that they will need to deliver more than food.
   a) realising   **b)** realised   **c)** realise

6 So, are European managers hopelessly outclassed by their American counterparts in the world of e-commerce? A year ago, many executives and analysts .... said 'yes'.
   a) shall have   **b)** should had   **c)** would have

7 Wanadoo, the Internet service provider, ... have a market value of more than € 15bn if its customers are valued at the same level as those of Club Internet.
   a) could   **b)** did   **c)** didn't

8 If the order .... made on-line to a US-based computer and paid in dollars, the transaction is not subject to French tax.
   a) be   **b)** is   **c)** will be

9 If the investors who bought the stock are unhappy, this .... require the company to buy the shares back.
   a) did   **b)** might   **c)** have

10 If people believe using technology will get them lower prices and better services, they .... use it.
   a) be   **b)** have   **c)** will

11 As one consultant pointed out, if you have to go to the post office to pick up a parcel, then the incentive to shop on-line rapidly ....
   a) drops   **b)** dropped   **c)** dropping

12 The level of understanding of e-commerce in Europe has increased dramatically over the last six to nine months. If you .... asked me nine months ago, I would have had significant worries.
   a) were   **b)** is   **c)** had

Reading

Read the website descriptions. To which website does each sentence 1–7 refer?

a) paralegal.com Fed up with paying exorbitant legal fees? Get leading-edge legal services at a fraction of the cost of going to a law firm. E-mail our legal team for low-cost advice on all aspects of company and tax law. Download specialist up-to-the-minute documents for a small charge. Conduct your own court cases with our help and save thousands of euros! No win, no fee!

b) bespontaneous.com Be spontaneous! Do something on the spur of the moment. Book otherwise impossible-to-get tickets to theatre and sports events. Ready to fly tomorrow? Take a break to one of our popular destinations: beach or city. Worry-free booking by credit card on our secure server. Next-day courier delivery of tickets to your door.

c) worldweather.com Want to see what the weather's like anywhere in the world? Come to worldweather.com! Consult free forecasts for 100 world cities. Download stunning satellite pictures of the world's increasingly unpredictable weather for free. Deluxe, framed versions of these pictures make beautiful gifts. Order on-line. Delivery within 48 hours.

d) goinggoinggone.com Consumer electronics products auctioned daily: computers, TVs, washing machines, you name it. It's so simple: put in your bid and we'll notify you by e-mail of the competing bids. You can raise your bid as many times as you like over a three-day period. If your bid is the highest at the end of three days, pay by credit card and goods are delivered to you within 24 hours.

1 You consult this site if you are not sure what clothes to take with you on a trip.
2 This site tries to reassure users who may be worried about giving their credit card details on-line.
3 This site mentions a delivery method that does not use the ordinary post office service.
4 This site does not mention physical delivery of goods or documents.
5 On this site, you can order a picture to put on your wall.
6 On this site, you can offer a price for something, but you won't necessarily get it.
7 On this site, there is a service that you may have to pay for or that may be free, depending on the results.

UNIT 8 Team building

None of us is as smart as all of us.
Japanese proverb

OVERVIEW ▼

☐ **Vocabulary**
Prefixes
☐ **Reading**
Successful teamworking
☐ **Listening**
Building a team
☐ **Language review**
Modal perfect
☐ **Skills**
Resolving conflict
☐ **Case study**
The new boss

Starting up

A What are the advantages and disadvantages of working in teams?

B For each box in the quiz below, tick the three statements that most apply to you. Then read the explanations on page 149.

What sort of team player are you?

Doers vs Thinkers	Details vs Ideas	Mind vs Heart	Planners vs Improvisers
a) I consider what I say.	a) I often come up with unusual solutions.	a) I like to think logically.	a) Meetings have to be prepared for carefully.
b) I contribute a lot in discussions.	b) It's important to be realistic.	b) I keep emotions out of decision-making.	b) I like surprises.
c) Action is more important than reflection.	c) People see me as a creative person.	c) I avoid confrontation.	c) I hate time-wasting at meetings.
d) I listen to others before I say anything.	d) I like practical solutions.	d) I sometimes tread on people's toes.	d) Too much time can be spent on preparation.
e) Discussion gives me energy and ideas.	e) You shouldn't overlook details.	e) Understanding people is as important as being right.	e) People say I'm a punctual person.
f) I don't say a lot at meetings.	f) You shouldn't get lost in details.	f) I care about other people's feelings.	f) I need a deadline to get me going.

C Work in groups and compare your answers. Then discuss these questions.

1 How important are thinking styles in effective teamwork?

2 Do you think your group would make a good team, based on the results of the quiz? Explain why or why not.

Vocabulary
Prefixes

A **Match the prefixes of these words to their meanings.**

Prefix	Meaning of prefix		
1 *mis*manage	**a)** not	**b)** badly	**c)** former
2 *pro*-European	**a)** opposite	**b)** in favour of	**c)** before
3 *pre*dict	**a)** not enough	**b)** against	**c)** before
4 *post*-industrial	**a)** after	**b)** too much	**c)** not enough
5 *dis*honest	**a)** two	**b)** former	**c)** not
6 *ex*-president	**a)** opposite	**b)** former	**c)** after
7 *under*developed	**a)** against	**b)** not enough	**c)** opposite
8 *anti*social	**a)** opposed to	**b)** two	**c)** before
9 *bi*lateral	**a)** against	**b)** after	**c)** two
10 *re*connect	**a)** again	**b)** former	**c)** after
11 *ir*responsible	**a)** again	**b)** not	**c)** against
12 *hyper*active	**a)** not enough	**b)** very	**c)** opposite

B **Complete these two short texts with some of the words above.**

The ....[1] of the United States was present at the signing of a ....[2] agreement between the USA and the EU on research into computer software. The agreement, which had been widely ....[3] for some time, came about through support from ....[4] senators.

Some of the ....[5] countries profiled last month have run into serious balance of payments problems. In each case this has been due to ....[6] of debts and ....[7] leaders who have run up enormous expense accounts.

C **Add prefixes to the words in the box to give their opposite meanings. Then use them to discuss the questions that follow.**

> communicative   decisive   efficient   enthusiastic
> flexible   focussed   imaginative   loyal   organised
> popular   practical   sociable   stable   tolerant

1 Who is the best person you have ever worked with? Who is the worst? Explain why.

2 What qualities could you contribute to a team? What qualities would the other members need to have to create an effective team?

Reading
Successful teamworking

A Read the article. Then match these headings with the sections marked 1–6.

- Open communication
- Measuring progress against goals
- Leadership

- Common goals with challenging targets
- Involvement of all team members
- Conflict resolution

Team building involves more than throwing a few people together

'Teamworking' has infiltrated every nook and cranny within just about every organisation. You can't get away from 'teams' that are supposed to be able to create something that is
5 greater than the sum of its parts. Or so the theory goes.

Yet the truth about teams is that the large majority of them do not achieve the synergies they could. For example, poor teamworking is
10 the culprit when meetings regularly overrun, when there are frequent arguments between team members or there is an unhealthy level of competition between individuals. Other signs of unproductive teamworking are people not
15 always completing tasks assigned to them or last minute panics to meet deadlines. More often than not, ineffective teams are the result of poor planning.

There are six measures that need to be taken
20 before you can get the most out of a team:

1 ....
In other words, a clear reason for the team to exist. But don't think of goals as wish lists – they have to be achievable, yet challenging
25 enough to motivate team members.

2 ....
Members must be able to express their opinions freely without fear of retribution, and feel that suggestions will be taken seriously. The
30 team might also need to agree whether politically sensitive topics of discussion in meetings should be kept within the confines of the team or shared with other employees.

3 ....
35 It is easy to think (albeit subconsciously) that a junior team member may have less to contribute than more experienced members.

This is not only demoralising, it also makes no sense – people that have nothing to contribute
40 should not have been selected for the team in the first place. You need to ensure that every member has an opportunity to add his or her thoughts to discussions.

4 ....
45 Disagreements are natural and, in fact, debate and discussion should be encouraged. A team made up only of 'yes men' can make disastrous decisions that few people honestly agreed with in the first place. Consequently, there should be
50 explicit rules on how lengthy disagreements should be tackled. For example, team meetings may not be the most appropriate place for a discussion that involves only two people, so the team could agree to certain issues being taken
55 'off line'.

5 ....
Most high-performing teams (whether it is in the workplace, sports or even in a pub quiz) have leaders. A good leader should be able to
60 play to individuals' strengths and compensate for their weaknesses. 'A good leader is critical,' says Gary Spellins, Managing Director of Managed Services, Lex Service plc, which delivers a range of outsourcing solutions to the
65 public and private sector. 'It should be someone who can act as a catalyst and a constant reminder of what the team needs to achieve.' The leader must, above all, be skilled in sharing responsibility and delegating work to others,
70 coaching them to achieve tasks, and providing constructive feedback on how the tasks went.

6 ....
Team members need to be able to see how they are doing against the objectives set at the beginning of the project.

From *Accountancy* magazine

B **Discuss these questions.**

1 What is meant to be the advantage of creating a team? (paragraph 1)

2 Which word means the same as the answer to question 1? (paragraph 2)

3 What are the five signs of unproductive teamworking that the article mentions?

C **There are a number of fixed phrases in English joined with *and*. These are called *fixed pairs*.**

1 Look at the first sentence of the text. Does *nook and cranny* mean:
   a) all the parts?
   b) the most important parts?
   c) the least important parts?

2 Complete sentences **a)–h)** with an appropriate *fixed pair* from the box. Use the words in brackets to help you.

| by and large | give and take | hard and fast | on and off |
| pros and cons | touch and go | ups and downs | wine and dine |

a) I've been writing this report .... (occasionally, not continuously) for the last two weeks, but it has to be in tomorrow.

b) There isn't any .... (strict, fixed) rule about how we are going to proceed in this negotiation.

c) You won't win this negotiation through bullying. There needs to be some .... (compromise).

d) We've had a few .... (mixture of good and bad things) in recent years.

e) It was .... (very unsure that something will happen) whether we'd get to the meeting on time.

f) If this contract is important, we'll have to .... (entertain) their management team.

g) Full employment was .... (mostly true, in general) achieved.

h) The union discussed the .... (advantages and disadvantages) of strike action.

Listening

Building a team

▲ Doug Cole

A 🎧 **8.1 Doug Cole runs team-building courses for managers. Listen to the first part of the interview and complete the key points below.**

• Know what your *strengths and weaknesses* are.

• Establish your baseline, where you are in terms of your
  ....

• Relate that to the ....

• Identify what the ....

• Build the team around what you need to ....

B 🎧 **8.2 Listen to the second part of the interview and answer these questions.**

1 When might you need someone to co-ordinate a team's activities?

2 What does co-ordination involve?

3 When might you need someone to drive the situation?

Language review
Modal perfect

- The modal perfect is formed using **modal verb + *have* + past participle**. *We **might have won** the contract.*
- Two uses of the modal perfect are:
  a) **criticising or commenting on past actions.**
  You should have told me the meeting was cancelled.
  She got there early. She needn't have allowed so much time to find the place.

  b) **speculating about the past.**
  He may have moved to another department.

 page 133

A Answer *yes*, *no* or *not sure* to each of the questions below.

1 *You should have chosen her for the team.*
  Was she chosen for the team?

2 *He must have made over 30 changes to the project.*
  Did he make over 30 changes to the project?

3 *They needn't have spent so much time on the report.*
  Did they spend too much time on the report?

4 *They could have prepared better if they'd had more time.*
  Did they prepare as well as they wanted to?

5 *The team would have been stronger without him.*
  Was the team as strong as it could be?

6 *Sylvia may have arrived by now.*
  Has Sylvia arrived yet?

7 *Thomas should have reached Barcelona by now.*
  Has Thomas reached Barcelona?

8 *They couldn't have done enough research as the launch was a failure.*
  Did the team do enough research?

B Which of these statements uses the modal perfect correctly? Suggest alternative modals for the incorrect statements.

1 It's too late to apply for the job now. You must have applied last month.

2 It was silly to leave your wallet in the hotel room. It would have been stolen.

3 The fire in our showroom last night could have destroyed all our merchandise.

4 He bought the land cheaply and sold it at a higher price to developers, so he needn't have made a lot of money.

5 Gerry wasn't at the meeting. He might have been delayed in traffic.

6 You couldn't have seen Mr Lebeau at the conference because he was in Hong Kong at the time.

7 He looked exhausted when he arrived. He should have had a bad flight.

8 He was charismatic and decisive. We must have made him team leader.

C Role play this situation in pairs.

A sales rep went on a three-day business trip. He/she:

- stayed in a five-star hotel
- phoned home from their room
- ordered breakfast in their room
- hired a top-of-the-range car
- drank most of the mini-bar
- had clothes dry-cleaned by the hotel.

After the trip, the Financial Director thinks the rep's expenses are excessive and refuses to pay them. The sales rep defends their actions.
The conversation begins as follows:
FD *You shouldn't have stayed in a five-star hotel.*
SR *There was no alternative. It was the only one that had a vacancy.*

Skills
Resolving conflict

A Read the suggestions below about ways of dealing with conflict. Put each of them under one of the following headings: either *Do* or *Don't*.

1 Be positive when handling problems.
2 Get angry from time to time with difficult members.
3 Delay taking action, if possible.
4 Try to see the problem from the point of view of the team.
5 Be truthful about how you see the situation.
6 Encourage open and frank discussion.
7 Try to ignore tensions within the team.
8 Bring potential conflict and disagreement into the open.
9 Give special attention to team members who are creating problems.
10 Persist with 'impossible people' – you may win them over.
11 Try to find 'win–win' solutions.
12 Make sure you know who the influential members are.

B Study the phrases in the Useful language box. Add one expression under each heading.

Useful language

Expressing your feelings
My main concern is ...

Showing sympathy
I know how you feel.

Making suggestions
One thing you could do is ...

Stating common goals
We've all got the same objective.

Expressing satisfaction
Yes, that would be very helpful ...

Identifying the real problem
What's really bothering you?

Expressing dissatisfaction
I don't think that would do much good.

Resolving the conflict
How do you think we should deal with this?

Agreeing action
OK, this is what we'll do.

Reviewing the situation
Let's meet next week and see how things are going.

C Work in pairs. Role play the following situation. Use phrases from the Useful language box above to discuss the problems.

A team of six multinational staff is managing a number of apartment blocks in Nice, France. However, one of the team is unhappy. The employee is difficult to work with and unco-operative.

Team leader turn to page 146.
Team member turn to page 155.

CASE STUDY

The new boss

NIGEL FRASER

Title: **Manager**

Nationality: **English**

Age: **32**

/// BES ///

NIGEL FRASER

A 'whiz kid'.
Previously worked for a business equipment chain. Ambitious and creative with a direct, 'no-nonsense' approach. Task-oriented, he sees his main objective as meeting sales targets. Very disappointed with current sales performance. Believes the team needs to be controlled more tightly and is underperforming because of bad habits acquired under Vanessa Bryant.

Background

Business Equipment and Systems (BES), based in Birmingham, England, sells fax machines, data projectors and slim plasma screens. Eighteen months ago, its national Sales Manager, Vanessa Bryant, moved to a senior management position. Her replacement, Nigel Fraser, has been told to increase turnover by at least 10% and to create a high-performing sales team. However, since Nigel's appointment the team has not been working effectively and morale is low. Last year's sales were over 20% below target. The sales team has a mix of nationalities because BES intends to enter other European markets in the near future.

Problems

1 Nigel has asked for more detailed sales reports from his team and wants to check their diaries every two weeks. The more experienced staff resent this.

2 To set clear objectives and improve communication, he holds more meetings. However, some staff are often late or don't attend, and two or three people dominate the discussions.

3 When targets are not met or customers complain, staff blame each other or other departments. They never take responsibility for mistakes.

4 Because of rivalry between individual members, they do not help each other. Some actively dislike each other.

5 The team become defensive if outsiders make helpful suggestions. They lack creativity and can't accept criticism.

6 Nigel often praises his previous company and colleagues, while the team talk about 'the good old days' when Vanessa was Sales Manager.

Task

You are directors of BES. Discuss the problems and consider:
a) what advice you should give Nigel.
b) what action, if any, you should take.

Use these questions as a guide.

1 Should Nigel approach team members individually? What should he say?

2 Should he remove one of the team? If so, who?

3 Should you replace Nigel with an existing team member?

4 How will you build on the team's strengths? How will you deal with its weaknesses?

5 Do the team get enough of a say in decision making?

Writing

Either:
Write a letter to the Managing Director of BES outlining your solution to the problems.

Or:
You are a sales manager. The behaviour of one of your salespeople is upsetting the others in the team. Write a letter warning them about their conduct and indicating where improvements should be made.

 Writing file page 138

The sales team

JOHAN NIEDERMEISTER

**Fax machines
Dutch, aged 35**

Calm, laid-back and very popular. A harmonising influence in the team. Missed his sales targets four times last year. Says competition is very strong in the fax machine market. A little inconsistent – makes a lot of calls one day, then relaxes the next. Gets on well with Nigel, who considers him a friend and a good team member.

ELIANA PETRIDES

**Data projectors, new products
Greek, aged 25**

One year's experience in BES. Always exceeds her monthly target. Hard-working, ambitious and talented. Rather aggressive. Everyone envies her success, except Johan. Some staff put her down at meetings and do not welcome her ideas. Feels demotivated. Wants to move to plasma screens. Thinks paperwork and training courses are a waste of time.

JEAN DUBOT

Plasma screens   French, aged 35

Extrovert, noisy. Gets up late. Calls on customers mostly between 11am and 3pm. Often exceeds sales targets. Earns good commissions. Well-liked by customers. Some colleagues think he is arrogant and boastful. Frequently late for meetings but always has an excuse.

NINA PERSSON

Fax machines   Swedish, aged 26

Reliable, quiet, hard-working. Starts early, finishes late. Missed her monthly targets three times last year. Contributes little to meetings, but has some good ideas. She is often 'put down' by Jean, although other members like her. Thinks commission should be based on the sales of the whole team.

BRUNA TARDELLI

**Fax machines
Italian, aged 34**

Dynamic, moody and a little insecure. Good sales record. Generally meets her sales targets. Can be aggressive if her ideas are not accepted at meetings. Gets on well with Robert. They always support each other at meetings and obviously like each other a lot.

ROBERT DRISCOLL

**Data projectors,
new products
English, aged 45**

The top salesperson, with 20 years' experience at BES. Strong character, sociable. Dissatisfied because of the atmosphere in the department. Great rivalry between him and Jean. They sometimes insult each other in meetings. Enjoys meetings and talks a lot. Can't see the point of paperwork. Talks a lot about the good old days.

DON MILLS

**Plasma screens
English, aged 35**

Volatile and unpredictable. Greatly exceeds his targets some months, then falls well below in others. Very talented salesman. Liked by most of his colleagues, but often clashes violently with Bruna. There are rumours that they were very 'close' friends in the past. He always makes his final call close to his home, which is not in the company's interests.

Raising finance

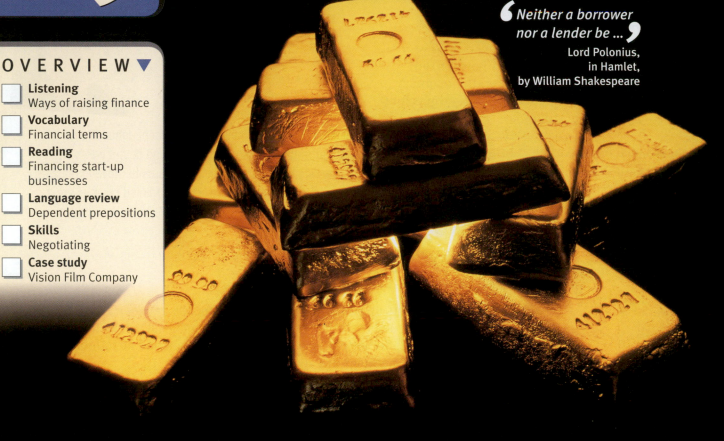

> Neither a borrower nor a lender be ...
>
> Lord Polonius,
> in Hamlet,
> by William Shakespeare

OVERVIEW ▼

Listening
Ways of raising finance

Vocabulary
Financial terms

Reading
Financing start-up
businesses

Language review
Dependent prepositions

Skills
Negotiating

Case study
Vision Film Company

Starting up

Discuss the following questions.

1 What are the advantages and disadvantages for a private individual of borrowing money from the following:
   a) a bank?
   b) a friend or colleague?
   c) a member of your family?
   d) a loan shark?
   e) a credit card company?
   f) another source?

2 Imagine you have just won $300,000. You want to use it to secure your long-term financial future. How would you invest the money?

3 Do you think it is good business practice for a company to pay its bills late?

4 'People with overdrafts are bad money managers.' Do you agree?

5 What do you think the following sayings mean? Do you agree with them?
   a) Time is money.
   b) Money is the root of all evil.
   c) A fool and his money are soon parted.
   d) Money can't buy you love.
   e) Love does much; but money does more.

Listening
Ways of raising finance

A 🎧 9.1 **Listen to the first part of an interview with Rosemary Leith, co-founder of the Internet business consultancy Flametree.com. What are the two commonest ways for businesses to raise finance?**

▲ Rosemary Leith

B 🎧 9.2 **Now listen to the rest of the interview and answer these questions.**

1 Are start-up companies more likely to raise money through debt or equity? What about growth businesses?

2 Why can debt be more expensive than equity?

3 Which method of raising finance did Rosemary's company choose?

4 What four factors does the process of raising money depend on?

5 What are the advantages of the way Rosemary's company raised money?

Vocabulary
Financial terms

A **Match the following expressions with the correct definitions.**

1 human capital	**a)** money to carry on production and keep trading
2 risk capital	**b)** money a company has raised from investors who bought shares
3 share capital	**c)** money invested in a project with a high chance of failure
4 venture capital	**d)** money a company borrows to start up a new business
5 working capital	**e)** the perceived value of people and their skills

B **Choose the correct word to complete each sentence. Use a good dictionary to help you.**

1 I took out a .... to extend the factory.
   a) credit   **b)** debt   **c)** loan

2 He offered his home as security or .... when he borrowed from the bank.
   a) collateral   **b)** deposit   **c)** warranty

3 The .... rate on the loan was 15%.
   a) charge   **b)** fee   **c)** interest

4 We have a(n) .... of $1 million to finance our three-month advertising campaign.
   a) budget   **b)** cost   **c)** expense

5 They have to pay the loan back over three years. The first .... is due in August.
   a) amount   **b)** instalment **c)** part

6 Our state-of-the-art machinery is our major ....
   a) asset   **b)** possession **c)** property

7 We want to find a partner who will take a .... in our business.
   a) risk   **b)** share   **c)** stake

8 Thanks to a government .... the firm was able to move to a new location.
   a) contribution **b)** subsidy   **c)** support

9 Money owed by a company to its suppliers forms part of its ....
   a) damages   **b)** liabilities **c)** losses

10 When the bank grants a business an .... facility, their current account can go into the red.
   a) overdraft   **c)** overhead   **c)** overpayment

Reading
Financing start-up businesses

A Scan the two articles on page 79 and match them to the following statements.

1) Emerging entrepreneurs will be essential to the future prosperity of the country.

2) With banks reluctant to lend, many entrepreneurs have looked to family and friends for help providing start-up capital.

B Work in pairs. Student A reads article A; Student B reads article B. Do not read your partner's article yet.

C Work in pairs to decide if the following statements about *both* articles are true or false.

1 In both countries entrepreneurship has always been an important part of the culture.

2 In both countries businesses usually start with finance from banks.

3 Risk money is available in Japan, but not readily available in Italy.

4 Families often provide finance for start-up companies in Italy and Japan.

5 Both governments want to promote schemes to encourage new businesses.

D Match the definitions below to words in the articles. Then use the words in sentences of your own.

Article A

1 something that causes an important change or event to happen   (para 1)

2 to encourage something to happen over a period of time   (para 3)

3 favouring people who want to start up new businesses   (para 3)

4 a company paid to do part of the work of another company   (para 2)

Article B

5 a company's business expressed as sales of goods and services over a period of time   (para 3)

6 shares that one company owns in another company   (para 5)

7 a loan which is not guaranteed by the borrower's assets   (para 5)

8 a bank that deals with businesses rather than the public   (para 2)

E Study the order of the underlined words in the sentence from article A. Then rewrite the sentences below beginning with the words in brackets. Discuss how the meaning of the sentence is affected in each case.

Only now is Japan starting to develop a business environment conducive to entrepreneurial growth.

1 (Seldom ...) We rarely have goods returned to us because they are faulty.

2 (At no time ...) He never apologised for his mistake.

3 (Under no circumstances ...) The budget must not be exceeded.

4 (Only by ...) We will increase sales significantly by spending more money on advertising.

5 (On no account ...) Private calls should not be made from the office.

Article A

Venturers who hope to be the business

By Michiyo Nakamoto and Naoko Nakamae

In the past few years, a new generation of Japanese entrepreneurs has emerged, boosting hopes that venture businesses are poised to become a new catalyst for the enfeebled Japanese economy.

Japan's small business sector already accounts for more jobs than the big corporations, such as Sony and Toyota, but a large proportion of smaller companies are subcontractors whose fortunes are totally dependent on big companies. Only now is Japan starting to develop a business environment conducive to entrepreneurial growth.

Of the three main ingredients needed to foster venture businesses – risk money, a structural framework and an entrepreneur-friendly culture – the country has attracted the first, is improving the second, but needs to move forward on the third.

'The reason why there is a business chance for us is because the social structure is changing as a result of the Internet,' says Hiroshi Mikitani, 34-year-old founder of Rakuten Ichiba, Japan's most popular Internet shopping mall. Old skills are becoming less important than Internet expertise and money is flowing to new businesses rather than mature industries, he says. Internet entrepreneurs are also leaving the relative sanctuary of larger companies to set up on their own, something which is still rare in Japan. Meanwhile the Japanese authorities have been scrambling to make the country's legal and structural framework more venture business-friendly.

In the past, Japan's reliance on indirect financing through banks also discouraged the development of risk capital. 'The head of a big bank may know what it's like to have difficulties in raising Y100bn but he doesn't know what it's like to try to raise Y500,000,' points out Masao Horiba, founder and chairman of Horiba, a leading manufacturer of measuring instruments.

But while the money flows in and structural change increases, the critical question is whether Japanese culture can change sufficiently to support more entrepreneurs. 'Japan's venture capital sector is like a brand new race track. The track and stands have been built, the gamblers have arrived – but there aren't any horses,' says Mr Horiba.

From the Financial Times

FINANCIAL TIMES
World business newspaper.

Article B

Businesses learn from past mistakes

By Ian Hamilton Fazey

As the UK looks for new ways to encourage entrepreneurship, Italy might be thought a good place to look for lessons. It has a highly successful scheme to help young people start businesses; entrepreneurship seems part of the culture; working for yourself commonplace. There is an assumption that if people fail – and 46 per cent do so within five years – they will learn from their mistakes and start again.

Few Italians start a business with bank support. They save their start-up capital, sometimes for years, and borrow from parents, other family members and friends. Italy has almost no merchant banks and the fragmented banking sector is tightly regulated because of past banking failures. Banks have therefore become risk-averse and reluctant to lend.

Of scores of entrepreneurs interviewed for the OECD evaluation, only two had successfully borrowed money from the bank under the government loan guarantee scheme, thus avoiding up to three years of saving to accumulate capital. The rest had started from their own or privately-borrowed resources and then used growing turnover to expand. This was found to aid survival, nurturing financially conservative entrepreneurs, who did not over-extend and calculated risks carefully.

Parallel to this is an outstandingly successful government-funded scheme to encourage young entrepreneurs under 24. Highly selective, the Youth Entrepreneurship Agency approved only 1,056 projects out of 4,603 applications in the first 10 years. Successful applicants are tutored and advised, and the survival rate is running at 82 per cent.

The agency is now allowed to take equity stakes in the most promising ventures. In addition, an unsecured 'loan of honour' – voluntarily repayable from future profits – has been introduced in southern Italy to help get over the problems of financing businesses in poorer areas where the banks really could not care less.

From the Financial Times

FINANCIAL TIMES
World business newspaper.

Language review
Dependent prepositions

Prepositions commonly occur after certain verbs, adjectives and nouns. Complete these extracts from the articles on page 79 with suitable prepositions. Then check your answers in the articles.

Verbs	Adjectives	Nouns
1 Japan's small business sector **accounts** _____ more jobs … 2 They **borrow** _____ parents, and friends. 3 They will **learn** _____ their mistakes …	4 … whose fortunes are **dependent** _____ big companies. 5 … develop a business environment **conducive** _____ growth. 6 **Parallel** _____ this is an outstandingly successful scheme …	7 … Japan's **reliance** _____ indirect financing… 8 … discouraged the **development** _____ risk capital. 9 … to have **difficulties** _____ raising Y100bn …

➡ page 134

A Complete this text with words and prepositions from the Language review box.

It is essential to our future progress that we ……………….[1] our mistakes. Our ……………….[2] a limited range of products has affected our performance. We are too ……………….[3] our number one brand. We need to concentrate on the ……………….[4] new products. If we do not do this we will experience ……………….[5] raising finance for our expansion programme. ……………….[6] our bank is not an option as we have already exceeded our credit limit.

B Join the halves of sentences below. They are all from newspaper articles.

1 She had a sound business specialising	a) on my investment.
2 Self-employment may be the only alternative	b) of the risks facing European companies.
3 Researchers say this results	c) of finance, beyond his grasp.
4 Why do women still have limited access	d) in lower failure rates.
5 Once you understand the mindset of your investors, you can profit	e) from their suggestions.
6 He can see opportunities which lie, through lack	f) in renovating and refurbishing buildings.
7 The document contained an assessment	g) to starvation in poorer countries.
8 I want a return	h) to venture capital?
9 We are very focussed	i) to any further investment.
10 They are strongly opposed	j) on transferring ideas from the hard world of industrial economics to the dot-coms.

C Why do people often find it difficult to get finance to start a business? Make a list of reasons.

Skills
Negotiating

A **Which of these negotiating tips do you agree with? Explain why or why not.**

1 In the early stages, you need to ask the other side a lot of questions.
2 Always interrupt if you don't understand something.
3 Never make a concession for free. Always get something in return.
4 Use simple, direct language and be open about your aims.
5 Signal what you are going to do. For example, say, 'I'd just like to clarify that'.
6 Summarise often so that everyone is clear when you reach agreement.
7 Adapt your language so that you don't appear aggressive.
8 Talk about your emotions and how you are feeling.

B **Research shows that skilled negotiators often use techniques 1–5 below to achieve their negotiating objective. Match the techniques to their definitions.**

1 Open questions
2 Closed questions
3 Softening phrases
4 Signalling phrases
5 Summarising

a) say what you are going to do before you do it.
b) modify language so that it does not appear too aggressive.
c) go over the points covered to highlight when agreement is reached.
d) gather information and explore the opposite number's views.
e) check understanding and ask for precise information.

C **Match the statements and questions below to the headings in the Useful language box. Then, make up two expressions of your own for each heading.**

1 Can you offer any collateral?
2 What sort of figure do you have in mind?
3 What sort of benefits are you looking for?
4 There seems to be a discrepancy in your figures.
5 Let me clarify my last point. What I meant was …
6 Can I just recap?
7 I'm afraid that doesn't solve our problem.
8 Could I make a suggestion? Why don't we renegotiate the loan?
9 When can you begin repayment?
10 Let's go over what we've agreed.

Useful language

Open questions
Why do you need a loan?

Closed questions
Do you have any other backers?

Softening phrases
I'm sorry we can't go that high.

Signalling phrases
I'd like to make a proposal. I think we should …

Summarising
Let's see what we've got so far.

D **Work in pairs. Role play the following situation.**

A financial manager learns that he/she has been posted to one of the company's subsidiaries in a developing country. He/she does not really want to take up the posting but cannot refuse because it will improve his/her career prospects. He/she meets the Personnel Director to negotiate better financial terms for the posting.

Financial Manager: turn to page 148.
Personnel Director : turn to page 155.

Vision Film Company

CASE STUDY

Background

Vision Film Company (VFC) was founded fifteen years ago by two Polish expatriates. Now based in Krakow, Poland, it has produced numerous television commercials and documentaries, some of which have won international awards for originality and creativity. It has a small, highly experienced production staff and depends on an extensive freelance staff for its projects.

The Director and Executive Producer of VFC now want to make a feature film. The film is a drama set in post-war Europe. VFC have presented their business plan to a Swiss film finance company, European Finance Associates (EFA).

EFA have provisionally agreed to finance the project with a budget limit of $10 million. They have asked for a second meeting next month (April) to negotiate the details of the finance package. Industry practice is for film finance companies to be repaid their investment, usually with interest, and receive a share of the film's net profits.

Here are some extracts from the VFC Business Plan.

Executive Summary

The extraordinary success of independent films in recent Academy Awards shows that there is a huge demand for dramatic human interest films, whether they are performed by unknown actors or by stars. This proposal is for an independent feature film with a budget of $5.5 million.

The Polish Affair is a romantic thriller about Alicia, a young Polish interpreter, and a British intelligence officer, Justin, who meet and fall in love in the chaos of Vienna at the end of the Second World War. Without warning Alicia disappears, and their brief, passionate relationship ends. When, ten years later, they meet again by chance in Berlin their feelings for each other are as strong as ever. However, as the mystery behind Alicia's disappearance unfolds it threatens to destroy them both.

This story will have great appeal to all age groups, but especially to film-goers in the 25–40 age group, who form a large segment of most countries' film-going audience.

Target audience

25–40 year olds; well-educated, frequent film-goers. The film will also appeal to older people.

Target market

Worldwide distribution.
Main markets: USA, Canada, Europe.

Promotion

To help the producer make deals with major film distributors, the film will be shown at key film festivals (e.g. Cannes and Berlin).

Production Schedule

This year

July	Complete financing and casting
December	Complete pre-production

Next year

March–June	Carry out principal photography
July	Complete laboratory work

Final year

January–June	Sundance Film Festival (US distribution deals) Berlin Film Festival Cannes Film Festival (European distribution deals) Publicity campaign
July	Release film in the United States and Europe

Draft Budget (key costs US$)

Story and script	400,000	
Producer's fee / costs	370,000	
Director's fee	120,000	
Principal artistes	140,000	
Total		**1,030,000**
Production unit	1,500,000	
Camera crews / equipment	290,000	
Artistes (other than principals)	280,000	
Music	450,000	
Travel and transport	230,000	
Hotel and living expenses	950,000	
Completion bond*	290,000	
Total		**3,990,000**
Other expenses	480,000	**480,000**
TOTAL COST		**5,500,000**

Three-year income projection summary: Gross revenues

Low: $15million   Medium: $25million   High: $40million

(*A *completion bond* is like an insurance policy. If a producer runs out of money or exceeds his/her budget, the completion bond provides the finance to finish the film.)

Task

Work in groups.

Group A: Director and Executive Producer of Vision Film Company (turn to page 153).

Group B: Directors of European Finance Associates (turn to page 150).

Read your role cards and prepare for the negotiation. Then hold a meeting and negotiate a suitable agreement.

Writing

As Executive Producer of Vision Film Company or as a Director of European Finance Associates, write an e-mail to all senior staff informing them of the results of the negotiation and indicating how the project will proceed.

➡ *Writing file* page 139

Reasons why "The Polish Affair" will appeal to audiences worldwide

- Outstanding script

- Romantic interest

- Exciting locations: Warsaw, Vienna, Berlin

- Dramatic tension

Customer service

'They usually have two tellers in my local bank.
Except when it's very busy, when they have one.'
Rita Rudner, American actress

OVERVIEW ▼

☐ **Listening**
New ideas in customer
care

☐ **Discussion**
Customer complaints

☐ **Reading**
Customer delight

☐ **Vocabulary**
Handling complaints

☐ **Language review**
Gerunds

☐ **Skills**
Active listening

☐ **Case study**
Hermes
Communications

Starting up **A** Which of the following irritate you the most when dealing with customer service departments?

On the phone	Face-to-face	Repairs and refunds
• Being put on hold • Speaking to a disinterested person • Having to dial several numbers before getting to the right person • Finding the Customer Service number is continuously engaged • Being cut off	• Unhelpful customer service personnel • Indifferent staff • Salespeople with poor product knowledge • Too few staff at peak times • No company policy on customer service or complaints	• Delays on repairs • Delays in getting one's money back • No replacement equipment while repairs are carried out

B How important to a company's success is customer care? Is it possible to have too much customer care?

Listening
**New ideas in
customer care**

A 🎧 **10.1** Chris Storey is Senior Lecturer in Marketing at the City University Business School in London. In the first part of the interview, Chris defines customer service as a) 'doing the right thing' and b) 'delighting customers'. What examples does he give to illustrate these two ideas?

B 🎧 **10.1** Why do some companies fail to answer their customers' e-mail queries effectively?

C ⌒ 10.2 **Listen to the second half of the interview and answer these questions.**

1 What are the advantages and disadvantages of 'call centres'?

2 Which statements below are true and which are false?
   a) Segmentation means dividing your market into different groups of people.
   b) Some people are prepared to pay for help and advice before buying a product.
   c) Everyone finds it easy to understand financial products like mortgages.
   d) Sophisticated consumers are able to buy cheaper mortgages.
   e) Companies are able to charge more when they deliver goods to customers in the evening.

Discussion

Customer complaints

Work in two groups, A and B. Choose the five best suggestions from your group's advice sheet. Then form new groups. Negotiate a single list of the six best suggestions from both sheets.

Group A Dealing with customer complaints

1 Show the customer you are listening by checking that you understand.
2 Allow the customer to show their emotions if they are upset or angry.
3 Say you are sorry that the customer is upset.
4 Admit that the problem was your fault as soon as possible.
5 Make sure you get full details of the problem.
6 Summarise and make sure that the customer understands what you have said.
7 Ask the customer to put the complaint in writing.
8 Be firm if you are sure of your facts.

Group B Dealing with customer complaints

1 Keep an open mind at all times.
2 Do not end up arguing with the customer. Do not be defensive.
3 Concentrate on the situation not the personalities.
4 Don't force your solution on the customer.
5 Try to find out what result the customer wants.
6 Tell the customer what you can and cannot do.
7 Never admit you are wrong.
8 Offer compensation of greater value than the goods or service complained about.

Reading
Customer delight

A Companies are increasingly aware of the importance of 'word-of-mouth' advertising – when customers talk to others about their experience of products or services. What do you think are the answers to the following questions?

1 How many other people do satisfied customers tell? Up to:
   a) 12?   **b)** 18?   **c)** 24?

2 How many other people do dissatisfied customers tell? Up to:
   a) 10?   **b)** 20?   **c)** 30?

3 What percentage of people stay loyal when they feel complaints are handled fairly?
   a) 40%?   **b)** 60%?   **c)** 80%?

B Now read the article and answer the questions that follow it.

Delighting in a superior service

By David White

In the increasingly competitive service sector, it is no longer enough to promise customer satisfaction. Today, customer 'delight' is the stated aim for companies battling to retain and increase market share.

It is accepted in the marketing industry, and confirmed by a number of surveys, that customers receiving good service will stimulate new business by telling up to 12 other people; those treated badly will tell their tales of woe to up to 20 people. Interestingly, 80 per cent of people who feel their complaints are handled fairly will stay loyal.

New challenges for customer care have come with the rapid growth in obtaining goods and services via telephone call centres and the Internet. Averting 'phone rage' – induced by delays in answering calls, being cut off in mid-conversation or left waiting for long periods – has been tackled by vast investment in information technology and training courses for staff.

OUR AIM IS A DELIGHTED CUSTOMER, SIR

FLIGHT DELAYED   FLIGHT DELAYED

'Many people do not like talking to machines,' says Dr Storey (Senior Lecturer in Marketing at City University Business School). 'Banks, for example, encourage staff at call centres to use customer data to establish instant rapport with them. The aim is to make the customer feel they know you and that you can trust them – the sort of reassuring feelings people have during face-to-face chats with their local branch manager.'

Recommended ways of inducing customer delight include: under-promising and over-delivering (saying that a repair will be carried out within five hours, but getting it done within two); replacing a faulty product immediately; throwing in a gift voucher as an unexpected thank you to regular customers; and always returning calls, even when they are complaints.

Aiming for customer delight is all very well, but if services do not reach the high level promised, disappointment or worse will be the result. This can be eased by coupling an apology and explanation of why the service did not meet usual standards with empathy ('I know how you must feel') and possible solutions (replacement, compensation or whatever fairness suggests best meets the case).

Airlines face some of the toughest challenges over customer care. Fierce competition has convinced them that delighting passengers is an essential marketing tool, while there is great potential for customer outrage over delays caused by weather, unclaimed luggage and technical problems.

For BA staff, a winning telephone style is considered vital in handling the large volume of calls about bookings and flight times. They are trained to answer quickly, with their name, job title and a 'we are here to help' attitude. The company has invested heavily in information technology to ensure information is available instantly on screen.

BA also says its customer care policies apply internally and staff are taught to regard each other as customers requiring the highest standards of service.

Customer care is obviously here to stay and it would be a foolish company that used slogans such as 'we do as we please and are answerable only to ourselves'. On the other hand, the more customers are promised, the greater the risk of disappointment.

From the *Financial Times*

FINANCIAL TIMES
World business newspaper.

1 Are the following statements true or false, according to the writer?
   a) In a competitive market a company must aim to satisfy the customer.
   b) Fast automated service is preferred to slower person-to-person service.
   c) Companies which promise the most have the most satisfied customers.

2 Why is customer care particularly important for airlines?

3 Why has BA spent a lot of money on information technology and training?

4 What approach to customer care does BA have within its organisation?

C The writer says that 'under-promising' and 'over-delivering' is a good way to please customers. Can you think of any risks associated with this strategy?

D The article gives airlines as an example of a sector where customer service is critical. What other sectors can you think of? Explain your answers.

Vocabulary
Handling complaints

A Complete the beginnings of sentences 1–5 with words from the box. Then finish each sentence using the sentence endings a)–e).

> standards   products   rapport   complaints   reassure

1 When you handle .... it is important ...
2 You can establish a .... with a customer if ...
3 A key element in customer care is to .... people ...
4 Companies which do not meet their .... of service ...
5 Many companies will replace .... free of charge if ...

a) ... when they are worried.
b) ... will lose customers.
c) ... they are faulty.
d) ... you know about their buying habits.
e) ... to be diplomatic.

B Match the idiomatic expressions 1–7 to their meanings a)–g).

1 pass the buck
2 get to the bottom of the problem
3 it was the last straw
4 got straight to the point
5 slipped my mind
6 ripped off
7 talking at cross purposes

a) forgot to do something
b) paid far too much for something
c) avoid responsibility
d) find the real cause of something
e) talked about the subject directly
f) the last in a series of irritating events
g) misunderstanding what someone else is referring to

C Use the idiomatic expressions to complete the sentences appropriately.

1 She was very helpful. She promised to .... and find a solution.
2 He's the person responsible. He shouldn't try to .... and blame others for his mistakes.
3 Several customers have complained about our service contract. They say they're paying far too much and feel they have been ....
4 I meant to send him a brochure but we were very busy and it ....
5 They wanted to place a larger order. I thought they wanted a bigger discount. We were ....
6 They ignored my complaints, but .... when they refused to refund my money.
7 I saw no point in arguing with him. I .... and said I wanted my money back.

Language review
Gerunds

- A gerund is formed from a verb but behaves like a noun.
- It can be the subject of a sentence or clause: ***Aiming*** *for customer delight is all very well …*
- It can be the object of a sentence or clause: *Many people do not like **talking** to machines …*
- It often follows a preposition: *Customers receiving good service will stimulate new business **by telling** up to 12 other people …*
- A useful way to use gerunds is in lists. (See paragraph 5 in the article on page 86.)
- Most gerunds are formed by adding *-ing* to the base form of the verb: *answer, answer**ing***   *handle, hand**ling***   *get, gett**ing***
- Some verbs are followed by either a gerund or an infinitive, but the choice can lead to a change in meaning:
  *He remembered **to reply** to the complaint. (He didn't forget.)*
  *He remembers **replying** to the complaint. (He has a clear memory of this.)*

 page 134

A The article on page 86 has many examples of the gerund used:
a) as the subject of a sentence / clause   b) following a preposition.
Find three examples of each.

B Each of the sentences 1–4 is naturally followed by another, a)–d). Match the pairs of sentences.

1 We mean to enhance our customer service policy this quarter.
2 The new customer care policy meant putting more time and effort into the Service Department.
3 The company has now stopped giving free three-year guarantees.
4 Before leaving the country, the CEO will stop to give a short speech at Head Office.

a) The extra cost involved significantly affected the budget.
b) It's been one of our objectives for some time.
c) She is expected to announce a major new investment for the group.
d) In future, customers will have to pay a premium.

C Complete the guidelines for improving customer service with suitable gerunds. Add some tips of your own.

Improving customer service
Recommended ways of improving customer service include:

1 ......*returning*...... calls promptly.

2 .... key customers special discounts.

3 .... research to find out what customers need.

4 .... staff training programmes in customer care.

5 .... procedures so they are customer-focussed.

6 .... clear performance targets.

7 .... results in order to review progress.

8 .... quickly with complaints.

9 .... the customer is happy with the outcome.

10 .... from complaints.

Skills
Active listening

A How do you know if someone is not listening to you? How does it make you feel?

B Which of the following do you do to show people that you are listening to them? Can you add any other suggestions?

- look people directly in the eye at all times
- nod your head often to show interest
- repeat what the speaker has said in your own words
- be aware of the speaker's body language
- interrupt the speaker often to show you are listening
- think about what you are going to say while the speaker is talking
- use body language to show you are attentive
- try to predict what they are going to say next
- ask questions if you do not understand
- say nothing until you are absolutely sure that the speaker has finished

C 🎧 **10.3** Listen to three conversations in which people are talking about customer service.

1 Make notes under the following headings:
   a) Product or service
   b) Reasons why service was good or bad

2 Listen again. Tick the words and phrases in the Useful language box that you hear. Then add other words and phrases of your own.

D Work in pairs. Describe two examples from your own experience where the service you received was:
a) excellent   b) poor.

When your partner is speaking, make an effort to listen actively. Use some of the language from the Useful language box.

Useful language

Showing interest
Really?
That's interesting.
Right / OK / Mmm / Yes / No

Showing empathy
I know what you mean.
How awful!

Asking for details
So what happened?
What did you do?

Clarifying
Are you saying ... ?
What (exactly) do you mean by ... ?
Could you be more specific please?

Summarising
(So) you think ...
(So) what you're saying is ...

Repetition / Question tags
A We've reduced customer complaints by 30%.
B 30%? / Have you?

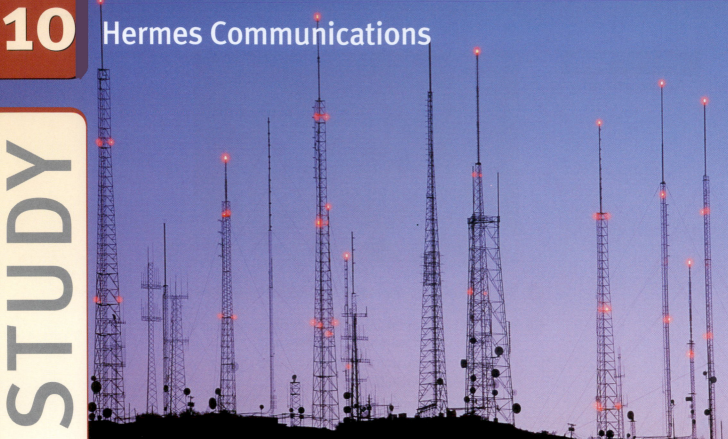

CASE STUDY

Background

You and some of your colleagues in the Customer Services Department at Hermes Communications are attending a course on how to deal effectively with customer complaints. You have been asked to do a number of tasks based on some correspondence, a telephone conversation and a recorded message which the course trainer has given you.

Task

1. 🎧 10.4 Read the written correspondence. Then listen to the telephone conversation and the recorded message and make notes. Because you are so busy, decide which complaints you will handle now as a priority, and which you will leave until later.

2. In groups, discuss how to deal with the complaints that you have prioritised. Then delegate writing tasks within your group and write replies to the complaints.

3. Exchange your replies with those of another group. Comment on the effectiveness of the various documents.

4. Work in pairs. Role play the following situation.
   Student A: You are the customer who wrote complaint 1. You have come to the regional office to complain in person.
   Student B: You are the Customer Service Officer at Hermes Communications' regional office. Read complaint 1 that the customer has sent. Then listen to their complaint. Deal with the problem as effectively as you can.

Writing

Following your attendance at the training course on how to deal with customer complaints, the Head of Customer Services asks you to write a memo giving your opinion of the training course and any suggestions for improvements to it. Your memo will be circulated to the Head of Training who likes to monitor all courses run by his department.

 Writing file page 140

Complaint 1

I'm writing to you because I've been trying to get through to your helpline unsuccessfully for the past three days. I've called at various times of the day and night and <u>never</u> get through. I wish to query something on my monthly bill. Is there any point having a helpline if it's always busy?

I intend to visit you next week to discuss this in person at your regional office.

Complaint 2

e-mail to Hermes Communications

To: Customer Services Dept.
From: Customer 567/001
Date: 24 November

Having finally got through to the helpline, I was passed from department to department and nobody wanted to deal with my problem. In the end, after twenty minutes, I gave up. It's not a helpline if no one wants to help you.

Complaint 3

To: Customer Services Dept.
From: AA Company
Date: 24 November

I'm writing to complain about your terrible customer service. I topped up my phone using my credit card on two occasions (£20 each time), however the amount wasn't credited to my account. It's not so much the loss of £40 which upsets me. I'm sure I'll get it back. But my phone didn't work when I needed it to make an urgent call to an important client. This is not the sort of service I expected from a company as well known as yours. I'd like to know how you're going to compensate me.

Complaint 4

• • • F A X   T R A N S M I S S I O N • • •

To: Customer Services Dept.
From: A Person
Date: 24 November

I became a subscriber to your service because you promised six months of cheap–rate calls to the US, where my daughter lives at present. So imagine my horror to find this service withdrawn, with no explanation from you, after only three months. Then you wrote to me asking for an extra £30 a month to maintain the previous level of service. I find this absolutely outrageous.

Complaint 5

As a mobile phone user and subscriber with your network for the past five years, I have been very pleased with the level of service provided.

However, recently, I've been experiencing headaches. After visiting my doctor, he informed me that this could be due to mobile phone use. As I am in sales and travel a lot, I am on the phone up to three hours per day. I was not previously aware of any health risk associated with mobile phones and am now very concerned about the long-term health risks of prolonged exposure to microwave radiation.

I've heard of other cases like mine and therefore I would like to know what your company is doing about this problem.

I look forward to hearing your comments with interest.

Crisis management

OVERVIEW ▼

Listening
Coping with crises

Reading
Airline crashes

Vocabulary
Noun phrases with and without *of*

Language review
Similarities and differences

Skills
Asking and answering difficult questions

Case study
Game over

Starting up

A **Discuss these questions.**

1 When, in your opinion, does a business problem become a crisis?
2 What crises that business managers have to face can you think of?
3 What sort of crisis might your own company or institution have to deal with?
4 What do crisis management teams do?

B **Crisis management experts have identified the following key steps for companies in a crisis. Use them to complete the table below. Then discuss your answers.**

1 Set up a crisis management team
2 Try to predict what crises could occur
3 Role play a potential crisis
4 Inform the directors
5 Disclose as much information as you can
6 Analyse the actions you took to deal with the situation
7 Write down and circulate your crisis management programme
8 Practise making decisions under stress
9 Work out an action plan to ensure the crisis does not happen again
10 Find out what happened and how it happened

Before the crisis	During the crisis	After the crisis

危机

When written in Chinese, the word crisis *is compounded of two characters – one represents danger, and the other represents opportunity.*

John F Kennedy (1917–1963), 35th US President

Listening
Coping with crises

▲ Jan Walsh

A Jan Walsh, a crisis management expert at British Telecom, is talking about the main crises facing managers today. Before you listen to the interview, discuss what you think she will say.

B 11.1 Listen to the first part of the interview and answer these questions.

1 What examples of crises does she give?

2 What is expensive?

3 Who are your stakeholders? What point does she make about them?

C 11.2 Listen to the second part of the interview and complete this extract of what Jan says.

Oh, be quick. Deal ....[1] with a crisis. If it's your fault, sometimes you know we make mistakes ... admit it. Admit it quickly, tell the public, tell your stakeholders ....[2], tell them what you're doing about it and keep ....[3]. The important thing is to keep communicating. If you don't, then that ....[4] of ....[5], the damage to your share price will follow. So you need to keep telling the public what is happening.

D 11.2 Summarise the example of Johnson & Johnson that Jan gives.

E 11.2 Why does she compare some companies to ostriches?

Reading
Airline crashes

A What actions does an airline's management have to take when one of its passenger aircraft crashes?

B Read the article. Then compare the actions it describes with your answers in Exercise A.

Handling a disaster

Moments that build or destroy reputations

When Swissair's flight 111 plunged into the sea off Nova Scotia, the tragedy bore several similarities to the loss of Trans World Airlines' flight 800 two years earlier.

Both jets crashed off the North American coast soon after leaving New York. Both were bound for Europe. Neither accident left any survivors. Neither has been fully explained. But the two disasters provoked sharply differing reactions. In the first, TWA was accused of incompetence and insensitivity for the way it responded to the needs of the victims' families. In the second, Swissair earned praise for its efficiency and compassion.

For TWA, the result has been lasting damage to its reputation. In contrast, Swissair's handling of the flight 111 crash has left confidence in the airline intact, and may even, conceivably, have enhanced it.

Richard George, Director of Public Relations for the Public Relations Society of America, says a crash is a 'defining moment' for an airline. 'In a matter of seconds, a reputation that has been built up over decades can be destroyed by making a mistake at that time,' he says.

So what lessons in crisis management emerge from the differing outcomes of the TWA and Swissair crashes?

Gary Abe, Deputy Director of the National Transportation Safety Board's office of family affairs, says the speed of an airline's response is one of the most important factors in determining how its behaviour is perceived.

'The first 24 hours following a disaster are critical for the airline involved. That is probably the only opportunity to build a trusting relationship with the family members,' he says.

TWA drew fury after the crash of flight 800 by refusing to produce a passenger list until it had determined exactly who was on the aircraft and notified their families – a process that took almost a full day.

Family members also complained that calls made to special toll-free telephone numbers went unanswered, that the flow of information was inadequate, and that insufficient attention was paid to their travel and accommodation needs.

Soon, politicians such as Rudolph Giuliani, New York's Mayor, started lambasting the airline for its handling of the disaster; the news headlines became critical; and TWA found itself portrayed as the company that could do nothing right.

Swissair's experience could hardly have been more different. Within hours of the loss of flight 111, a passenger manifest had been issued, fully-functioning hotlines had been set up, and hundreds of crisis counsellors had arrived in New York, ready to receive the grieving families. Soon afterwards, flights to the crash site at Peggy's Cove were being planned.

Friends and relatives were grateful for the way Swissair kept them informed of unfolding events, and appreciated the airline's offer of $20,000 (about £12,000) for each family to cover immediate expenses. Mr Giuliani praised the airline, and favourable headlines flowed.

One factor that worked in Swissair's favour was legislation passed by Congress requiring airlines to be much more responsive to the needs of victims' families after crashes. The Aviation Disaster Family Assistance Act – passed after a series of air crashes – required domestic carriers to file detailed plans for providing accurate passenger manifests, issuing toll-free telephone numbers, returning victims' personal effects and helping families with their travel and personal needs.

'That forced the airlines to have a good, effective manifest procedure,' says Mr Abe. 'Some of them didn't do that in the past. They just didn't care about their manifests, so they never really knew who was on the plane.' That legislation was not in place before TWA's flight 800 went down.

Swissair also benefited immeasurably from its code-sharing agreement with Delta Air Lines, the third biggest US carrier, under which the two sell seats on each other's flights as if they were their own.

By that agreement, Delta treated the loss of flight 111 as if it had been the loss of a Delta aircraft, and deployed the full weight of its resources in the crisis management effort. At times, the hundreds of Delta care-givers in New York and Peggy's Cove outnumbered the victims' relatives and friends. In contrast, TWA – twice bankrupt, and now a relatively small carrier – was on its own.

One obvious lesson from these disasters, as from any others, is that companies should rehearse for the worst, and rehearse often. A less obvious moral may be that no expense should be spared in helping the victims' families – if not out of compassion, then out of respect for the bottom line.

From the *Financial Times*

FINANCIAL TIMES
World business newspaper.

C Information about the TWA crash is summarised in the table below. Copy the headings and complete your table with corresponding information about the Swissair crash.

Crash site / Destination	North American coast / Europe
Casualties	No survivors
Cause of crash	Not fully explained
Public perception of airline	Incompetent / insensitive
Effect on reputation	Lasting damage
Production of passenger list	Slow
Telephone communication	Calls not answered
Treatment of relatives	Insufficient attention to travel / accommodation needs
Political reaction	Criticised by New York's Mayor
Press reaction	Critical
Legal obligations	No legislation at time of crash
Agreements with other airlines	None

D Why was Swissair able to respond more effectively than TWA in the hours immediately after the crash?

Vocabulary

Noun phrases with and without *of*

A Match words from each box to make word partnerships, adding the word *of* if necessary. For example, *action plan, admission of liability*.

~~action~~ ~~admission~~ contingency
damage flow legal loss
press press speed

action conference confidence
information ~~liability~~ limitation
plan ~~plan~~ release response

B Complete these sentences with the word partnerships above.

1 How quickly a crisis is reacted to is known as the ....

2 In a breaking crisis, management may speak to the media in person at a(n) ....

3 Alternatively, they may have a written statement which is given to the media in the form of a(n) ....

4 During the crisis, management may choose to keep customers or employees up to date with a regular ....

5 A strategy for dealing with a crisis is a(n) ....

6 A backup strategy is a(n) ....

7 The risk of being taken to court is the threat of ....

8 An acceptance of responsibility in a crisis is a(n) ....

9 Following a crisis, a company may suffer a decline in loyalty from its customers, or a(n) .... in its product or service.

10 Minimising the negative effects of a crisis is known as ....

Language review
Similarities and differences

The article on page 94 describes similarities and differences in two crises:
- **Similarities**
  Both jets crashed off the North American coast …
  Neither accident left any survivors.
  There were no survivors in either crash.
- *Differences*
  But the two disasters provoked sharply differing reactions.
  In the first, TWA was accused … In the second, Swissair earned praise …
  In contrast, Swissair's handling of the flight 111 crash …
  Swissair's experience could hardly have been more different.
  Calls to TWA were not answered, whereas Swissair set up telephone hotlines.
  Swissair's reputation was enhanced. On the other hand, TWA's was damaged.
- We use **modifying adjectives, adverbs and adverbial phrases** to comment on how big a difference is:
  Swissair's response to the crisis was much faster than TWA's.

see page 135

A Work in pairs. Look at the table on page 95 and your own table about Swissair. Talk about the similarities and differences they describe.

B Choose the most appropriate modifier to complete these sentences.

1 Swissair handled the crisis *quite / easily / far* better than TWA.

2 Swissair paid *even / much / many* more attention to people's accommodation needs.

3 Going by car is *nowhere near as / quite as / even less* safe as travelling by air.

4 Some passengers feel *virtually / slightly / nearly* more confident if they can have a drink before flying.

5 There was a(n) *minimal / equivalent / substantial* difference in the way the airlines handled the crises.

6 In the 1950s, aircraft were *nothing like / just / at least* as fast as they are today.

C Work in pairs. Use the notes below to write a short news article highlighting the similar and different ways in which the companies handled their crises.

Company: Clearwater	Company: United Drinks
last year had to withdraw its mineral water from all overseas markets	last year had to recall a batch of its soft drinks from the US market
drink had become contaminated at its source	drink had become contaminated during the manufacturing process
reacted immediately and issued a statement	delayed a month before informing its customers
admitted its mineral water was impure	said its soft drink was not a health hazard
at a press conference made every effort to answer journalists' questions honestly	at a press conference evaded reporters' questions on the nature of the problem
allocated $50m to recall its products	allocated $5m to deal with the crisis
some months later customers had regained confidence in the product – sales had increased	a few months later sales had fallen dramatically – customers had lost confidence

Skills
Asking and answering difficult questions

A The Chief Executive of a pharmaceutical company is answering questions at a press conference. The company is accused of offering bribes to doctors and medical staff in order to increase sales.

Read the questions and statements from journalists. In each case decide whether it is:

a) neutral / polite   b) forceful / aggressive.

1 Could you answer my question?

2 Would you mind answering my question? What is your policy about gifts to customers?

3 Could you please tell me how many sales staff you employ?

4 Could you tell me how many sales staff you employ?

5 Do you deny that bribery is a common sales strategy of your company?

6 Could I ask why you are replacing your Sales Director?

7 Do you mind if I ask how many letters of complaint you have had from doctors?

8 I'm interested in knowing whether you consider yourself an ethical company.

9 Isn't it true that you don't care how your staff behave as long as they meet their sales targets?

10 May I ask why you didn't investigate the allegations more quickly?

11 Surely you're not saying that no payments were made?

12 Could you clarify what gifts can be offered to customers?

B 🎧 11.3 Now listen to the questions above being spoken. Do you want to change any of your answers to Exercise A?

C The responses below are from a speaker at a press conference. Decide whether the speaker is answering a question which is:

a) neutral / polite – one which helps them to explain their message.
b) forceful / aggressive – one which they can't or don't want to answer.

1 I'm afraid I'm not in a position to comment on that.

2 That's a very good question. Let me explain.

3 I'm sorry, I can't possibly comment on that.

4 I'm afraid I don't know the answer to that one.

5 Sorry, I don't have any information on that at the moment.

6 No comment.

7 I'll be happy to answer that.

8 I've no idea off the top of my head.

9 I'm pleased you raised that point.

10 I'm glad you asked me that.

11 Sorry, I'm not prepared to answer that at the moment.

12 Can I get back to you on that one?

D Role play the following situation.

A mobile phone company has been attacked in several newspapers for using 'dishonest' methods to sell its phones. The managers arrange a press conference to defend their company's reputation and answer questions.

Managers turn to page 148.
Journalists turn to page 152.
Read your role cards, then hold the press conference.

CASE STUDY

Background

The article below appeared in today's edition of *Euronews*, a weekly newspaper published in English throughout Europe.

High Street Retailer in Pirated Goods Row

Retailing chain Target Stores was accused last night in a TV documentary of selling illegal software products. The documentary claimed that pirated copies of the best-selling computer game 'Race against Time' were flooding the market in Europe.

According to the programme, in the last three months Target Stores have sold approximately 50,000 games, said to be illegal copies from a supplier based in Hong Kong. It was alleged that the copies had been bought at a heavily discounted price and were 'selling like hot cakes' because the price was so low.

Target's Chief Executive, Penny Taylor, insisted the accusation could not be true, saying 'Target Stores is known for its integrity and high ethical standards. We price our products competitively and offer top quality goods. We have a skilled and committed workforce in whom we have great confidence.'

A company employee who does not wish to be named said that Target Stores have had problems in their buying department recently. Staff turnover in the department has been high. This has affected employees' morale and efficiency.

🎧 **11.4** Listen to part of a conversation between Carla Davis, Director of Public Relations for Target Stores, and Hugo Stern, an independent crisis management consultant.

Company profile

 TARGET STORES

Based in Dublin, Ireland, Target Stores is a major retailer with stores in most European cities. The company started by selling stationery, books and greeting cards, later branching out into magazines and music products. Because of fierce competition it has repositioned itself, concentrating on computer products, especially computer games.

Its merchandise appeals particularly to teenagers and young adults. The chain prides itself on providing quality products at affordable prices. It is known for its high ethical standards. Its mission statement begins, 'We put people first'.

Key figures	
Workforce	8,000
Sales	€ 720m
Pre-tax profits	€ 90m

Key
- ▪ Computer software / games
- ▪ Stationery and cards
- ▪ Books and music
- ▪ Office equipment
- ▪ Other

Task

Because of the serious allegations and the effect on the company's image and share price, Target Stores decide to hold a press conference. This will enable them to defend the company, explain how they are dealing with the crisis and answer questions from journalists.
You are either:
a director of Target Stores (turn to page 146)
or a newspaper journalist (turn to page 151).
Read your role card and prepare for the press conference. Then hold the press conference.

Writing

One of the objectives of the Society for the Prevention of Software Fraud (SPSF) is to eliminate software piracy. Its members include over 1,000 UK companies, some of them leading software publishers. It is highly respected and has the power to impose large fines in cases of extreme malpractice. Any warnings or sanctions it issues in such cases can damage a company's reputation.

Journalists

The head of the SPSF has asked you for a report on the Target Stores crisis. It should include the following information:

- the background to the crisis
- an analysis of the actions the company took to deal with it
- recommendations about what action you think the SPSF should take, if any.

Target Store Directors

The head of the SPSF has asked you for a report on the recent crisis. It should include the following information:

- the background to the crisis
- an explanation of the actions you have taken to deal with it.

You need to put up a good defence as a strong sanction from the SPSF will further damage your company's reputation.

 Writing file pages 144 and 145

Management styles

"Management is tasks. Management is discipline. But management is also people."

Peter Drucker, Austrian–American management guru

OVERVIEW ▼

☐ **Vocabulary**
Management qualities

☐ **Listening**
Management styles and qualities

☐ **Reading**
Who would you rather work for?

☐ **Language review**
Text reference

☐ **Skills**
Putting people at ease

☐ **Case study**
Zenova

Starting up

A **Which of these statements do you agree with? Explain your reasons.**

A manager should:

1 know when your birthday is.

2 know where you are and what you're doing at all times during working hours.

3 not criticise or praise.

4 not interfere in disagreements between members of staff.

5 not ask people to do things they're not prepared to do themselves.

6 be available at all times to give staff advice and support.

7 keep their distance from staff and not get involved in socialising outside work.

8 use polite language at all times.

9 work longer hours than their staff.

10 comment on the personal appearance of their staff.

B **Mothers and fathers often have different ways of managing their families. How would you describe the management styles of your parents? If you have children, what about your own style?**

Vocabulary
Management qualities

A Complete column 2 of the table with opposite meanings. Use the prefixes *in-*, *ir- un-*, *il-* or *dis-*. Then complete column 3 with the noun forms.

1 Adjective	2 Opposite adjective	3 Noun form
considerate	*inconsiderate*	*consideration*
creative		
decisive		
diplomatic		
efficient		
flexible		
inspiring		
interested		
logical		
organised		
rational		
responsible		
sociable		
supportive		

B Choose the four best qualities of a manager from the list above and rank them in order of importance. Then choose the four worst qualities and rank them (1 = worst).

C Discuss your answers to Exercise B. What other management qualities or weaknesses can you add?

D Match these pairs of contrasting management styles.

1 autocratic	**a)** collaborative
2 centralising	**b)** controlling
3 directive	**c)** delegating
4 empowering	**d)** democratic
5 hands on	**e)** people-orientated
6 task-orientated	**f)** laissez-faire

E Different business situations call for different management styles. Which kinds of situation need to be tightly managed and which loosely managed?

F Which management styles have you experienced? Which do you prefer? If you are a manager, how would you describe your own management style?

Listening
Management styles and qualities

A 🎧 12.1 Listen to the first part of an interview with Stuart Crainer, who has written many books on business and management. What four qualities for an ideal manager does he talk about? What additional quality does he mention?

B 🎧 12.2 Listen to the second part of the interview. What does Stuart say about management styles at the following companies?

1 General Electric
2 Virgin
3 Body Shop
4 IKEA
5 Nokia

C 🎧 12.3 Listen to the last part of the interview. What, according to Stuart, is the key to managing globally?

▲ Stuart Crainer

Reading
Who would you rather work for?

A Discuss these questions.

1 Which would you prefer to work for?
   a) a male boss
   b) a female boss
   c) either – you don't have a preference

2 Do you think your response to question 1 is a typical one?

B Read the first paragraph *only* of both articles. What is the main point made by the writer in each case?

C Work in pairs. One of you reads article A. The other reads article B. Summarise each paragraph in a single sentence of no more than 15 words. Then give an oral summary of the whole article to your partner.

Article A

Who would you rather work for?

Women are more efficient and trustworthy, have a better understanding of their workforce and are more generous with their praise. In short they make the best managers, and if men are to keep up they will have to start learning from their female counterparts, a report claims today.

The survey of 1,000 male and female middle and senior managers from across the UK is an indictment of the ability of men to function as leaders in the modern workplace.

A majority of those questioned believed women had a more modern outlook on their profession and were more open minded and considerate. By way of contrast, a similar number believe male managers are egocentric and more likely to steal credit for work done by others.

Management Today magazine, which conducted the research, said that after years of having to adopt a masculine identity and hide their emotions and natural behaviour in the workplace, women have become role models for managers.

The findings tally with a survey of female bosses carried out in the US. A five-year study of 2,500 managers from 450 firms found that many male bosses were rated by their staff of both sexes to be self-obsessed and autocratic. Women on the other hand leave men in the starting blocks when it comes to teamwork and communicating with staff.

In Britain more than 61% of those surveyed said men did not make better bosses than women. Female managers use time more effectively, with many of those surveyed commenting that juggling commitments is a familiar practice for women with a home and a family.

Female managers also appear to make good financial sense for penny-pinching companies: most people, of either sex, would rather ask for a rise from a man.

'If men want to be successful at work they must behave more like women,' said the magazine's editor, Rufus Olins. 'Businesses need to wake up to the fact that so-called feminine skills are vital for attracting and keeping the right people. In the past women who aspired to management were encouraged to be more manly. It looks now as if the boot is on the other foot.'

From the *Guardian*

Article B

Which bosses are best?

How do you like your boss? Sympathetic, empowering and not too busy, probably. They will be aware of the pressures of your job, but delegate responsibility where appropriate. They will be interested in your career development. Oh, and, preferably, they will be male.

In a survey for Royal Mail special delivery, a quarter of secretaries polled expressed a preference for a male boss. Only 7% said they would prefer a woman. The future of management may be female, but Ms High-Flier, it seems, can expect little support from her secretary.

One should not, of course, assume that all secretaries are female, but women still make up the overwhelming majority. So it makes uncomfortable reading for those who like to believe that a soft and cuddly sisterhood exists in the previously macho office environment, where women look out for their own. The findings also raise questions about neat predictions of a feminised future for management, where 'womanly' traits such as listening skills, flexibility and a more empathetic manner will become normal office currency.

Business psychologist John Nicholson is surprised by the survey's findings, asserting that 'the

qualities valued today in a successful boss are feminine, not masculine'. He is emphatic that women make better bosses. 'They listen more, are less status-conscious, conduct crisper meetings, are much more effective negotiators and display greater flexibility.'

They are also considerably more common than they used to be. According to information group Experian, women are no longer scarce in the boardroom – they occupy a third of the seats round the conference table. Women directors are still relatively uncommon in older age groups, but among young directors the proportion is growing.

Anecdotal evidence suggests that a reluctance to work for a woman may be more a question of management style than substance. 'It's just women bosses' attitude,' says Martha, a PA for 25 years who has worked predominantly for women, including a high-profile politician. 'It's something women have that men don't. When they are critical they are much more personal, whereas men sail through not taking a blind bit of notice.'

Sonia Neill, a former secretary at Marks and Spencer, has experienced power struggles between women even where there was a significant disparity in status. 'Women either find it awkward to give you work or they try to assert themselves by giving you really menial tasks. Men never do that.'

From the *Guardian*

D **Find words in the articles with the following meanings.**

Article A

1 people with the same jobs as each other (paragraph 1)

2 a clear sign that a system isn't working (paragraph 2)

3 thinking only about yourself (paragraph 3)

4 giving orders without asking others for their opinions (paragraph 5)

5 wanted to achieve an important goal (paragraph 8)

Article B

6 aspects of a person's character (paragraph 3)

7 absolutely convinced (paragraph 4)

8 based on stories about personal experience (paragraph 6)

9 a difference between things (paragraph 7)

10 behave in a determined way (paragraph 7)

E **From the two texts, find as many characteristics as possible that are attributed to female managers.**

F **Which ideas expressed in the two articles do you agree with? Do you find any of the ideas surprising?**

Language review
Text reference

- In written English, we often use pronouns to avoid repeating words and phrases when it is already clear what we are talking about. For example, *We need the report urgently — it's got to be sent to head office.*
- Writers sometimes use *we* to refer to themselves and the readers together. For example, *As we saw in Chapter 2 ...*
- We sometimes use *it* as an 'empty' subject with no real meaning. For example, *It's raining.*
- We can use *it, this, that, these* and *those* to refer back or forward to something in a text, or outside the text itself.
- We can use *they* to avoid saying *he* or *she*, especially after indefinite words like *anyone, no one, somebody,* etc. For example, *Someone's been trying to send us a fax but they can't get through.*

➡ **page 135**

A **Look at article B on page 103 and answer these questions.**

1 Find the word *boss* (line 1). Then find three references to *boss* in the same paragraph.

2 Find the word *women* (line 39). Then find six references to *women* in paragraphs 4, 5, 6 and 7.

3 What do the following words refer to?
   a) it   (line 15)
   b) it   (line 21)
   c) those   (line 23)
   d) He   (line 39)
   e) It's   (line 60)
   f) It's   (line 64)
   g) it   (line 74)
   h) that   (line 77)

B **Paragraphs 8 and 9 of article B, which are not included on page 103, are given below. Complete them using the pronouns in the box.**

it	them	we	they	their	they	they

A particular bugbear is secretaries who have moved up the ladder. 'You expect ....¹ to be more sympathetic because ....² know what ....³ is like being at the bottom, but instead ....⁴ seem desperate to prove a point.'

Marilyn Davidson, Professor of Management Psychology at UMIST, suggests national assumptions on gender and status are more tenacious than ....⁵ might like to think. 'I interview women in managerial positions who've advertised for secretaries and when the secretary realises ....⁶ boss is female ....⁷ have walked out.'

From the *Guardian*

Skills
Putting people at ease

A **Discuss these questions.**

1 What is *small talk*?

2 What topics are appropriate for small talk in your country? List five topics.

3 What topics are definitely not suitable?

B **To which questions might the following be answers?**

1 Terrible. There was a lot of turbulence and several people were sick.

2 Yes, several times.

3 Right in the centre.

4 Very comfortable, and the service is first class.

5 They're all well, thanks very much.

6 I enjoy tennis, when I get the time.

7 I'm really impressed. The architecture is fascinating. I hope I have time to take it all in.

8 By all means.

C **Discuss these questions.**

1 What ways could you use to put people at ease in the following situations:
   a) entertaining socially with friends
   b) business entertaining with colleagues
   c) entertaining foreign visitors

2 Do you feel comfortable when there is silence in a group?

3 Do you feel more comfortable:
   a) in a small group or a large group?
   b) with members of your own sex or with the opposite sex?
   c) in a formal situation or an informal one?

D **The Managing Director of a large American company made the suggestions on the left for putting people at ease. Match them to the comments on the right.**

1 Use informal greetings when you meet people.

2 Find out about who you're going to meet.

3 Share something of a personal nature.

4 Pick a topic which isn't work-related.

5 Use open questions rather than statements.

a) 'I'm a bit stressed – we've got builders in our house!'

b) 'Did you see the football last night?'

c) 'Hi, I'm John.'

d) 'How are you finding the conference?'

e) 'You must be Dan Jervis. Weren't you with Datacom?'

E **Which would be appropriate in your culture? What other things do you say to put people at ease?**

F **You are about to meet a foreign business contact socially for the first time. Choose four of the topics below and prepare to talk about them.**

- cars
- families
- food and restaurants
- hobbies
- holidays
- how you travelled here
- IT topics
- jobs
- places of interest in your town / country
- the building you are in
- the stock market
- the weather

CASE STUDY

Background

Zenova is based in Hamburg, Germany. It is a multinational conglomerate which makes pharmaceuticals, health and beauty products, have recently initiated a global Customer Care Policy.

Six months ago it assembled a project team of 250 staff drawn from subsidiaries in Europe, America and Asia to work on the policy's implementation. The multinational team has 12 managers who each manage 10–30 staff. The working language used in the project team is English.

Recently however, it has become clear that the different management styles within the team are causing problems. Many staff are unhappy with the way they are being managed and morale is generally poor. If the situation continues, the project will not be completed within its scheduled two-year period.

As a result, Zenova's Communications Director sent a questionnaire to all 250 staff inviting them to assess their managers. In addition, a cross-section of staff were interviewed. The findings will be used by the twelve project team managers to discuss ways to achieve more effective management styles.

Task

🎧 **12.4** You are managers in the project team. Study the questionnaire findings.

Then listen to the interview extracts of staff comments and note any useful information.

Hold a meeting to discuss what the feedback reveals about the management styles within the team. The checklist on page 107 may be useful as a guide for your discussion.

Finally, suggest ways in which you could achieve a more consistent management style and improve the team's morale and efficiency.

Summary of questionnaire findings

Number of questionnaires sent out: 250   Number of questionnaires completed: 171

		% Very Often	% Often	% Sometimes	% Never
1	Are you involved in decision-making?	41	12	31	16
2	Does your manager give you clear goals?	8	10	70	12
3	Does your manager give clear instructions?	11	14	56	19
4	Are you allowed to use your initiative?	18	35	15	32
5	Is your manager accessible?	28	11	54	7
6	Does your manager offer support and listen to your problems?	28	11	26	35
7	Does your manager praise your work, when appropriate?	12	10	31	47
8	Are you offered constructive feedback?	22	18	47	13
9	Does your manager accept that you will sometimes make mistakes?	23	15	41	21
10	Are you given career advice and training?	3	7	11	79
11	Does your manager present himself / herself as a positive role model?	35	21	13	31

Evaluation of findings: Checklist

Delegation	Do we provide enough decision-making opportunities for our staff?
Feedback	Do we devote enough time to providing it?
Briefing	Do we make company objectives clear enough, often enough?
Troubleshooting	Do we help solve problems effectively?
Teambuilding	Do we do enough to create team spirit?
Coaching	Do we show a caring attitude and help employees to realise their career aspirations?
Motivation	Do we help employees to achieve a sense of fulfilment? Do we make them feel that their contribution is valued by the company?

Writing

As a manager in the project team, write the action minutes for the meeting you have just attended. These will be sent to all the participants and senior management. The minutes should contain the following:

- a summary of the discussion for each item on the agenda.
- action required and who will carry out each task.

 *Writing file* page 143

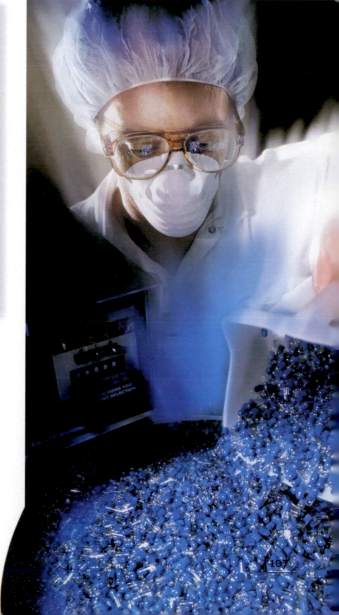

UNIT 13 Takeovers and mergers

You cannot buy a company merely by buying its shares.

Sir James Goldsmith (1933–1997)
Anglo–French financier

Vocabulary
Describing takeovers and mergers

Listening
Making acquisitions

Reading
Why mergers fail

Language review
Headlines

Skills
Summarising in presentations

Case study
Group Bon Appetit PLC

Starting up

A Think of a recent takeover or merger. What kinds of business were involved? Were both companies successful before it happened? What about now?

B What are the advantages and disadvantages of:

a) takeovers? b) mergers?

Think about the companies involved, their employees and the consumer.

C Studies show that 65% of mergers do not achieve their expected results. What are the reasons for this, do you think?

Vocabulary

Describing takeovers and mergers

A Match the terms on the left to the definitions on the right.

1 alliance
2 joint venture
3 LBO (leveraged buyout)
4 MBO (management buyout)
5 merger
6 takeover / acquisition

a) getting control of a company by buying over 50% of its shares
b) two or more companies joining to form a larger company
c) a business activity in which two or more companies have invested together
d) when a company's top executives buy the company they work for
e) buying a company using a loan borrowed against the assets of the company that's being bought
f) an agreement between two or more organisations to work together

B Make as many expressions as you can from the words in the box. For example, 'to *take a stake* in a business'.

> acquisition   bid   hostile   launch   make
>
> stake   take   takeover   target

C Complete the following newspaper extracts with words from Exercises A and B. There may be several possible choices for each gap.

1   Investors dismissed Lafarge's £3.4 billion ....
.... for Blue Circle yesterday, rejecting the offer on the
grounds that it was 'wholly inadequate'.   (The *Times*)

2   The Boards of Glaxo Wellcome and Smithkline Beecham announce
that they have unanimously agreed the terms of a proposed
.... of equals to form Glaxo Smithkline. The new
company is expected to generate substantial operational synergies.
(Press release)

3   Sotheby's, the auction house, is forming a ....
with Amazon.com, the Internet retailer, to create a new on-line
auction service. As part of the deal Amazon.com will
.... in Sotheby's.
(The *Economist*)

Listening
Making acquisitions

A Match these words with their meanings

1 asset
2 cost structure
3 integration
4 momentum
5 projections
6 synergy

a) an organisation's different costs and the way they are related to each other
b) advantage produced when two organisations combine resources
c) calculations about, for example, what the size, amount or rate of something will be in the future
d) something belonging to a business that has value or the power to earn money
e) combining two companies so that they can work closely and effectively together
f) the ability to keep increasing, developing or being more successful

▲ Nigel Portwood

B 🎧 13.1 Listen to the first part of an interview with Nigel Portwood, President and Chief Executive Officer at Pearson Education.

What essential preparatory steps should a company take to make a successful acquisition?

C 🎧 13.2 Now listen to the second part of the interview. What three things need to be done to ensure the successful integration of a newly acquired business?

D 🎧 13.3 Listen to the last part of the interview. What are the five key questions for judging whether an acquisition has been successful?

Reading
Why mergers fail

Ⓐ Before you read the article, discuss these questions.

1 Whose shareholders benefit more in a takeover: those of the acquiring company or those of the one that is being acquired?

2 What is corporate culture? How might it affect the success or failure of a merger?

Ⓑ Read the article. Then answer these questions.

1 According to the article, whose shareholders benefit most in a takeover?

2 Why do so many mergers fail, according to the article?

3 What do acquiring companies need to do to ensure success?

Ⓒ Choose the answer.

1 If your reputation is *tarnished* (line 3), it is
   a) improved.
   b) made worse.

2 If a merger suffers from *poor implementation* (lines 45–46), it is
   a) badly planned.
   b) badly put into practice.

3 If two organisations are *compatible* (line 75), they are
   a) able to have a good relationship with each other.
   b) able to be divided into smaller groups.

4 If you have *complementary businesses* (lines 80–81), are they businesses
   a) that offer different products in the same range.
   b) that offer free products.

5 If you *pay a premium* (lines 107–108), you
   a) pay a higher than usual price.
   b) pay a lower than usual price.

6 If something is difficult to *replicate* (line 149), it is difficult
   a) to find.
   b) to copy.

7 If the *odds are stacked against* you (lines 160–161), you are
   a) likely to succeed.
   b) likely to fail.

Ⓓ Complete these sentences with some of the italicised words and phrases above. Then make sentences of your own with the remaining italicised words.

1 We need to make sure that the software is .... with our computer applications.

2 Successful businesspeople have a will to succeed even when the .... them.

3 The new manager's skills are .... to those of the existing team members.

4 We won't be able to .... this level of sales next year.

Marrying in haste

Mergers and acquisitions continue apace in spite of an alarming failure rate and evidence that they often fail to benefit shareholders, writes **Michael Skapinker.**

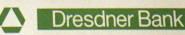

The collapse of the planned Deutsche–Dresdner Bank merger tarnished the reputation of both parties. Deutsche Bank's management was exposed as divided and confused. But even if the takeover had gone ahead, it would probably still have claimed its victims. Most completed takeovers damage one party – the company making the acquisition.

A long list of studies have all reached the same conclusion: the majority of takeovers damage the interests of the shareholders of the acquiring company. They do, however, often reward the shareholders of the acquired company, who receive more for their shares than they were worth before the takeover was announced. Mark Sirower, visiting professor at New York University, says surveys have repeatedly shown that about 65 per cent of mergers fail to benefit acquiring companies, whose shares subsequently underperform their sector.

Why do so many mergers and acquisitions fail to benefit shareholders? Colin Price, a partner at McKinsey, the management consultants, who specialises in mergers and acquisitions, says the majority of failed mergers suffer from poor implementation. And in about half of those, senior management failed to take account of the different cultures of the companies involved.

Melding corporate cultures takes time, which senior management does not have after a merger, Mr Price says. 'Most mergers are based on the idea of "let's increase revenues", but you have to have a functioning management team to manage that process. The nature of the problem is not so much that there's open warfare between the two sides. It's that the cultures don't meld quickly enough to take advantage of the opportunities. In the meantime, the marketplace has moved on.'

Many consultants refer to how little time companies spend before a merger thinking about whether their organisations are compatible. The benefits of mergers are usually couched in financial or commercial terms: cost-savings can be made or the two sides have complementary businesses that will allow them to increase revenues.

Mergers are about compatibility, which means agreeing whose values will prevail and who will be the dominant partner. So it is no accident that managers as well as journalists reach for marriage metaphors in describing them. Merging companies are said to 'tie the knot'. When mergers are called off, the two companies fail to 'make it up the aisle' or their relationship remains 'unconsummated'. Yet the metaphor fails to convey the scale of risk companies run when they launch acquisitions or mergers. Even in countries with high divorce rates, marriages have a better success rate than mergers.

Mark Sirower asks why managers should pay a premium to make an acquisition when their shareholders could invest in the target company themselves. Mr Sirower denies he is saying companies should never make acquisitions. If 65 per cent of mergers fail to benefit shareholders, 35 per cent are successful.

How can acquirers try to ensure they are among the successful minority? Ken Favaro, managing partner of Marakon, a consultancy which has worked for Coca-Cola, Lloyds TSB and Boeing, suggests two conditions for success. The first is to define what success means. 'The combined entities have to deliver better returns to the shareholders than they would separately. It's amazing how often that's not the pre-agreed measure of success,' Mr Favaro says.

Second, merging companies need to decide in advance which partner's way of doing things will prevail. 'Mergers of equals can be so dangerous because it is not clear who is in charge,' Mr Favaro says. Mr Sirower adds that managers need to ask what advantages they will bring to the acquired company that competitors will find difficult to replicate.

Managers need to remember that competitors are not going to hang around waiting for them to improve the performance of their new acquisition. Announcing a takeover will have alerted competitors to the acquiring company's strategy. Given how heavily the odds are stacked against successful mergers, managers should consider whether their time and the shareholders' money would not be better employed elsewhere.

From the Financial Times

FINANCIAL TIMES
World business newspaper.

Language review
Headlines

Newspaper headlines are often written in a special style which can make them difficult to understand. They often:

1 contain groups of several nouns: *software company takeover battle*
2 leave out articles and the verb *to be*: *Wal-Mart and Asda close to deal*
3 contain simple tenses instead of progressive or perfect forms, and use the present simple for past events: *Shell confirms China stake*
4 contain words used both as nouns and verbs: *French company targets UK media group; UK media group becomes takeover target*
5 refer to the future with infinitives: *Wal-Mart to acquire Asda*

 see page 136

A Look at these headlines. Which of the features described in the Language review box do they show? (Some headlines show more than one feature.)

1 Renault on brink of two alliances
2 Moulinex and Brandt near merger deal
3 Austin Reed rejects offer as unwelcome
4 Biotech groups agree merger
5 Wal-Mart in £6.7bn bid for Asda
6 Melrose to raise £5.8m via London flotation
7 Rivals in final United Biscuits fight
8 Takeover target Esat hints at a white knight
9 AOL deal calls rivals' web plans into question
10 United News to dispose of US magazines

B Write out the headlines above in full. For example, *Renault is on the brink of two alliances.*

C Certain words are used more commonly in headlines, often because they are shorter or more dramatic than their alternatives. Match the italicised words in the headlines on the left to their meanings on the right.

1 Renault on *brink* of two alliances
2 Mannesmann investors *split* over bid
3 Banks in merger credits *deal*
4 KPN seeks new partners after Telefonica *blow*
5 Deutsche chief criticised *over* Dresdner deal
6 Rivals study EMI–Warner *link*
7 Treasury seeks peace deal in takeovers *row*
8 Wickes fights hostile *bid*
9 Brussels pressed to *block* merger
10 Aircraft group *seeks* £300m merger savings
11 WPP and Y & R set to *unveil* $4.4bn merger
12 Takeover *backing* for Union Fenosa

a) offer to buy a company
b) connection
c) about, concerning
d) edge
e) announce
f) disagree
g) agreement
h) support
i) look for
j) disagreement
k) obstruct
l) bad news

Skills
Summarising in presentations

A Jeremy Keeley, an independent management consultant, is giving a presentation to a board of directors involved in a takeover. Before you listen match these words that he uses to their meanings.

1	pitfalls	a)	things that limit your action
2	rigorous	b)	thorough
3	constraints	c)	to work together to produce something
4	confidential	d)	unexpected difficulties
5	hamstrung	e)	those who try to please important people
6	sycophants	f)	competing for
7	vying (for jobs)	g)	intended to be kept secret
8	collaborate	h)	prevented from doing something

B 13.4 You will hear part of the final section of Jeremy's presentation. He is giving a summary of common mistakes that managers make. Which of the four points in his presentation notes below does he *not* make?

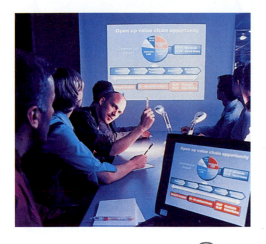

Avoiding the pitfalls
- *Recognise the constraints*
- *Pay attention to the cultural differences*
- *Beware of the sycophants*
- *Refer to core meaning/purpose*

C 13.4 Study the Useful language box. Then listen again and tick the phrases that you hear.

Useful language

Referring back
As I mentioned earlier in my presentation …
So as you were saying a few minutes ago …

Making points in threes
You really have to plan carefully, be rigorous in your analysis and be flexible …
It's a long process. It's expensive. It can also be very profitable.

Asking rhetorical questions
What are the advantages of the merger?
But what are the sort of things that the experts forget generally?

Ordering
Firstly …, then …, finally …
There are three things in my mind and the first thing is …

Using emotive language
Beware of the sycophants in your organisation …
It is commercial suicide …

Repetition
They're going to be saying Yes! Yes! Yes!
It won't work. It just won't work.

Exemplifying
For instance…
… for example, caring as their primary task.

Asking for feedback
Is there any area I haven't covered?
What's missing?

D Work in two groups, A and B. Group A discuss some of the advantages of takeovers and mergers. Group B discuss the problems associated with them.

Then form pairs – one from Group A and one from Group B. Give a short presentation summarising the points you discussed in your group.

Group Bon Appetit PLC

Background

Last year, Group Bon Appetit PLC acquired Innovia Cafes after a bitterly fought takeover battle. Bon Appetit won by offering Innovia's shareholders 20% over the market price for their shares. At the time, Bon Appetit stated: 'Our objective is to double our business within the next five years'.

Shortly after the takeover, the group's share price reached a peak of almost 400 pence. But then it began to decline dramatically to a low of less than 50 pence. Recently it has risen to 80 pence because of strong interest from a powerful predator, the restaurant chain Icarus.

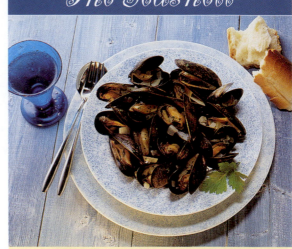

The Seashell

- Middle-income groups, 25–60 year olds, mixed clientele
- Seafood a speciality
- £15–£30 per person

Group Bon Appetit PLC

Innovia Cafes

- All income groups, all ages, family-orientated clientele
- Good food and drink at affordable prices
- £5–£10 per person

Group Bon Appetit PLC

Bon Appetit

- Higher-income groups, 25–50 year olds, loyal clientele
- Top-class cuisine
- £30–£60 per person

Group Bon Appetit PLC

Group Bon Appetit: Key facts

Three restaurant chains in London and South East England

■ Bon Appetit	22 restaurants
■ The Seashell	10 restaurants
■ Innovia Cafes	16 cafes

Planning a nationwide expansion

- ■ 10 new restaurants next year
- ■ A further 20 within the next three years

We are continuing to look for suitable acquisitions in order to create a more diversified group and to widen our customer base. The purchase of Innovia Cafes takes us into a new market segment, the £5–£10 a head market. We expect Innovia Cafes to contribute significantly to our profits in the future.

(Extract from Annual Report – Group Bon Appetit PLC)

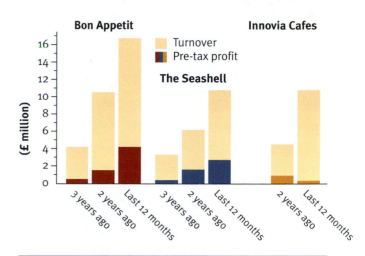

Debt ratio*

2 years ago	Last year	This year
30%	55% (includes cost of Innovia acquisition)	70% (includes cost of *proposed* El Morito acquisition)

(*Debt ratio: a company's debt in relation to the amount of share capital it has.)

Major shareholdings

• Directors of Bon Appetit	12%
• Weinburg Investments (venture capitalists)	20%
• Restaurant chain, Icarus	10%
• Private shareholders	58%

Recent developments

Financial experts in the City of London no longer have confidence in the group's strategy, for the following reasons:

1 Innovia Cafes have performed badly. There is strong competition from US chains, such as Starbucks.

2 Bon Appetit is closely controlled from head office. Innovia's managers, however, are used to a relaxed management style. Many have left because of the 'bureaucratic' culture.

3 Staff turnover among Innovia's other workers is also high and customer service is poor.

4 Bon Appetit has agreed to buy the El Morito chain of 12 Mexican-style restaurants for £14m. Experts believe that the group is overstretched and losing focus.

5 The powerful national restaurant chain, Icarus, has taken a 10% stake in Bon Appetit and says that Bon Appetit would be an excellent addition to its business.

Task

The directors of the venture capital firm Weinburg Investments, a major shareholder in Bon Appetit, are concerned about the threat of takeover. They have asked the directors of Bon Appetit to attend a meeting to consider:

1 What actions must Bon Appetit take to avoid the threatened takeover by Icarus?

2 How can Bon Appetit improve the performance of Innovia Cafes?

3 Should Bon Appetit reconsider the proposed takeover of El Morito?

4 Should Bon Appetit's overall business strategy be revised?

Form two groups:

a) Directors of Bon Appetit

b) Directors of Weinburg Investments.

Discuss the questions above. Then hold the meeting.

Writing

Directors of Bon Appetit

Write a report on your company for a financial group who are interested in investing in your business. Your report should give background information as well as information about recent developments. It should present the company in a positive light.

Directors of Weinburg Investments

Write a report on Bon Appetit. The report should give background information as well as information about recent developments. It should analyse the company's performance and indicate whether Weinburg Investments should sell their stake in Bon Appetit.

 Writing file pages 144 and 145

The future of business

'What we anticipate seldom occurs; what we least expected generally happens.'
Benjamin Disraeli (1804–81),
British Prime Minister

OVERVIEW ▼

☐ **Listening**
Changing customer needs

☐ **Vocabulary**
1) Expressions about time
2) Describing the future

☐ **Reading**
Products and services of the future

☐ **Language review**
The language of prediction

☐ **Skills**
Getting the right information

☐ **Case study**
Yedo Department Stores

Starting up

A The business world has changed dramatically in recent times. Which of the following do you think could happen within the next 50 years? Explain why.

1 People will have more leisure time.

2 Public telephones will disappear.

3 There will be cities of 100 million people.

4 There will be a world stock market.

5 Cash won't be used any more.

6 People will live and work in space.

7 Trade unions will disappear.

8 It will be possible for human beings to live to 150.

9 Men and women will understand each other better.

10 Traffic congestion in major cities will improve.

B What other changes do you think are likely?

C How optimistic are you about the future of business in your own country? Explain your answer.

Listening
Changing customer needs

A 🎧 14.1 **Martin Phelps, Business Director at the advertising agency Ogilvy and Mather in London, is talking about how customer needs are changing. There are eight factual mistakes in the interview summary below. Read the summary. Then listen to the interview and correct the mistakes.**

> **The changing needs of customers**
>
> Customer needs are changing because of developments in three key areas: environmental issues, technology and time.
>
> The change in social environment concerns the type of households that we live in. The classic family unit – mother, father and family pets – only constitutes about 50% of the UK population, and is being replaced by a variety of other forms. These include single-person households, single-parent households, and households where children share a house – but live as individuals rather than as a single family.
>
> The changes caused by technological developments are being driven in particular by the rapid expansion in the use of e-mail and the growing importance of household appliances.
>
> Finally, as our lives become less busy, customers are starting to expect 'value for time' when making a purchase. This can mean *saving* customers' time, for example through Internet shopping; or, on the other hand, creating an environment where shopping is treated as a business transaction that customers actually want to *spend* time on and enjoy.

B **Discuss these questions.**

1 What does the Henley Centre do?

2 Amazon.com and the bookshop chain Waterstones both offer 'value for time' but in different ways. What are the differences?

3 Which is more important to you when making a purchase: 'value for time' or 'value for money'? Why?

Vocabulary 1
Expressions about time

A **Complete the phrases below with words from the box.**

> art   ~~date~~   date   edge   fashioned
> forefront   forward   minute   past   times

1 up-to- *date*
2 a thing of the ....
3 at the ....
4 old- ....
5 state-of-the-...................................
6 the way ....
7 out of ....
8 up to the ....
9 at the leading ....
10 behind the ....

B **Use some of the expressions above to comment on products or companies that you are familiar with. For example,** *Public telephones could become a thing of the past.*

A Discuss these questions.

1 How important is it for companies to anticipate future trends in consumer behaviour? What methods can they use to do so?

2 The article below predicts possible changes to products and services by the year 2030. What do you think it might say? Brainstorm ideas in the following areas:

a) clothing   c) refrigerators   e) food

b) retirement homes   d) pharmaceuticals   f) toys

B Now read the article. Compare its predictions with your own ideas.

Cashing in on a tailor-made world

Predicting which products are going to be in demand is big business, writes **Helen Jones**

Retirement homes for cats and dogs, snacks to combat depression, clothing with an in-built massage facility, and sleep machines to provoke intense dreams. These are some of the products and services 21st-century consumers can look forward to, according to futurologist Marian Salzman.

Ms Salzman is head of the Brand Futures group at advertising agency Young & Rubicam and travels the globe spotting consumer trends for clients which include Ford, Sony, PepsiCo and Citibank.

Her aim is to provide an 'early warning system' for companies, keeping them up-to-date on consumer behaviour and identifying the way in which changing lifestyles could affect their brands in the future. New trends are identified through interviews with academics and scientists, as well as groups of consumers judged to be at the cutting edge of fashion.

'Marketers have always needed to understand consumers' current concerns and experiences with their brands. But if they are to thrive in the years ahead, they must anticipate where technology, social trends and myriad other change agents are leading, so that they will have a place in the consumer future,' she says.

One of the most important emerging trends is that 'mass marketing is becoming obsolete in high-tech cultures. As consumers we are being led to expect products that meet our specific needs – Levi's makes computerised-fit jeans to your exact measurements, for instance. And parents can buy personalised storybooks and videos for their children. Demand for these types of products will soar,' she forecasts.

'Entrepreneurial companies will find plenty of business opportunities if they target the increasingly ageing population', she says. By 2030, approximately 20 per cent of the US population will be over 65 and this group will influence everything from financial products to easy-to-open packaging.

'We will see great shifts in attitude regarding age. This group's power will increase, images of the elderly as victims will become historical, and they will increase their economic power as they move into their second half-century of life. Expect to see them driving top-of-the-range cars,' she says. Meanwhile, the 'oldest olds' – those in their nineties and beyond – will be looked after at day-care centres, along with under-fives and pets, while the economically active are at work.

Demand for food with added health benefits will also rise as the world's population ages. Ms Salzman says in the US a third of consumers regularly eat foods recommended for specific health conditions and half want food that can boost the immune system. Snacks which claim to influence mood are already on sale in the US and Asia. Personality Puffs, for example, contain a blend of plant extracts which includes St John's Wort and ginkgo biloba to fight depression and improve memory, while Kava Corn Chips claim to aid relaxation.

But it is not just the elderly who will demand new goods and services – parents will be a prime target for marketers with bright ideas. 'Today's parents are faced with unique pressures – and conveniences – of raising children in the digital age.

'Expectations are high, resources are plentiful, but time is limited,' Ms Salzman says. Anxious parents will not only feed their children 'nutraceuticals' to make them healthier and more intelligent, they will also invest in anti-bacterial toys, educational products and organic cotton clothing.

Members-only parks, beaches and theme parks which promise to keep out undesirables will spring up in affluent areas, and trendy loft-living couples will call in teams of 'baby proofers' to make their high-tech homes child-friendly.

Labour-saving gadgets and services will become vital as increasingly harried consumers have less time to shop, cook and clean for themselves.

'Intelligent refrigerators will track consumption, printing a shopping list on demand or transmitting it electronically to a home delivery service, smart cookers will know how you like your eggs, meal trucks will circle neighbourhoods at dinner time, offering complete meals, and you will get your personal shopper to pick out everything you need from clothing to food,' says Ms Salzman.

But she warns that for an emerging underclass of technological have-nots, the future looks bleak.

'The chasm between those who do and do not have access to new technologies (particularly the Internet) will be far more significant than separations caused by age, geography, sex or lifestyle. Those who aren't wired will be blocked from an entire universe of information, communication and community,' she says.

From the *Financial Times*

FINANCIAL TIMES
World business newspaper.

C Are the statements below true or false, according to the article?

1 The best way to predict the future is to analyse technological and social trends.

2 The demand for mass-produced jeans, storybooks and videos will grow rapidly.

3 Marketing people will focus on the needs of both the old and parents.

4 Products aimed at children's health and diet will be a major growth area.

5 Because consumers are under greater pressure, there will be greater demand for labour-saving devices.

6 Differences in age, geography, sex or lifestyle will affect people more than lack of access to new technology.

D Choose the best definition for the following phrases from the article.

1 'consumers judged to be at the cutting edge of fashion' (lines 32–34)
   a) people who are the last to buy popular products
   b) people who buy the latest products before they are generally popular

2 'mass marketing is becoming obsolete' (lines 50–51)
   a) mass marketing is becoming old-fashioned and no longer useful
   b) mass marketing is becoming more common and more important

E Which of the predictions in the article are most likely to happen, in your opinion? Which do you think will still be science fiction by 2030? Why?

Vocabulary 2
Describing the future

A The article on page 118 states that for some people 'the future looks *bleak*'. The adjectives in the box can also be used to talk about the future. Use them to complete the table below.

> ~~bleak~~   bright   brilliant   depressing   dire   doubtful
> dreadful   great   magnificent   marvellous   promising
> prosperous   rosy   terrible   uncertain   worrying

very bad	⟹	bad	⟹	good	⟹	very good
bleak						

B Discuss the short- and long-term futures for some key industries in your country. Combine adjectives from the table with words like: *possibly, potentially, probably, certainly, undoubtedly*. For example, '*The future for shipbuilding is potentially very bright*'.

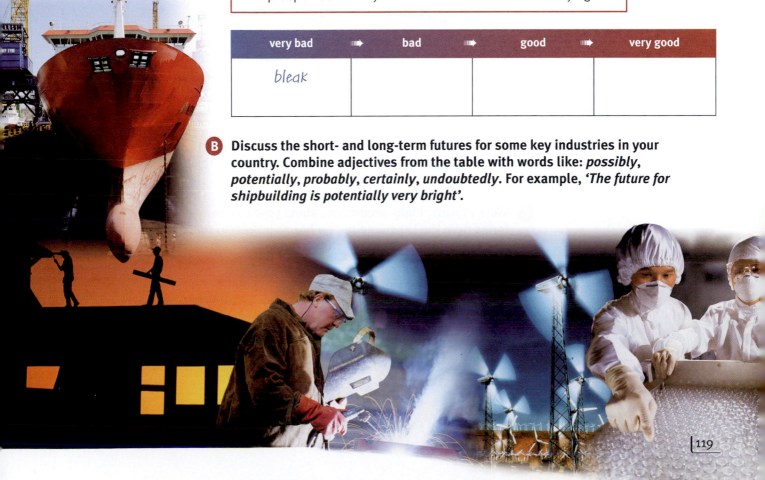

Language review
The language of prediction

To make a prediction we usually use *will* or *going to*.

'Demand for food with added health benefits **will** also **rise** as the world's population ages.'

'Based on our income and expenditure figures, we are **going to** make a profit of nearly £3m next financial year.'

Underline the correct choice of words in the following rule.
We use *will / going to* when there is present external evidence for a future event and *will / going to* when we state our own intuitions.

Here are some other ways of making predictions. Examples are given in Exercise A below.

a) future continuous
b) lexical future
c) *may / might / could* + infinitive
d) *be + about to* + infinitive

e) future perfect
f) conditional *will* + present simple
g) *would*

 see page 136

A **Match the predictions below to a)–g) in the Language review box.**

1 It would have an instant effect on the share price if the news got out.

2 There is speculation that widespread redundancies are about to be made.

3 Oxygen bars and smart alcohol are just around the corner.

4 Entrepreneurial companies will find plenty of business opportunities if they target the increasingly ageing population.

5 They may have to design cars that are easier to get into and out of and are easier to drive.

6 In ten years, mobile phones will be waking us up in the morning, reading out our e-mails, ordering our groceries and telling us the best route to work.

7 Work will not have disappeared 100 years from now.

B **Look at the following sentences and say whether they are correct or incorrect. If they are incorrect, correct them.**

1 In the near future we will be moving to a new factory.

2 Sometime in the next decade they will be taken over.

3 By the end of this century electric cars are about to become common.

4 By the end of next year we will be in business for 25 years.

5 In the next five years our profits will increase significantly.

6 By this time next year we would pay off this loan.

7 We won't be entering new markets in the foreseeable future.

8 Within the next 20 years the industry will be dominated by a few large companies.

C **Work in pairs. Make predictions about your company or country. Use as many forms from the Language review box as possible. You may also find the phrases in the box below useful.**

In my lifetime …	Over the next decade …
Before long …	By this time next year …
In the near future …	By the end of this century …
In the next … years	Sometime in the next decade / century

Skills
Getting the right information

A 🎧 14.2 **Listen to each dialogue and answer the questions. Then listen again and tick the expressions in the Useful language box that you hear.**

Dialogue 1
1 Why does Carla have difficulties contacting Li Wang?
2 Who helps her with her enquiry?

Dialogue 2
1 Why is Michael Bishop angry?
2 How does the person he calls deal with the situation?

Dialogue 3
1 What caused the breakdown in communication?
2 What do the two speakers do to understand each other?

Dialogue 4
1 Why does the caller telephone the supplier?
2 How did the problem arise?

Useful language

Making contact
Could you put me through to Mr Li Wang please?
You seem to have got the wrong extension.
Can you transfer me to his extension?

Asking for information
Could you give me a few details?
When did you give us the order?
Can you tell me what the order number is?

Asking for repetition
Sorry, I didn't hear what you said.
I'm sorry, I didn't catch that.
What did you say the reference number was?

Checking information
Fine. Shall I just read that back to you?
Let me just check. What you need is ... Is that right?
Could you spell that please.

Clarifying
What exactly do you mean by ... ?
Sorry I don't follow you.
Are you saying that ...?

Confirming understanding
Right, I've got that.
Fine / OK / Right.

Confirming action
I'll check it out right away.
I'll get on to it immediately.
I'll call you back as soon as I can.

B **Role play these situations in pairs.**

1 A Marketing Director is due to attend a meeting with an overseas customer. He/she phones to confirm the arrangements.

Marketing Director
You are phoning to confirm details of a meeting which was arranged by a colleague two weeks ago. You want to meet half an hour earlier, if possible. Also, check the date, time, day and venue of the meeting. Your colleague left you a message with these details:

Time	14:30
Date	Tuesday, 13 November
Venue	Metropolitan
Contact at hotel	Karen

If you cannot agree on a suitable time and date, suggest alternatives.

Overseas customer
You receive a call from the Marketing Director who wishes to confirm details of a meeting arranged by his/her colleague. You have the following information in your diary.

Time	4.30pm
Date	Thursday, 30 November
Venue	Metropole
Contact at hotel	Kieran

• Confirm the arrangement for the meeting.
• Ask the Marketing Director to bring samples of his / her company's latest products.
• If you cannot agree a suitable time and date, suggest alternatives.

2 A customer telephones the Sales Manager of a German kitchen equipment manufacturer. The customer has ordered some microwave ovens which are more than a month overdue.

Customer turn to page 149. Sales Manager turn to page 150.
Read your role cards, then role play the telephone conversation.

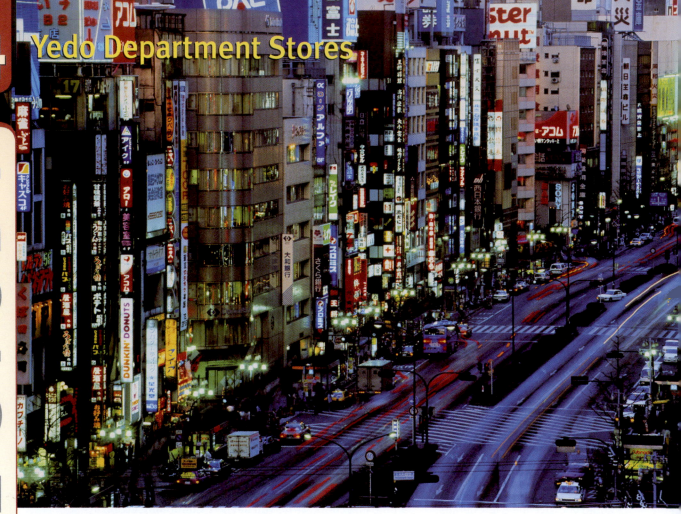

Yedo Department Stores

Background

Yedo is a successful Tokyo-based department store chain with six outlets in Japan and two more in London and New York. It has an excellent reputation for high-quality goods. Yedo also offers outstanding service and a large number of sales staff. Many lifts have uniformed attendants.

Yedo's strategy – to offer a wide choice of products and personalised service – has worked well until recently. Last year, however, profits fell sharply and results for the first six months of this year have been disappointing. As a result, several similar famous store groups are now heavily in debt.

Market research

Yedo's management has asked an international marketing agency, TWCB, for advice on how to maintain and increase profitability.

Yedo Department Stores: fact file

Founded	1895
Staff	Approximately 3,200 (mostly full-time)
Opening hours	7 days 10am – 6pm (Fridays 7pm)
Location	Usually near major railway stations
Core customers	Well-off, brand-conscious; over 80% female
Discount policy	Discounts only available during regular January and July sales
Décor	Traditional / Old-fashioned
Parking	Very limited
Special services	Classes in foreign languages and leisure activities; Travel service

Yedo Department Stores: extract from TWCB's market report

3 Competition

3.1 Convenience stores

These appeal to all groups, including housewives. They offer a much wider range of goods and services than they used to, and respond quickly to demand. Conveniently located, they often operate round the clock.

3.2 Discount stores

Prices in these stores are 20%–30% below the manufacturers' recommended level. Also, stores which price all products at ¥100 have become popular in Japan.

3.3 Speciality stores

Stores such as Muji and Fast Retailers sell good quality, 'no-brand' products at low prices, backed up by sharp advertising. Fast Retailers has opened 430 stores in Japan and plans another 80 to 100 each year. Muji has 251 stores in Japan, and appeals mostly to young shoppers.

3.4 Foreign retail chains

Following deregulation in the retail industry Carrefour from France, and the American chain Wal-Mart, plan to open in Tokyo.

4 Trends

4.1 As the Japanese population ages, older groups will provide opportunities for sales growth.

4.2 Japanese consumers want value for money and to feel they have got a bargain.

4.3 The Japanese are less brand-conscious now. Sales of 'no-brand' goods are increasing.

4.4 Japan is moving from a luxury culture to a convenience culture. People want services which make life easier or save time.

4.5 Women are marrying later in life.

Discussion questions

1 Should Yedo continue to position itself as an up-market store selling exclusive products?

2 Should Yedo try to appeal more to older or younger people? What products and services should it offer to appeal to these target customers?

3 What are the advantages and disadvantages of renting parts of the store to other businesses? Should Yedo be doing this?

4 Should Yedo expand overseas, with more stores abroad? If so, what countries would be suitable for overseas expansion?

5 Should Yedo use the Internet? If so, how can it use the Internet effectively?

6 How can Yedo compete against the convenience stores?

7 How do you see the Yedo Department Store group developing in the future?

Task

You are members of the marketing agency, TWCB. An informal meeting has been arranged to discuss ways of maintaining and increasing Yedo's profitability. Yedo's CEO has prepared some discussion questions for you to consider. Hold the meeting and note down your best ideas, which will be incorporated into a report.

Writing

As head of TWCB, write a report for the Chief Executive of Yedo, Kazuo Yamashiro, on your agency's ideas.

➡ *Writing file pages 144 and 145*

Revision

8 Team building

Fixed pairs

A Match the two parts of the expressions.

1	boom		**a)** bolts
2	hard		**b)** bust
3	loud		**c)** clear
4	nuts	and	**d)** cons
5	pros		**e)** fast
6	touch		**f)** go
7	wax		**g)** wane

B Now use the expressions to complete these sentences.

1 As the country's economic fortunes .... , graduates have more or less difficulty in finding jobs.
2 I hear you .... , and understand your worries.
3 In selling, there are no .... rules and no easy answers.
4 In the course, the trainer covers both advanced theoretical issues and some practical .... questions.
5 In the past, the UK housing market was subject to regular .... cycles, with periods of rapidly rising prices followed by sudden falls.
6 The negotiations were extremely difficult, and some delegates said it was .... whether overall agreement could be reached by the deadline.
7 We discussed the .... of doing it in-house or using outside suppliers.

Modal perfect

Read this article about hindsight: understanding a situation only after it has happened. In each of lines 1–8 there is one wrong word. Write the correct word in the space provided.

Hindsight is a great thing. It's so easy to be wise after the event, and newspapers and
1 management books are full of advice to managers about what they should had done in   ....
2 different situations. A merger is badly managed. Some say that it must have worked if it   ....
3 had been handled better. Others say that the merger would not have gone ahead at all, and   ....
4 that it would not have working even if it had been handled differently. A new product is   ....
5 launched and it fails. Some commentators say that the firm would have succeed if the   ....
6 product had had different features, a lower price, or if it had be distributed in a different way.   ....
7 A company chooses a new CEO and she leaves after three months. What might had   ....
8 happened if the firm had use a different selection procedure? But every situation is new. The   ....
'lessons' from other situations, even if they seem similar, may not be applicable in new
contexts. And the 'experts', writing from the comfort of their business schools and
newspaper offices, are not the ones who have to take the decisions.

9 Raising finance

Negotiating expressions

Put each expression 1–7 into one of the categories below. Then match the expressions 1–7 with the possible responses a)–g).

- Pre-negotiation small talk
- Closed questions
- Signalling phrases
- Open questions
- Softening phrases
- Summarising

1 I'm afraid we can't consider an agreement for longer than two years.
2 It might be useful at this point to outline what we've decided so far.
3 Did you find us OK?
4 Can you give me a general idea of your requirements?
5 Let me make you an offer you can't refuse. We'll order 20% more if you can give us a 5% discount.
6 Do you have a list of recent customers you can give us?
7 I realise this is difficult for you, but we really need a lead-time of two weeks.

a) Yes, I can even put you in touch with one or two of them.
b) No problem, but the traffic was awful.
c) Yes, that would be helpful.
d) OK. Let's stick to two years, for the moment at least.
e) Well, the sort of thing I had in mind was …
f) It is going to be difficult, but we'll see what we can do.
g) We can manage a reduction of 3 per cent, but any more and we'll be losing money.

Reading

Read the passages about negotiating styles. To which style does each sentence 1–7 refer?

a) **The Clarifier**
Clarifiers like to structure the negotiation process. They frequently point out the progress that has been made, the issues that remain to be settled, the time this is likely to take, and so on. There are negotiators who find this helpful, but some find it irritating if it happens too often. They say that if there are real, irreconcilable differences between the two sides, structuring language in itself will not be enough to bridge them.

b) **The Empathisor**
Empathisors are good at understanding the needs and objectives of the other side. They show this in the language they use: 'I can see that's important to you' is a phrase they might use. The other side are pleased that their needs are being addressed, and they then forget that the empathisor does have his or her own objectives. It is important to remember this, and try to understand what the empathisor's objectives might be.

c) **The Stonewaller**
Stonewallers are great believers in the take-it-or-leave-it approach. In pay negotiations, for example, there are employers who make an offer and say that it is non-negotiable: all that the company can afford. The danger here is that workers go on strike and the management's previously non-negotiable offer then improves. This damages the stonewaller's credibility in future negotiations.

d) **The Dissimulator**
In a commercial negotiation, dissimulators might pretend that price is the key issue, when in fact the delivery date is. In wage negotiations, dissimulating employers might pretend that limiting salary increases is important, when really they are keen on reducing staff numbers. Dissimulators are good at disguising their priorities, making the other side think that important priorities are unimportant to them, and vice versa.

1 The description of this negotiator makes use of two examples.
2 This negotiator may have trouble being taken seriously in future negotiations.
3 This negotiator tries to make the other side believe that only their objectives are being considered.
4 Some people criticise this negotiator, saying that words are sometimes not enough to settle real differences.
5 This negotiator tries to impress and intimidate the other side by saying that no negotiation is possible.
6 This negotiator might typically say, 'I can see where you're coming from'.
7 This negotiator plays down their real objectives and plays up unimportant ones.

10 Customer service

Idioms

Correct the mistakes in italics in the sentences below, using idioms containing the words in the box.

| bottom | buck | court | light | mind | point | straw |

1 They've backed out of the negotiations and it's up to them to make the next move. *The ball is in their field*.

2 I bought it two years ago. The electric windows stopped working; the car soon needed new brakes, and then came *the final string* – the car broke down on a busy motorway.

3 I had an appointment for a check-up at the dentist, but it completely *slipped my memory*.

4 Robert Evans, Chief Executive, was confident his company was 'close to seeing *day at the end of the tunnel*'. But financing has been delayed.

5 Prison officials should take responsibility for the escapes rather than *pass the bucket* to the guards.

6 I'll get *straight to the dot*. We're broke.

7 An independent inquiry into the accident is beginning after the minister promised to '*get to the base* of what went wrong'.

Reading

Choose the best word from the list below to complete what this professor of marketing says about customer service.

Let me tell you a story. It's about the local manager of an overnight courier company. The company promised to deliver all packages by 10.30 the following morning. The local manager knew that the ....[1] drivers were not able to do this, so he regularly had a large ....[2] of deliveries made by taxi. When managers at head office found out what the local manager was ....[3], they were furious. The local manager thought he was doing his best to delight customers, but he had also turned his area into a loss- ....[4] operation. His special efforts showed that there was a basic problem in the company's business ....[5]: either there were not enough delivery drivers, they were not ....[6] managed properly, or they were not doing their delivery rounds in the most efficient way. ....[7] for customer delight is all very well, but where delight is being provided in a way not specified in the company's business plan, profitability will ....[8].

1 **a)** deliver   **b)** delivers   **c)** delivery   **d)** delivered
2 **a)** party   **b)** quota   **c)** ration   **d)** proportion
3 **a)** do   **b)** doing   **c)** done   **d)** did
4 **a)** make   **b)** making   **c)** have   **d)** having
5 **a)** mode   **b)** kit   **c)** model   **d)** dummy
6 **a)** be   **b)** being   **c)** been   **d)** was
7 **a)** Aim   **b)** Aimed   **c)** Aiming   **d)** Aims
8 **a)** suffer   **b)** suffers   **c)** suffered   **d)** suffering

11 Crisis management

Comparisons

Match the beginnings of the extracts on the left with their endings on the right.

1 Intershop expects revenues of € 120m this year, whereas

2 Results showed a loss of 25 cents per share, a slight improvement on the 26 cent loss reported a year before, and far better than

3 The best-performing Asian economy during periods of low interest rates has tended to be Hong Kong;

4 E-sure is planning to launch a new car insurance service;

a) are more or less comparable with conventional models.

b) but it was nothing like as bad as independent television.

c) but the outlook is nowhere near as gloomy as some others have suggested.

d) Taiwan, on the other hand, has historically been the worst performer during such periods.

e) analysts' expectations of a 33 cent loss.

5 With a price-tag of around £17,000, these battery-powered cars

6 The survey reported a drop in consumer confidence,

7 Newspapers certainly saw a decline in advertising,

f) it will be a telephone rather than Internet-based service.

g) Broad-vision, the US-based leader in the sector, will have sales of about $400m.

Writing

You are a crisis management consultant. Recently, there was an incident in which one of Serene Cruises' liners broke down in the middle of the Caribbean and 1,200 passengers and crew had to be lifted off by helicopter. No one was hurt, but the incident was handled badly from the communications point of view, and Serene's image has suffered.

Another company, Carefree Cruises, has commissioned you to advise on what it should do if something similar happens to one of its ships: an incident where there are no deaths or injuries, but where the cruise has to be ended early. Write a summary of 140–180 words, containing the key recommendations in your plan.

Your summary should include:
- who will be responsible for dealing with the press, issuing statements, etc: Carefree's press office or an outside organisation specialising in crisis management
- whether passengers' families will be contacted and, if so, who should handle it
- compensation to passengers: money, another cruise, etc.
- consequences of not having an efficient contingency plan: refer to Serene's bad experience

12 Management styles

Opposites

A **Find the opposites of the adjectives 1–6, using the prefixes in the box.**

| dis-　il-　im-　in-　ir-　un- |

1 fair　2 formal　3 legal　4 obedient　5 patient　6 responsible

Now form nouns related to the opposites, using the suffixes below.
- -ence (2 nouns)　• -ity (3 nouns)　• -ness (1 noun)

B **Use the nouns you formed in Exercise A to complete these extracts.**

1 In the Air Force you have to do what you're told: .... is not tolerated.
2 Employees should be able to draw attention to malpractice, law-breaking and other .... in their organisations without being victimised.
3 The trade talks are continuing, but France has shown .... with the slow rate at which they are progressing.
4 Lima is a mixture of formality and ....; a combination of old world courtesy and entrepreneurial dynamism.
5 Indifference, ... and incompetence in dealing with the country's problems: that is how people assess the current government.
6 Tax rules that try to avoid all .... tend to be impossibly complicated.

Text reference

Read this extract about the merger between BTR and Siebe to form Invensys, and the role of Allen Yurko, Invensys's CEO. Use four of the sentences a)–e), to complete the article.

There's more to making the merger work than closing down the odd underperforming plant. Invensys has a 'Lean Enterprise' programme which sends statistical engineers, called Blackbelts, to underperforming parts of the business to map out why they are not working. ....[1] The idea was conceived in the middle of the last decade at Siebe to ensure some named individuals took responsibility for cutting costs. ....[2]

Combined with these Blackbelt teams is what Mr Yurko calls his 'simultaneously loose and tight' management approach. It's loose in that managers have plenty of responsibility and freedom to make their own decisions. ....[3]

'There's one strategic planning meeting, one budgeting meeting and ten performance reviews a year for each manager,' he says. 'We get to talk about pure operating performance down at the plant level, measuring productivity, customer service and the like; ....[4]'

From the *Independent*

a) They make presentations and if the guy's got a problem with a major customer we'll fix it right there.
b) Invensys now has one thousand of them poring over many of the underperforming businesses acquired in the merger.
c) The Blackbelts stick around until they are fixed.
d) Statistical engineering is a very complex subject.
e) It's tight in that Mr Yurko visits middle-tier managers ten times a year to check on them.

13 Takeovers and mergers

Reading

Read this short article about takeovers and mergers. In most of the lines 1–5 there is one extra word that does not fit. One or two of the lines, however, are correct. If a line is correct, put a tick in the space provided. If there is an extra word in the line, write that word in the space.

Smithson doesn't believe in growing internally: it's a very acquisitive company. It often
1 follows the same strategy. It builds up over a stake in a company it's interested in   ....
2 acquiring. Then it launches off a full takeover bid for the target company. At first, ...
3 the bid may be described as hostile and unwelcome, but eventually the share-   ....
4 holders usually accept to it. Smithson's CEO holds a press conference and talks   ....
5 about the benefits gained up by the acquisition. But the target company's   ....
employees are nervous. They know what usually happens when Smithson takes over another company, and they start looking for jobs elsewhere.

Presentation language

Identify the types of phrases used in this presentation about modern architecture by matching a)–h) with the items 1–8.

1 Referring back
2 Making points in threes
3 Asking rhetorical questions
4 Ordering
5 Using emotive language
6 Repetition
7 Exemplifying
8 Asking for feedback

a) Getting planning permission for futuristic office towers can be an absolute nightmare.
b) For instance, the Channel 4 building in London really helped to reinforce the Channel 4 brand.
c) Is there anything you'd like me to discuss that we haven't looked at so far?
d) These are the key factors in assessing property values: location, location, location and location.
e) There are four things we have to bear in mind, and the first is the demands that technology makes on modern buildings.
f) Using modern design, there are cost benefits, there are advantages for corporate image, and there are pluses for employees.
g) But what do we really mean by modern architecture?
h) As I was saying earlier, the property market is extremely cyclical.

14 The future of business

Reading

Read the passages about different groups of people. To which group does each sentence 1–7 refer?

a) **Rosy futurists** have a positive view of the future, but they are not obsessed by technology or the environment. They are more interested in social and political trends. They believe that human behaviour will continue to improve, with fewer undemocratic regimes, greater emphasis on human rights and more participation by ordinary people in the political decisions that affect them.

b) **Catastrophists** are extremely pessimistic. They think that the Earth is on the brink of environmental collapse, with rapidly rising temperatures and sea levels bringing permanent flooding of heavily populated coastal areas in places like Egypt and Bangladesh. They believe that it is now too late to do anything to avoid this disaster and, even if it is not, there is no political will to do anything about it.

c) **Technophiles** believe that technology will provide answers to everything. They believe that as technology gets cheaper, its benefits will spread to all classes of society. They point out that even 'poor' people in advanced countries now have mobile phones and colour TVs. They think technological advances will, eventually, reach the population of most of the world. They believe that this process will improve people's lives far more than any political decision.

d) **Technophobes** think that technology is dehumanising. They see a future of walled communities, with the people in them leading more and more unnatural, technology-driven lives. In the future people may possess machines to give them intense dreams, but technophobes say the machines are more likely to induce nightmares. Technophobes think that there will be more and more people who choose to live 'outside the walls' with alternative lifestyles that are less dependent on technology.

1 This group is more concerned by the environment than anything else.
2 These people think that technical progress is less important than politics in bringing about social change.
3 These people think that access to technological innovation will not be limited to the well-off.
4 These people are more interested in politics than anything else.
5 The description of this group gives examples of technical advances that they think have improved people's lives.
6 The description of this group gives examples of countries that will be badly affected by climate change.
7 The description of this group gives an example of a device that may have negative effects.

Writing

You are a futurologist working for a think-tank, an organisation whose experts predict what will happen in particular areas in the future and make recommendations to companies, political parties and so on. You have been commissioned to write a report of 180–220 words on 'The World in 2050'.

You have been asked for your views on the following:
• housing
• work
• transport
• food production
• leisure
• overall quality of life

Grammar reference

1 Idioms

In the language of business, idioms and metaphors are often used with reference to the domains of sport, war and gambling.

Sport

I don't know the exact price but $500 is a good **ballpark figure**. (= estimate).

She's smart and really **on the ball**. (= quick to understand).

Follow his advice and it'll be **plain sailing**. (= easy to do or achieve).

You don't know where you stand, they keep **moving the goalposts**. (= changing their aims or decisions).

There must be no unfair competition in the EU and we shall continue to stress the need **for a level playing field**. (= a situation that gives no one an advantage)

War

Bill's **on the warpath** *again* (= very angry) – *there are mistakes in the publicity material we sent out.*

You may have to **do battle with** (= fight it out) *the insurers because they won't want to pay up.*

Manufacturers often feel they are **fighting a losing battle** (= making no progress) *against counterfeiting.*

If you can convince the commercial attaché here, that's **half the battle** (= the rest is easy).

I've been **fighting a running battle** (= having a series of arguments) *with the financial department but they won't give us the money.*

She may want to convince you otherwise but you should **stick to your guns** (= maintain your point of view).

She's **up in arms** (= very angry and ready to fight) *about the lack of safety procedures.*

Gambling

We are trying to **hedge our bets** (= reduce our chances of failure) *and not put all our eggs in one basket.*

The odds are stacked against us (= there are many difficulties) *but we're determined to succeed.*

It **makes no odds** (= makes no difference) *whether we get permission or not, we'll go ahead anyway.*

They're paying **over the odds** (= more than it's worth) *for the site but it's a prime location.*

We had our doubts about Susan but she has really **come up trumps** (= produced good, unexpected results).

If you **play your cards right** (= do the right thing) *you'll get the promotion.*

2 Noun compounds and noun phrases

1 When two nouns occur together, the first noun is used as an adjective and describes the second noun. The first noun answers the question 'what kind of?'

   a manufacturing subsidiary
   a draft agenda
   a phone conversation
   a network operator

2 Noun + noun compounds can often be transformed into structures where the second noun becomes the subject:

   an oil refinery (= a refinery that produces oil)
   company executives (= executives that work for the company)
   a travel agency (= an agency that sells travel)

3 They may also be reformulated using a preposition:

   market research (= research **into** markets)
   rail transport (= transport **by** rail)
   leisure activities (= activities **for** leisure)
   a web page (= a page **on** the web)
   their Paris store (= their store **in** Paris)
   income distribution (= distribution **of** income)

4 The first noun is usually singular:

   five-star hotel (*not* five stars)
   consumer-purchasing behaviour (*not* consumers)
   risk assessment (*not* risks)
   brand names (*not* brands)

   However, some words retain the plural form:
   sales policy
   newsletter
   needs analysis

5 Sometimes three or more nouns occur together:

   line management system
   production research centre
   travel insurance claim form
   Motorola's software development establishments

6 Noun compounds can be modified by adjectives and adverbs:

   inspiring *team leadership*
   international *business development directors*
   extremely boring *conference presentation*
   increasingly volatile *mobile phone market*

3 Multi-word verbs

Multi-word verbs are formed when a verb is followed by one or more particles. Particles can be prepositions or adverbs.

The meaning of a multi-word verb is sometimes very different from the meanings of the two words taken separately.

*How are you **getting on**? (get on is not the same as get + on).*

There are two different types of multi-word verbs.

1 Intransitive: without an object

*The plane has just **taken off**.*
*She **turned up** unexpectedly.*
*What time did you **set off**?*

2 Transitive: with an object

*We will **set up** a new subsidiary.*
*They have **called off** the strike.*
*She has **handed in** her resignation.*

- With two particles:

*I'm **looking forward to** seeing you.*
*She's trying to **catch up with** her work.*
*We need to **make up for** lost time.*

- Multi-word verbs are either separable or inseparable.

An adverb particle can come before or after the object if the object is a noun.

*We've **put by** some money.*
*We've **put** some money **by**.*

- But you cannot put a pronoun after the particle:

*She's **switched off** the computer.*
*She's **switched** the computer **off**.*
*She's **switched** it **off**.*
*(NOT *She's switched off it.)*

- If the particle is a preposition, the verb and particle are inseparable:

*Can you **cope with** your work?*
*(NOT *Can you cope your work with?).*

- We do not normally separate multi-word verbs with two particles. However, there are some transitive three-word combinations that allow separation. For example:

*Multinationals can **play** individual markets **off against** each other.*
*She **puts** her success **down to** hard work.*
*I'll **take** you **up on** that suggestion.*

4 Present and past tenses

1 The **present simple** is used to make true, factual statements.

*Established customers **tend** to buy more.*
*Nokia **sells** mobile telephones.*

2 Verbs relating to beliefs, being, knowledge, liking, perception and appearance are normally only used in the simple form.

*I **understand** what you **mean**.*
*It **depends** on what the chairman **wants**.*
*I **appreciate** your concern.*

3 The **present continuous** is used to refer to events in progress and temporary or changing situations.

*'I'll be back late, I**'m sitting** in a traffic jam'.*
*They**'re installing** a new switchboard.*
*The world **is getting** smaller.*

4 The **past simple** is used to refer to events completed in the past. We frequently use a time expression to say when the event took place.

*In the late 1940s Ford **decided** it needed a medium price model to compete with General Motors.*
*2001 **was** a good year for our firm.*

5 The **past perfect** sequences two or more past events.

*Before he joined this firm **he had** worked for two competitors abroad.*

6 The **present perfect** is used to say that a finished past action is relevant now. There cannot be any specific reference to past time.

*They **have changed** the address of their website.* (it's new)

*The share price has **plummeted**.* (it is lower than before)

7 The present perfect covers a period of time starting in the past and continuing up to the present. An appropriate time expression takes us up to now.

*So far, the company **has defied** predictions that its rivals will catch up.*
*Stella McCartney **has been** one of the leading fashion designers since the mid-1990s.*
*He**'s been** acting strange lately.*
*Over the last few years e-commerce **has become** fashionable.*

5 | Passives

We use the passive when the person who performs the action is unknown, unimportant or obvious.

*The file **was stolen**.*
*The roof **was damaged** during the storm.*
*She**'s been given** the sack.*

1 The passive can be used in all tenses and with modal auxiliaries.

*A new fitness centre **is being built**.*
*The job **was going to be done** on Friday.*
*He **had been asked** to do it twice before.*
*She **may be required** to work on Sunday.*
*The best employees **should be given** a performance bonus.*
*He **would have been told** eventually.*

2 If we know who performed the action (the agent) we use 'by':

*The file was stolen **by** a secret agent.*

3 In a passive sentence, the grammatical subject receives the focus:

a) *Giovanni Agnelli **founded** Fiat in 1899.*

b) *Fiat **was founded** by Giovanni Agnelli in 1899.*

In a) our attention is on the agent – Giovanni Agnelli. In b) it is Fiat rather than Agnelli that is the topic of the sentence.

4 The subject of the sentence can be a pronoun.

*We **were informed** that the firm was going to be taken over.*

5 Passive constructions are common in formal contexts, for example in reports or minutes, and help to create an impersonal style. Using 'it' as a subject enables us to avoid mentioning the person responsible for saying or doing something.

***It was felt** that the system needed to be changed.*
***It was decided** that expenditure would be limited to $250,000.*
***It was suggested** that staff be given stock options.*
***It was agreed** that the proposal should be rejected.*

6 | Intensifying adverbs

1 If we want to amplify the quality an adjective describes we use an intensifying adverb. These are some of the most common:

*The presentation was **really** / **very** good.*
*She's **dead** certain to get the job.*
*The new design looks **pretty** good.*
*I was **extremely** surprised by her reaction.*
*She's a **thoroughly** efficient organiser.*

2 The relative strength of adverbs is shown on this scale:

Strong: *absolutely, altogether, awfully, completely, greatly, highly, quite, terribly, totally, very*
Moderate: *fairly, mildly, moderately, partly, quite, reasonably, somewhat*
Weak: *a bit, a little, marginally, poorly, slightly.*

*The whole thing is **quite** amazing.*
Note that quite also means fairly:
*The restaurant is **quite** cheap but the food isn't wonderful.*

*The goods are **reasonably** cheap.*
*I was **slightly** surprised by what she said.*

3 Intensifying adverbs modify adjectives that are **gradable** – that is, they can signify degrees of a given quality. Adjectives that are not gradable or identify the particular class that something belongs to are not normally used with intensifying adverbs. We cannot say:

(NOT* a very unique idea)
(NOT* a fairly free gift)
(NOT* a very impossible solution)
(NOT* some slightly financial news)

4 However, you can use an adverb such as *absolutely* or *utterly* with an ungradable or classifying adjective to show that you feel strongly:

*It doesn't cost anything – it's **absolutely** free.*
*The task is **utterly** impossible.*

7 Conditionals

1 We use conditional sentences to make hypothetical statements and questions.

*We'll deliver within 24 hours **if** you **order** on-line.*
If *we order now,* **will** *you* **give** *us a discount?*

The use of *it + will +* verb suggests that these arrangements are feasible.

2 If the proposal is more tentative and possibly less feasible *would +* past verb forms are used.

*I'**d need** some venture capital **if** I **was** / **were** to start my own business.*
If *I* **got** *a guarantee for the loan, I* **would lend** *them the money.*
If *I* **had invested** *my savings in the firm I* **would have made** *a fortune.*

3 If the verb is *had, were* or *should,* we can leave out *if* and put the verb at the beginning. The sentence is now more formal.

Had *it not been for his help, we would not have survived.*

Were *it not for Patrick, we'd be in a terrible mess.*

Should *you require any further information, do not hesitate to contact me.*

4 These words are also used in conditional sentences.

We'll meet tomorrow **providing** / **provided (that)** *no one has an objection.*
Even the best management teams won't be successful **unless** *they are given the resources.*
You can say what you like **as long as** *you don't make any criticisms.*
Supposing (that) *we decide to use the Topsite service, how much would it cost?*

5 Mixed conditionals follow a variety of patterns.

If you need help, just **ask**. *(an offer)*
If Peter **wants** *to see me,* **tell** *him to wait. (an instruction)*
If you **hadn't invested** *in e-commerce our sales* **would be** *much lower. (this is true now, so* wouldn't have been *is inappropriate)*
I **would** *be grateful if you* **would** *give me an early reply. (a polite request)*

8 Modal perfect

1 We use past modals to speculate about events in the past.

I thought I saw Yolanda in the car park but it **may / might / could have** *been someone else.*
The project **might / could have** *been a terrible failure but turned out to be a great success. (we know it was a success, therefore* **may** *is not possible here).*
I wasn't there myself but from what I hear it **must have** *been a very stormy meeting.*
She says she met me in Brazil but it **can't have** *been me because I've never been to Brazil!*

2 Past modals can also be used to express irritation.

She **could / might have** *given me the information but she didn't bother.*

3 Missed opportunities are also expressed using *could* or *might.*

She **could / might have** *had a brilliant career but she gave it all up for love.*

4 *Would have* and *wouldn't have* are used to make hypotheses about the past.

The team **would** *have been stronger if she had been with us.*
We **wouldn't have** *achieved such good results if we hadn't worked together as a team.*

5 *Should have, shouldn't have* and *ought to have* are used to criticise.

The report **should have** *been submitted a lot earlier.*
He **shouldn't have** *resigned without having another job to go to.*
You **ought to have** *made a reservation – there are no seats left now.*

6 Note the difference between *needn't have* and *didn't need to.*

I **didn't need** *to come into the office because there was no work for me to do, so I stayed at home.*
I **needn't have** *gone into the office because there was no work for me to do when I got there.*

9 Dependent prepositions

1 Here is a list of common verbs and the prepositions that follow them:

complain about	*insure against*	*react against*
hint at	*account for*	*hope for*
long for	*opt for*	*pay for*
strive for	*emerge from*	*stem from*
suffer from	*invest in*	*result in*
bet on	*insist on*	*rely on*
amount to	*lead to*	*object to*
refer to	*relate to*	*resort to*
associate with	*contend with*	*sypathise with*

2 Some verbs may be followed by more than one preposition, with a corresponding change in meaning.

How did you learn of his sudden departure?
I hope you will learn from your mistakes.
The team consists of two Americans and two Japanese. (= is made up of)
For her, job satisfaction consists in having almost no work to do. (= is based on)

3 Here is a list of common adjectives and the prepositions that follow them:

lacking in	*aware of*	*capable of*
representative of	*contingent on*	*intent on*
reliant on	*conducive to*	*essential to*
parallel to	*prone to*	*susceptible to*
vulnerable to	*compatible with*	*filled with*

4 This is a list of common nouns and the prepositions that follow them:

admiration for	*aptitude for*	*bid for*
demand for	*need for*	*remedy for*
respect for	*responsibility for*	*room for*
search for	*substitute for*	
ban on	*comment on*	*constraint on*
curb on	*effect on*	*tax on*
access to	*alternative to*	*contribution to*
damage to	*exception to*	*introduction to*
reference to	*resistance to*	*solution to*
threat to		
contrast with	*dealings with*	*dissatisfaction with*
involvement with	*relationship with*	*sympathy with*

10 Gerunds

1 The gerund is the *-ing* form of the verb used as a noun, either as the subject or object of the verb.

Selling *is all about persuasion.*
Getting through to *the right person isn't always easy.*
My idea of relaxation is **going to** *a fitness centre.*

2 Gerunds follow prepositions:

We are committed <u>to</u> **giving** *the highest quality.*
We depend <u>on</u> **having** *fast communications.*

3 They are often used to begin an item in a list.

Good leaders are skilled at:

- **fixing** goals
- **motivating** people
- **producing** creative ideas

4 Gerunds can be made negative, used in the passive, and with past verb forms.

It's wonderful **not having** *to get up early for work.*
Being kidnapped *is not a pleasant experience.*
He mentioned **having met** *our main competitor.*

5 Many verbs are followed by a gerund (e.g. *admit, avoid, consider, deny, dislike, involve, mention, recommend, risk, suggest*)

He denied **fiddling** *his expenses.*
I dislike **having** *to eat at my desk.*
She suggests **raising** *the price.*

6 Some verbs are followed by either a gerund or an infinitive. The choice of one or the other usually leads to a change in meaning.

Increased production may **mean taking** *on extra staff at the weekend. (= involve)*
I didn't **mean to** *cause any offence. (= intend to)*
He remembered **to buy** *his wife a present.*
   (= he didn't forget)
He remembers **buying** *his wife a present.*
   (= he has a clear recollection of this)

11 Similarities and differences

1 We use *both either* and *neither* when only two people or things are involved:

   Both *BMW and Mercedes are German makes.*
   Either *she goes or I do, but we can't both go. And, in any case,* ***neither*** *of us wants to.*

2 Numbers can be used in comparisons to rank things:

   We are ***the second largest*** *supplier of circuit boards in the world.*
   Last year our dividend to shareholders was ***three times as*** *much as the year before.*

3 We can link two comparisons using *the … the …*

   The earlier *you detect a problem* ***the easier*** *it is to find a remedy.*
   The larger *the organisation* ***the more difficult*** *it is to manage.*

4 We can indicate the degree of difference by adding a modifier such as *much* or *far*.

   She's ***much more*** *intelligent than him.*
   They do ***far more*** *business in Europe than in the US.*
   I see ***even less*** *of her nowadays.*
   We've performed ***considerably better*** *this year.*
   Our products are ***by far the best*** *on the market.*

5 After the verb *to be* we can modify a comparative adjective with *a good / a great deal.*

   It would be ***a good / great deal*** *easier if meetings were not so long.*

6 There are a number of expressions used to make contrasts and highlight differences.

   In some cultures promotion is based on merit ***whereas*** *in others it is based on seniority.*
   On the one hand *he says he wants the company to grow but* ***on the other hand*** *he doesn't want to invest.*
   Though *he's lived in Spain for years he hasn't mastered the language.*

7 This can be reformulated as:

   Despite *having lived in Spain for years he hasn't mastered the language.*

12 Text reference

Read the following text and note how certain words refer forward and back to other words in the text.

Although more *women* are becoming sales managers, *they*'ll have to tailor *their* management styles to the gender of their employees if *they* want to have continued success. According to a *study* carried out by John Doyle and Jill Harris of the University of Hull, both female and male sales personnel welcome the newcomers. But *it* also points out that there can be a difference between *the management style* males prefer and *the one* that elicits their best performance.

In particular, the researchers wanted to discover differences in satisfaction and variations in sales performance under female supervision. Two management *styles* were identified. A transactional style is the more traditional of *the two*. Male managers are hands-off until something goes wrong. The philosophy is 'When *you*'re doing OK, *you* won't even know *I*'m around. But, when *you* mess up, *I*'ll be right next door.

Women take a more hands-on approach. A transformational mode encourages a more hands-on individual-orientated manner. *Women* more than *men* tend to motivate by encouragement and personal attention. *The former* relate to their staff emotionally and tend to foster new ways of thinking whereas *the latter* rely on rewards and punishments.

Grammatical reference

In paragraph 1:
they, their, they, refer back to, *women, it* refers back to *the study*
the one refers back to *the management style*
In paragraph 2:
the two refers back to *styles*
you, you, you, refers back to any employee working under a male manager
I, refers to the male manager
In paragraph 3:
the former refers back to *women*
the latter refers back to *men*

Lexical reference

Very often in texts, words belonging to the same family and synonyms and antonyms occur closely together.

gender … men ≠ women, male ≠ female
John Doyle and Jill Harris … the researchers
the newcomers … women sales managers
employees … personnel … staff
differences … variations
hands-off … hands-on
something goes wrong … you mess up ≠ do OK
style … mode … approach … manner
individual … personal
encourages … motivate … foster
encouragement … rewards ≠ punishments

13 Headlines

The headlines in English-language newspapers can be difficult to understand as they are often written in a special style, with some specific rules of grammar, and words that may be used in unusual ways.

1   They are not always complete sentences:
    Challenge for Euro

2   They may contain strings of three or more nouns:
    Takeover bid drama
    Office staff pay deal row

3   They omit articles and the verb *to be*:
    Orange CEO likely to quit

4   They use simple forms and an infinitive refers to the future:
    Nokia chief to stand down

5   If a continuous form is used *be* is omitted:
    Prices going through the roof

6   Short words are used to save space. Here are some examples:

    Axe = abolish, abolition, close down, closure
    RST to axe 100 jobs
    Chairman axed in boardroom clash

    Blow = bad news
    Peace talks blow

    Flak = criticism
    PM faces opposition flak

    Hail = welcome
    Bosses hail interest rate cut

    Slam = criticise
    Unions slam jobs plan

    Top = exceed
    Exports top $5bn

14 The language of prediction

1   A number of modal verbs are used to make predictions. The modal indicates the speaker's degree of certainty.

    *They **will** be there by now* (100% certain)
    *They **won't** have any trouble finding our office, they've been here many times* (100% certain)
    *They **must** have arrived by now* (80% certain)
    *They **can't** have arrived yet* (80% certain)
    *They **should** have arrived by now* (60% certain)
    *They **may / could have** arrived by now* (40% certain)
    *They **might** have arrived by now* (20% certain)

2   Conditional statements contain hypotheses about the way the future may turn out:

    *If you break off negotiations they'**ll probably go** on strike.*
    *If you try harder you **would be able to** do it.*

3   The future perfect and the future continuous predict what will be in progress or will have been accomplished in the future:

    *By 2050 businessmen **will be taking** orders from the moon.*
    *By 3000 scientists **will have discovered** how to transmit objects by fax.*

4   There are a number of lexical expressions of likelihood. These include:

    about to   bound to   going to
    (un)likely to

    *He's tapping his glass, I think he's **about to / going to** make a speech.*
    *She's **bound to** be late, she always is.*
    *The market is stable, it's **unlikely to** change much.*

5   Note too these phrases:

    *He's suffering from stress – he's **on the point of** collapse.*
    *He says that recession is **around the corner**.*
    *With an election **in the offing / on the horizon** the Prime Minister is anxious to maintain his popularity.*

Are you in danger of burning out?

Do the quiz and discuss your answers with a partner. Then check your result on page 155.

You're turning up for meetings at the right time but in the wrong week. You're pouring milk into the waste paper basket rather than your coffee. You've lost your temper with half of the office, and the other half are cowering under their desks. You could be suffering from burnout, a debilitating condition caused by working too hard for too long and failing to prioritise. Try this quiz to see if you are in danger of self-combusting.

1 Your boss asks if you can work late for the third night in a row. Do you:

a Say yes without giving it a second thought?

b Laugh politely and close the door on your way out?

c Say yes, but feel like crying?

2 Some of your colleagues want to play a practical joke on your boss for April Fool's Day. Do you:

a Organise a brainstorming session to select the best idea?

b Tell them that there are more important things to be done?

c Go to your boss and tell them what they are planning to do?

3 You arrive home one Friday night with a pile of work only to discover that your partner has arranged a surprise weekend away. Do you:

a Leave the work behind and take Monday off to catch up?

b Tell them that you're sorry, but you can't afford the time?

c Agree to go but insist on taking the work with you?

4 There is a rumour going around that a proposed company merger may mean some job losses. Do you:

a Take a cursory glance at the job adverts in the paper and look for your CV?

b Bite your nails until your fingers hurt?

c Find yourself hyperventilating?

5 It's bedtime and you are exhausted after a stressful day at the office. Do you:

a Lie awake for two hours, then make a start on next week's assignment?

b Lie awake for five minutes, then sleep right through until morning?

c Lie awake for one hour, then read for a while until you fall asleep?

6 A colleague asks if you could help them with a problem but you're in the middle of a project with a tight deadline. Do you

a Schedule some time in your diary to work with them when you're free?

b Agree to help, but become irritated when they don't grasp the solution straight away?

c Tell them to speak to someone who cares?

7 There are a lot more things on your 'To Do' list than you realistically have time for. Do you:

a Divide the items into urgent and important and start with the urgent things?

b Pick out the easy tasks and start with them?

c Work overtime until they're all done?

8 An old friend you haven't seen for ages asks you to go out for a meal with them. Do you:

a Have a fantastic evening of reminiscence?

b Refuse the invitation as you are always too tired to go out on weekdays?

c Accept the invitation, and spend the evening telling them all about your job?

From the *Guardian* website:
http://www.workunlimited.co.uk/quiz/questions

Writing file

Letters

TM Breweries GmbH

Baubergerstr 17
80991 Munich

Ms Teresa Winch
Vending Machines Inc
Box 97
New York

19 February

Dear Ms Winch

South East Asian opportunities

I was very pleased to have met you again at the open day we held in our Munich brewery last week. I hope you enjoyed yourself and felt that your visit was useful.

I found our discussion about the activities of your organisation in Korea very interesting. It seems to me that there are a lot of ways in which our organisations could work together to our mutual advantage in South East Asia. I have enclosed a brochure with further information about our products. I propose that we get together soon to discuss the matter in more detail.

I hope this suggestion is of interest and look forward to hearing from you.

Yours sincerely

Katherine Sell

Katherine Sell
Sales Manager

Encl. product brochures

Salutation

When you don't know the name of the recipient:
Dear Sir/Madam (BrE)
Ladies and Gentlemen (AmE)

When you know the name of the recipient:
Dear Mr/Mrs/Ms/Miss Winch (BrE, AmE)

Note: In the US Mr. and Mrs. include a full stop/period e.g. Mr. Winch

Endings
When you don't know the name of the recipient:
Yours faithfully (BrE)
Sincerely yours (AmE)

When you know the name of the recipient:
Yours sincerely (BrE)
Sincerely (AmE)

Sign the letter, then print your name and position under your signature.

Common abbreviations
Re.   regarding
pp.   (on behalf of) when you sign the letter for another person
encs. documents are enclosed with the letter
cc   copies, the names of the people who receive a copy are included in the letter

e-mails

e-mails have two distinct styles: a semi-formal business style and a more informal personal style.

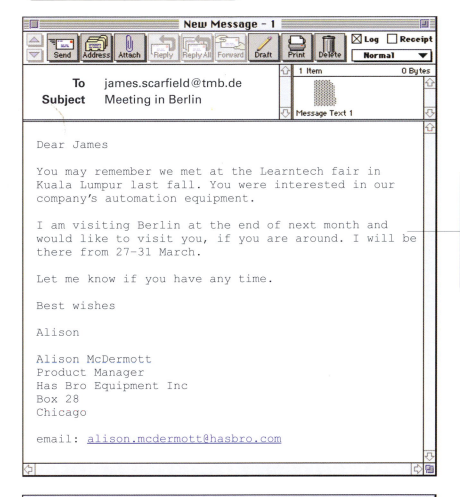

The semi-formal style is similar to a business letter, but less formal and shorter. A likely ending is *Best wishes* rather than *Yours sincerely*. This style is best used for e-mails to people outside your company, or who you do not know well. The emphasis is on the efficient provision or exchange of information.

The informal style is suitable for e-mails within your company and for people whom you know well. The greeting is often *Hi, Hello* or even *How are you?* The style is much closer to spoken than written English.

Faxes

J.D. Kingsland Ltd

Fax Transmission

To	Jenny Duncan
From	Zofia Nadstoga
Fax No	0044 1483 740675
Date	7 April
No of pages (including this)	1
Subject	Various

Jenny

Further to my message on your answering machine, I thought it might be helpful if I faxed you the points we need you to clarify on Monday:

1 Contacts inside Sataier-Bucht AG
We need to know what exactly we can say about your proposal to our contact inside the company. We have to ensure we do not breach any confidentiality agreements.

2 Technical documentation
Can you inform us about the technical documentation needed for the new equipment? Should it be in German as well as English?

3 Translator
Christine needs to give us more information about the technical writer required (French to English). The agency want an exact job description.

Regards

Zofia

Zofia Nadstoga
Office Manager

> Faxes may contain the following headings: To / From / Fax numbers / Date / Number of pages / Subject

> The style of the fax can be formal, as in a business letter, or more informal as here, depending on the subject and recipient.

> Points can be numbered for clarity.

Memos

MEMO

To:	**All Staff**
From:	**Melanie Jury**
Date:	**15 July**
Subject:	**Purchase orders**

Please note that a purchase order (copy attached) must be completed for all purchases over €50.

Complete purchase orders should be passed to Christine Hantke to agree terms of payment with the supplier, and then sent to the Woking office for final approval.

Purchase orders under €50 can be paid for from the petty cash account.

Many thanks for your co-operation.

MJ

> Memos are usually for internal communications.

> They should include the following headings: To / From / Date / Subject

> They should be short and include only relevant information.

> Points should be arranged in logical order. In longer memos, it is common to number points.

> The tone of a memo may be formal or neutral.

> It is usual to end with your initials rather than a signature.

Press releases

Press Presse Prensa

Automatix plc,
Semi Conductor Division

For the trade press
21 December

Opening of new production facilities in Johor Fahru, Balanesia.

At a ceremony attended by Automatix Chairman, Rocco Truffaldino, and the British Ambassador to Balanesia, Sir Edward Faulkner, Automatix plc's new semi-conductor chip facilities were opened in Johor Fahru on Wednesday.

'The new facilities represent our commitment to expanding our production of advanced memory chips. We aim to be the supplier of choice for the world's leading electronics companies, without damaging the environment' said Mr Truffaldino.

A special feature of the plant is the clean, no-waste production process, which aims to have zero impact on the environment.

For additional information visit our website
www.pr.automatix.co.uk
or contact Jerry Turner +44 (0) 1792 536012 (phone),
+44 (0) 1792 536723 (fax).

Date: 21 December
Title: Opening of new production facilities in Johor Fahru, Balanesia
Addressed to: The trade press
Author: Kylie Dawson

The header for a press release should make clear who it comes from, what the subject is and which part of the press it is aimed at.

The subject should be put in bold print so that the journalist can see immediately if it is relevant to him/her.

The main body should have a short introduction with names of people who might be interesting for the press, some description of what is new or interesting for the public and – if possible – a good quote which the newspaper could print.

The style should be formal and concise, with nothing irrelevant to the particular story.

Always include some information as to how the journalist can get more information about the subject if they want it.

Agendas

Management Committee Meeting

Agenda

Date:	7 April
Time:	14.00
Venue:	Building B Room 10–213
Participants:	JS, AH, RG, PK, TB

1. Apologies, minutes of last meeting and matters arising.

2. Sales projections for next quarter.

3. Recruitment and capital expenditure required for no. 2.

4. Company bonus scheme.

5. A.O.B.

6. Date of next meeting.

> Always put the date, time and venue (place). It is also usual to include the initials of the participants.

> The first point on the agenda is usually handled by the chairperson. He/she will explain why anybody is absent, check through the minutes from the last meeting, and allow participants to briefly comment on anything relating to the previous meeting (matters arising).

> The points are then worked through. They should be arranged so that they lead logically into each other, if possible.

> A.O.B. means *any other business*. This is for other relevant issues that were not included in the agenda.

Guidelines

Westpak Ltd
Company Guidelines

Welcome to Westpak, the company that cares!

As a new employee you probably have many questions that you wish to ask about your new position. To help you settle in quickly, here are answers to some of the most frequently asked questions.

1. How does the flexi-time system work?

All employees at Westpak are individuals with their own particular circumstances. We believe that it is your responsibility to work out with your supervisor a schedule that is fair to both you and the company. As long as your work is done as efficiently as possible, you can do it when you like. That is why our offices are staffed 24 hours a day.

2. How should I dress?

Most of you will be in regular contact with customers. It is important that they should feel confident about the service they will receive from Westpak. We suggest that you dress in a way which is smart and business-like as a mark of respect to our clients.

3. How are interpersonal problems dealt with?

Teamwork has always been the key to success at Westpak and anything which is likely to damage co-operation between team members has to be dealt with as quickly as possible. If you feel that efficient …

1

> Guidelines vary enormously from company to company and industry to industry. It is important to distinguish between guidelines and regulations.
>
> Regulations are required for ensuring the legally correct handling of a contract, or the safe operation of a piece of machinery, for example. The language used in regulations is therefore much more directive.
>
> Guidelines are also important for ensuring the smooth operation of the company, but they often touch on areas of human behaviour where it is not easy to dictate to people. The language must therefore be more persuasive and less directive, or else personnel will object.

Action minutes

Minutes of the Management Committee Meeting

Date: 7 April
Venue: Building B Room 10–213
Participants: Jim Scarfield, Andrea Hevitsun, Robbie Gibson, Paul Keown. Apologies: Tony Barton

Point	Discussion	Action
1. Management pay review	We agreed changes to the management pay review. AH will include these when the review is presented at the next meeting of the finance committee.	AH 26 April
2. Sales projections next quarter	We agreed that we need to produce better sales figures for the next quarter after the poor results so far this year. JS and PK will spend the next month personally visiting our top clients to check the reasons for the business downturn.	JS and PK
3. Recruitment and capital expenditure	We decided not to do any recruiting over the next quarter. However, we will buy the new accounting software to increase our efficiency in invoicing customers, if we can get a bigger discount from the software supplier.	RG
4. Company bonus scheme	Because of the present financial situation a bonus scheme can only work if it is linked to productivity. AH will review different possibilities for discussion with the finance committee, and report to us at the next meeting.	AH 3 May

Next meeting: 3 May 14.00
Venue: Building B Room 10–213

Always put the title, date, time and venue (place) of the meeting, plus the names of the participants.

The minutes can be an important record of what was really discussed at a meeting, so it is important to make sure that the summary of each point is as accurate as possible.

Initials are used to refer to participants.

The 'action' column is important for showing who is supposed to do what by when.

If you are a participant at a meeting always make sure you check the minutes when they have been written up. If you think something has not been accurately reported then have it corrected.

Reports

Parry, Parry & Gibson

Site accident report

Executive summary

Damage has been caused to the emergency generator on the Witherby power plant site. It was caused by a fire started by the electrical contractors Mullet & Sons. Although the packing material that caught fire was left by another subcontractor, the personnel from Mullet started work before clearing the waste matter away, in contravention of contract regulation 2.3.8. Mullet & Sons should therefore pay for the replacement of the damaged equipment.

Introduction

This report will look at:

- the sequence of events
- the subcontractors involved
- the responsibilities of the subcontractors
- the financial compensation from the subcontractors
- recommendations to avoid future incidents of this nature

Findings

1. Fire broke out at 17.30 on Friday 13 October in the working area around the emergency generator. All personnel were cleared from the site and the fire service informed by 17.45. The fire service arrived at 18.00 and the blaze was extinguished by 18.30.

2. The electrical contractors Mullet & Sons started the fire accidentally when carrying out the connection work of the generator to the main power line. Packing material left on the ground by another subcontractor Harvest Macdougall plc caught fire and this quickly spread.

3. Although Harvest Macdougall are obliged to remove any packaging material they bring with them it seems that the electricians from Mullet told them to just leave it. We assume they wanted to get their own work done as quickly as possible so that they could finish for the weekend. Starting welding work without first making sure there is no inflammable material around is in direct contravention of contract regulation 2.3.8.

Conclusion

Mullet & Sons must pay for the replacement of the generator (€90,000) as they are solely responsible for the damage.

Recommendations

1. Mullet & Sons should not be offered any more work on site if they do not accept these terms.
2. Harvest Macdougall should receive a formal warning.
3. All subcontractors must be reminded of their obligation to follow all fire and safety regulations.

Normal Poole
Site Manager
19 October

1 A report should be well organised with information presented in a logical order. There is no set layout for a report. The layout will depend on:
   a) the type of report
   b) the company style.

2 The format used for this example is common for many formal reports:
   • Title
   • Executive summary
   • Introduction
   • Findings
   • Conclusion
   • Recommendations

3 Another possible structure would be:
   • Title
   • Terms of reference
   • Procedure
   • Findings
   • Conclusions
   • Recommendations

4 The *executive summary* is a summary of the main points and conclusions of the report. It gives the reader a very quick overview of the entire situation.

5 The *introduction* defines the sequence of points that will be looked at.

6 The *findings* are the facts you discovered.

7 The *conclusion* is what you think about the facts and how you interpret them.

8 *Recommendations* are practical suggestions to deal with the situation and ideas for making sure future activities run more smoothly.

Activity file

6 Risk, Skills, Exercise C, page 51

Manager A
You are not in favour of sending the executives to the area. You think the risk is too great. They could be kidnapped, or war could break out at any moment. Both executives are your personal friends and you fear greatly for their safety. If they did go, the company would have to hire an armoured car for them, at great cost. Try to persuade your colleagues to give up the idea of sending them.

11 Crisis management, Case study, page 99

Directors, Target Stores
Your objectives are:
a) to defend Target Stores' reputation
b) to explain what you are doing to deal with the crisis
c) to handle the journalists' questions.

Your team will be lead by the Chief Executive of the company and could include: Director of Public Relations; Director of Human Resources; Head of Legal Department; Marketing Director; Consultant (crisis management firm).

1 Hold a meeting to discuss what actions you will take to deal with the situation.
2 Try to predict what questions the journalists will ask and prepare answers to them. You may be surprised by some of their questions as they have been carrying out some investigations to find out the truth.

You have made your own enquiries into the matter.
- You contacted your chief buyer. He says no one knows who placed the original order. According to him, it could have been a buyer who has left the company.
- You contacted the manufacturer of the game 'Race against Time'. They were not helpful. They said they were still considering what action to take regarding the illegal copies.
- Staff turnover in Target Stores has been high during the last two years. Because the company has suffered fierce competition, you have had to make over 2,000 employees redundant. You have to increase profits because the share price has been declining and shareholders are becoming restless.

8 Team building, Skills, Exercise C, page 73

Team leader
You meet a member of your team who is unco-operative and unhappy.
- Find out what the problems are.
- Try to offer solutions so that the employee performs better as a member of your team.

3 Building relationships, Skills, Exercise D, page 27

Sales manager
You are sales manager for a sports goods company. You are at a conference and see someone who you met briefly last year at a trade fair.
a) Reintroduce yourself.
b) Find out if the person is interested in becoming an agent for your company.

4 Success, Case study: Camden FC, page 36

Camden FC negotiating team
You have other companies interested in sponsoring the club if the negotiation with United Media fails. However, United Media are an international company with good management and a high profile in the business world. You want:

1 A four-year contract
The contract should have a total value of £40m, with no conditions attached. £20m should be paid within the first year as you need money to enlarge the stadium's seating capacity.

2 Limited advertising
Advertising of United Media at the club ground should be limited. You want the ground to keep its identity and intimate atmosphere. Too much United Media advertising will upset the fans.

3 Limited promotion by players
Players' appearances and promotional activities should be limited. Too much time doing promotion work affects performance on the field. If the team is knocked out of the European Cup though, you could increase players' availability.

4 Paolo Rosetti to stay at the club
You want to keep Paolo Rosetti at the club. Cristos and the head coach think he is a fine player who could play another three years at this level.

5 An additional payment
United Media should pay an additional £8m towards the cost of buying two star players. Cristos says this is essential to Camden's success in the European Cup.

6 Diversification into other areas
You have contacted baseball clubs in the United States. They are interested in renting the ground during the summer to play exhibition matches and promote baseball.

7 A deal with a football boot manufacturer
You want to make a deal with Sprint plc, a football boot manufacturer. Sprint have offered you £200,000 to be the official sponsor of the players' boots.

8 Perks
Try to get as many perks as possible from United Media, for example, £10,000 for each goal that a player scores over his individual target of 20 goals. Also, free cars for players, memberships to clubs, etc.

You can offer United Media
- the advantage of being linked to the most exciting young team in English football.
- the opportunity to work with one of the best managers in the Premier League.
- the benefit of working with a brilliant Commercial Director, Sophie Legrange.
- the possibility of becoming well known in China and the Far East.
- the use of a hospitality box with space to seat ten people.

9 Raising finance, Skills, Exercise D, page 81

Financial Manager

You do not really want the posting for these reasons:

- In your opinion, the salary offered is far too low. Your present salary is $80,000 p.a. You will receive $90,000 p.a. in your new posting.
- The posting has come at an inconvenient time. You have just bought an expensive apartment which you are currently re-decorating.
- Your partner will have to give up a good job to accompany you.
- You have a ten-year-old child who is a slow learner and needs to attend an expensive private school.
- The climate is very hot and humid in the country you have been posted to. You think it will almost certainly damage your health.

Try to persuade the Personnel Director to offer a higher salary and financial compensation for the problems you face as a result of the posting.

11 Crisis management, Skills, Exercise D, page 97

Managers

You should defend your company's sales methods and persuade the journalists that your business has high ethical standards. The information below will help you to answer the journalist's questions.

- Your marketing strategy is to target older people (over 60s) because they need phones more than young people. Most phones are sold by phoning potential customers.
- Your sales staff phone potential customers in the evening because customers are usually at home then. Your staff ask for the customer's credit card details to check the customer's financial status.
- Your sales staff say that the monthly payment is £14 for the black, economy phone. Other models of phone are more expensive. Customers must pay extra for a small device that increases the volume of the voice they hear on the phone.
- Sales staff are trained to maximise sales revenue by offering the customer extra accessories, for example leather cases, straps, etc.
- They can also increase sales revenue by offering to 'adapt' the phone to a customer's requirements, e.g. by keying in numbers frequently called.
- Sales staff are encouraged to send phones quickly when the customer shows interest in buying a phone.
- Your sales staff are motivated, dynamic and enthusiastic. Some of them may occasionally try a little to hard to increase sales!

6 Risk, Skills, Exercise C, page 51

Manager B

You are very keen to send the executives because a sales office there would be highly profitable – there is a huge demand for mobile phones in the area. You don't think the risk is very great. The government control the area firmly. There have been a few terrorists incidents, but that's to be expected. The executives can get advice before they go on what precautions to take (for example where to live, changing routes when they return home, locking their car doors, being alert at all times).

8 Team building, Starting up, Exercise B, page 68

Score 1 point for *each* of the following answers:

Doers vs Thinkers:	**a), d), f)**
Mind vs Heart:	**a), b), d)**
Details vs Ideas:	**b), d), e)**
Planners vs Improvisers:	**a), c), e)**

Score 2 points for *each* of the following answers:

Doers vs Thinkers:	**b), c), e)**
Mind vs Heart:	**c), e), f)**
Details vs Ideas:	**a), c), f)**
Planners vs Improvisers:	**b), d), f)**

18–24 points
You are definitely a creative type. You value original ideas over detailed planning. You are likely to show consideration for others. You can get bored easily and sometimes need to be under pressure to get results.

12–17 points
Clear thinking and careful planning are of great importance to you. You are not afraid of challenging others in order to get results. You are likely to be ambitious and well organised.

14 The future of business, Skills, Exercise B2, page 121

Customer
It is 5 January. You ordered 20 microwaves from the German manufacturer on 4 December. You are very angry because the delivery is so late. These are the details:
- Order number BJP 201
- Model MX14
- Colours: black and cream
- Discount off list price: 4%
- Delivery: Two weeks from date of order

You wanted the microwaves for your pre-Christmas sale. Try to persuade the seller to give you a discount of at least 10% because of the late delivery.

4 Success, Skills, Exercise D, page 35

Chief Buyer (Retailer)
You want the shoe manufacturer to agree to the following:

Delivery time	One week after receiving order
Place of delivery	to individual retail outlets (20 around the country)
Price	Knee-length boots € 280
	Ankle boots € 160
Colours	Black, brown, green and red
Payment	60 days after delivery
Discount	6% for orders over 200
Returns	All unsold boots returnable up to one year after order

14 The future of business, Skills, Exercise B2, page 121

Sales Manager
You receive a call from an angry customer who has not received the consignment of microwave ovens ordered the previous month. Try to deal with the situation diplomatically and calm the customer down.
- Get full details of the order.
- Explain that there was an unexpected increase in demand for the product so not all customers could be supplied on time.
- Promise to give the customer a firm delivery date after you have talked to your production manager.
- Say that you will call back as soon as possible.

9 Raising finance, Case study: Vision Film Company, page 83

Directors of European Finance Associates

1 **Financial terms**
   You want to be repaid 120% of your investment ($6.6 million) within five years of the launch of the film, plus 70% of the net profits of the film. Your reasons are: it is a high risk investment; the producer and director have no track record in making feature films; they want to use unknown actors.

2 **Payment of instalments**
   You want to pay the loan to Vision Film Company in the following way:
   a) Pre-production (September)   10%
   b) Before the principal photography (March)   40%
   c) At the end of the principal photography (June)   35%
   d) When laboratory work is completed (July)   15%

3 **Choice of director**
   You do not believe that the present director has suitable experience for this film. You want to appoint someone with a good track record in feature films and offer that person a salary, plus a share of the profits.

4 **The leading actors**
   You feel strongly that two European stars should have the principal roles. They would greatly increase the profit potential of the film and also attract major distributors.

5 **Distribution**
   The director and producer of VFC do not understand that it is difficult to sign up distributors, especially when they do not have a track record in feature films. To do deals, you need contacts and skills. You can help VFC to make the necessary deals, but this will involve time and money!

6 **Artistic independence**
   The film makers can have a great deal of independence – you will not interfere. However, they should bear in mind the following:
   a) the film must have a happy ending. Film-goers do not like to leave a cinema feeling sad.
   b) the film should contain some 'flashback' war scenes involving Alicia and Justin in order to attract younger film-goers.
   c) There should be few, if any, erotic scenes as the film needs to appeal to a wide range of adults in various age groups.

7 **Launch date**
   March (final year) at the latest, to follow up its expected success at the Sundance Film Festival.

11 Crisis management, Case study, page 99

Journalists

Your objectives are:

a) to ask probing questions so that you get the true facts and find out how the company is dealing with the crisis

b) to gather information so that you can write a powerful and accurate article for your newspaper.

1 Work in small groups. Prepare some questions which you would like to ask the Company's representatives.

2 Work as one group. Choose the best questions and decide who will ask each one.

3 When you ask your questions at the press conference, make sure you ask 'follow up' questions if you are not satisfied with the answers you receive.

You have made some enquiries and found out the following:

- The owner of the firm in the Hong Kong which sold Target Stores the games was investigated five years ago for selling counterfeit toys, but was not charged.
- Two other games, manufactured by the firm which made 'Race against Time', have also been sold by Target Stores in small quantities (approximately 200 each). The games 'Space Gladiators 4' and 'Endgame' are also illegal copies supplied by the same company in the Netherlands.
- For the last two years, Target Stores have been reorganising their business. They have reduced their workforce by making 2,000 staff redundant. Employees who left the company accused the management of being 'ruthless and dictatorial'.

4 Success, Discussion, Exercise A, page 31

New Coke for Old

By 1979 Coca-Cola's lead in the US soft drink market was down to 4% although it was spending $100m more on advertising than its great rival Pepsi. So, after 99 successful years Coca-Cola decided to change its original formula and launch New Coke. Coke spent two years and $4m on new flavour research. By 1984 their market lead was down to 2% but in blind taste tests people seemed to prefer New Coke to Pepsi and in the biggest test 61% preferred it to original Coke.

Within 24 hours of its launch on 23 April 1985, 81% of the US population knew of the change to New Coke. However, once it was realised that New Coke was to replace rather than to be available as well as original Coke, the complaints started. By the middle of June there were 8,000 a day. Coke also received 40,000 letters. On 11 July Coke executives apologised, admitted their mistake and re-introduced original Coke as Coca-Cola Classic.

The failure of New Coke had cost more than $4m. Sales of New Coke continued to fall while sales of Classic rose. Loyalty to the original was stronger than ever and Coca-Cola regained its place as the nation's favourite soft drink.

11 Crisis management, Skills, Exercise D, page 97

Journalists

Many readers have complained to you about the dishonest methods used by the phone company. The complaints are related to selling by telephone. Use the information below to question the managers closely about their sales methods. Try to persuade them to offer financial compensation to all dissatisfied customers.

Readers say that the company's sales staff:
- target old people, using high-pressure tactics to persuade them to buy a phone.
- always phone late in the evening when people are tired and vulnerable.
- trick customers into immediately giving their credit card information.
- say monthly payments are only £14, then send bills for much higher amounts.
- persuade people to buy accessories, such as leather cases, which they don't really need or want.
- send mobile phones to people before they have decided to buy them, and include an invoice in the package.
- usually send the expensive deluxe models.
- promise that the customer can send back the phone if not satisfied. But when customers phone the company, they can't get through.

3 Building relationships, Starting up, Exercise D, pages 22–23

Key

1	a) 2	2	a) 2	3	a) 2	4	a) 2	5	a) 1	6	a) 1	7	a) 2	8	a) 2
	b) 1		b) 1		b) 1		b) 1		b) 2		b) 2		b) 1		b) 1

8–10 Building relationships is not easy for you. Communication is the key. Make the effort to talk to people about problems. Ignoring them won't solve them and practice makes perfect.

11–13 You are making the effort to build good relationships but are you trying too hard? It might be better to spend more time developing the relationships you have rather than going out to meet more people.

14–16 Congratulations. You obviously enjoy good relations with many of your business associates. Can you use your skills to help those who work with you improve their business relations too?

6 Risk, Skills, Exercise C, page 51

Manager C

You can't decide whether the executives should go or not. On the one hand, the area has great sales potential and the company would be the first mobile phone operator to set up an office there. Also, at the moment, there is no terrorist activity. On the other hand, there is a real risk because in other areas of the country, executives have died as a result of terrorist activity or war. If they did go, you think they should have a special bodyguard at all time. This would, of course, be very costly.

9 Raising finance, Case study: Vision Film Company, page 83

Director and Executive Producer of Vision Film Company

1 **Financial terms**

After repaying 100% of EFA's investment ($5.5 million) you will then share the net profits of the film on a 50/50 basis.

2 **Payment of instalments**

You want the loan to be paid in the following way:

a) On signing the financing contract (April/May)   25%

b) Before the principal photography begins (March)   50%

c) At the end of the principal photography (June)   15%

d) When the laboratory work is completed (July)   10%

3 **Choice of director**

Director: you have a brilliant track record in the advertising sector of the film business. You have also written the remarkable script for the film. Try to persuade EFA that you are the right person to direct this film.

4 **The leading actors**

You want to use two unknown actors in the main roles. They have agreed to perform in the film and you believe they have great 'star potential'. If you have to use established stars, this could add $1–2 million to your costs – perhaps even more.

5 **Distribution**

You are confident of signing up major distributors once the film is made and its quality is apparent to everyone (good story, wonderful script, plus your technical skills).

6 **Artistic independence**

You want complete independence when making the film, especially in two matters:

a) the film must contain several erotic scenes featuring the two lovers so that it will appeal to contemporary audiences' tastes.

b) it will have a sad ending which will highlight the high moral standards of the two main characters.

7 **Launch date**

Preferably July (final year).

A three-month publicity campaign immediately after the Sundance Film Festival is essential for the film's success in the United States.

4 Success, Skills, Exercise D, page 35

Sales Manager (Shoe manufacturer)

You want to the retailer to agree to the following:

Delivery time	Four weeks after receiving order
Place of delivery	To the retailers' main warehouses in Frankfurt and Munich
Price	Knee-length boots €320
	Ankle boots €200
Colours	Black and brown
Payment	30 days after delivery
Discount	3% for orders over 100 pairs
Returns	Black boots only (easy to resell)

4 Success, Case study: Camden FC, page 36

United Media negotiating team

Your negotiating objectives are listed below. Keep them in mind when you plan your strategy and tactics. You want:

1 A four-year contract worth £30m

In addition to £30m in sponsorship, you could offer Camden an additional £10m if the club wins the European Cup. Decide how much you wish to pay each year and when payments will be made. If Camden are relegated to Division 1, the sponsorship deal should be renegotiated.

2 Maximum advertising at the football ground

- Four huge posters advertising the company at the sides and ends of the ground.
- The company's logo on flags at all entrances.
- The main stand to be renamed 'The United Media Stand'.

3 Maximum promotion by players of United Media

- Players wear the company's logo on their shirts.
- The team's shirts and shorts should have a blue strip – United Media's corporate colour.
- The two top goal scorers should do a minimum of 25 days promotional work a year for United Media (other players 15 days).

4 Discussion of Paolo Rosetti's behaviour

The player's behaviour is seriously damaging the club's reputation. If he continues to behave in this way, he will damage United Media's reputation too.

5 Approval of Camden's new ventures

If Camden FC wants to diversify into other businesses, United Media should be consulted. The new ventures must be in keeping with the company's image.

6 Cancellation of Camden's deal with Sprint plc

You have learned that Camden FC plan to make a sponsorship deal with Sprint plc, a football boot manufacturer. Sprint would become the official sponsor of the team's boots. You are against this deal because Sprint is owned by United Media's chief rival, Euromedia Group.

7 Use of a hospitality box

A hospitality box at the ground should be provided for the exclusive use of United Media staff and guests. There should be space for at least 30 people.

You can offer Camden

- a sponsorship package worth a maximum of £40m.
- perks, for example:
  - a car with the company logo on it.
  - free travel to holiday destinations.
  - cheap loans for apartment / house purchase.
- training courses for players to improve their presenting and interviewing skills.
- financial help for older players to attend coaching courses or obtain academic qualifications.
- a financial contribution towards the cost of a new player to replace Paolo Rosetti – £2m maximum?

3 Building relationships, Skills, Exercise D, page 27

Sports goods wholesaler

You have a wholesale business specialising in sports goods. You are at a conference and you see someone you think you recognise, but are not sure. When they introduce themselves:

a) show some interest

b) try to find out if there is any possibility of working together in the future.

Are you in danger of burning out, page 137

Key

1	a) 2	2	a) 3	3	a) 3	4	a) 3	5	a) 1	6	a) 3	7	a) 3	8	a) 3
	b) 3		b) 2		b) 1		b) 2		b) 3		b) 2		b) 2		b) 2
	c) 1		c) 1		c) 2		c) 1		c) 2		c) 1		c) 1		c) 1

19–24

The Olympic Flame is more likely to burn out than you. You glow gently when necessary, but rarely get above Gas Mark three. This is because your stress levels are comfortably low and you know what to do at the first sign that things are getting on top of you.

11–18

You are smouldering slightly, and any spark could set you off. You may not think that you are a candidate for burnout, but you are heading in that direction. Try to develop your life outside work, and if it's the job itself that's causing the problem, think about looking for a new one.

10 or less

It is simply a matter of time before there is a little pile of white ash on the chair where you used to sit. Take some positive action to prevent total burnout before it's too late. Prioritise, delegate, improve your time management and above all, ask for help immediately.

9 Raising finance, Skills, Exercise D, page 81

Personnel Director

You know that the Financial Manager is unwilling to take up the posting. You expect him/her to ask for financial compensation for the inconvenience caused by the posting. Be sympathetic and helpful, but bear in mind the following:

- The local salary rate for the position of Financial Manager is $60,000 p.a.
- The company will consider any request for financial compensation if the request is reasonable. However, it expects staff to make some sacrifices when they take up a posting.
- Overseas postings are essential for staff who wish to fill senior positions in the company. They are a testing ground to find out whether managers have the mental and physical strength for top jobs in the organisation.

8 Team building, Skills, Exercise C, page 73

Team member

You meet your team leader to discuss your performance at work. You are unhappy for the following reasons:

- You feel you are working harder than everyone else. You are always the last to leave work.
- Your hard work is not recognised and appreciated by the team.
- You recently married and are missing your partner and young child.
- You do most of the boring paperwork for letting the apartments while your colleagues are given more face-to-face contact with clients. You are not happy with how the workload is being distributed.
- You think the team leader is too young and inexperienced, and is not managing the team well. This is the main reason why you are unhappy.

Audio scripts

1 Communication

🎧 1.1 (I = Interviewer, PL = Penny Logier)

I   Is communication between companies and their customers better now than in the past and are there ways of improving it further?

PL   Tremendous in-roads has been made over the last two to three years, in terms of communication, and it's been principally down to two quite distinct things. The first is new technology and the second is the grasp that education and training is very, very important. In terms of new technology, erm, such things as e-mail, that now the majority of people are on, makes it that we can actually talk to our clients electronically, very quickly. We can get response back from them in terms of approvals, if we need to say let's have budgets signed off, or indeed if we want to debate something electronically in terms of the schedule or indeed a proposal. Er, this can only get better. Erm, people are now feeling far more confident in the way that they're using e-mail. As it gets more sophisticated, so we can actually attach far more detailed structures to them and they, again, can respond back and understand what we're trying to do with them.

I   Can you give us examples of some really good communication between companies and their customers?

PL   Yes, one of our key customers is the Volkswagen Group (or VAG) erm, who are international. It was very important when we began a trading relationship with them to get communication lines very clear. To that end, we set up an Intranet site between the two companies. Very briefly, Intranet is an extension of the Internet which means that we can communicate with each other via an … almost an Internet site, but on a daily basis and it is purely for those two companies to trade from. In other words, it has no access from outside, so confidentiality is, of course, kept. Er, this delivers to our client immediate access to any work that's in progress. They can therefore comment very quickly on changes that need to be made and we, in turn, can respond back with speed.

I   Can you think of any examples of when a breakdown in communication has seriously affected a business?

PL   Yes, I can think of a number of instances where we, as a company, have nearly lost clients because there's been a fundamental breakdown in communication. What I mean by that is that you've got two individuals who are not really either hearing or listening – for want of a better word – to what the other is saying. In other words, there's been a breakdown in understanding. Education, learning is very, very key in this in that we have to understand that quite often we talk in jargon. This has to be actually cut out because it's very important that clients understand the basic essence of what an argument is, otherwise, commercially, it can be disastrous.

I   And finally, is it possible to be a good manager but a poor communicator?

PL   No. Communication is key. Er, people have to understand what you're trying to tell them to do. They have to have a long-term strategy in terms of their career development. You must make it clear, as a manager, what those aims are. Verbal is more important than written. People can talk to you on a one-to-one basis. You actually encourage confidence then and you actually get a rapport and a relationship with the individual.

🎧 1.2 (C = Customer, S = Supplier)

C   Hello, Elena Roca here.

S   Hi Elena. How's everything going?

C   Not too good, I'm afraid. We've got a problem with those air conditioners. They haven't arrived yet and our customer wants to know what's going on. What's happening your end, Martin? Why haven't we received them?

S   Sorry, Elena. I meant to call you. There's so much going on at the moment, it slipped my mind. We've got a labour problem here. There's a dispute over pay rates. Our people refuse to work overtime and it's affecting production.

C   I see, but when can you get the goods to me? The customer's really breathing down our necks.

S   Erm, I don't know, to be honest. You may get them by the end of the month, but I'm sorry, I can't promise anything.

C   End of the month? I don't believe it! We can't wait that long. Surely you can give our order priority.

S   I'm sorry, we've got several urgent orders to fulfil before we deal with yours. I can't let you jump the queue, Elena, it wouldn't be fair to the others.

C   Well, it just isn't good enough. And you know it. We've been one of your regular customers for years. We should get special …

S   Hold on, there is a solution. How about this? There's a German firm I know, they sell similar air conditioners to the ones you ordered. You might have to pay a little more for them, but they can deliver within two weeks. They're very efficient.

C   Mmm, that's worth checking out. Can you give me a few details?

S   I don't have them to hand, but I could easily get them for you. Shall I call back in a few minutes' time?

C   Please do. I'll be waiting to hear from you.

🎧 1.3 (M = Manager)

PA   Hello Patricia. How are things going?

M   There's a problem, I'm afraid. My plane's been delayed. They've rescheduled the flight for 11 o'clock, so I won't get back in time to chair the budget meeting.

PA   Oh dear! Do you want me to cancel it?

M   Well no, not if we can avoid it. All the papers have been circulated, everyone's fully briefed. It's just that I can't make it by eleven.

PA   Well, why don't you get someone else to chair it, and you take over when you get back.

M   That's a good idea. We could rearrange the agenda and start with some of the less important points. With a bit of luck, I'll be back by lunchtime.

PA   OK. Then you could chair the afternoon session on the budget.

M   Exactly. So who's the best person to run the morning session, I wonder.

PA   Well, how about Rachel?

M   Rachel? Yes, you're right, she should be OK. Thanks for the suggestion.

PA   Right, if you're happy, I'll call her and put her in the picture. I'm sure she'll agree.

M   OK. And if she can't do it, give me a call on my mobile. I'll jot down one or two other names in case that happens.

PA   Right. Bye for now, and good luck with your flight.

2 International marketing

🎧 2.1 (P = Paul, S = Stephanie, C = Courtney)

P   OK, thanks for coming along this morning. Erm … as I said in my e-mail, er the purpose of meeting this morning is for us to brainstorm ideas, promotional activities that we're going to carry out to make sure that the launch of the Business Solutions website is a success from the start. I'm going to open up to you … er … to come up with the ideas that you've formulated over the past couple of weeks. Erm … anything goes, we've got no budget at the moment but, you know, fire away.

S   Oh great, no budget constraints.

C   That's great! Television and radio.

S   Well, it's starting big.
P   Excellent!
C   Well, we have no budget, erm, well, I think we'd reach a wide audience, something like that, and erm, we could focus on some of the big, sort of business, financial, network television. Er. If we want to reach a global market and, if that's what were working to do, and extending to all areas I think …
S   Yeah, that's been quite successful for some of the banks and stuff hasn't it.
P   That's right, but definitely focussed – focussed advertising.
C   Focussed on specific networks that would reach, … that businessmen are watching, network television.
S   Well, I've been working more on cheaper solutions than that, just in case there are budget problems. I thought we could do some effective on-line promotion, which is actually very cheap, and I think we should aim to do that anyway. Direct mailing but also register the site effectively with search engines so anybody who goes on to the Internet and is looking for business solutions would come up with our website.
C   Yeah. Well, yes, we should definitely do some of that.
P   Absolutely! Yeah.
C   What about press advertising? Traditional newspapers, business magazines, journals?
P   Yes.
S   Yes, great, I mean we've done that very effectively in the past.
P   Yes, we've had some good response rates to the ads we've placed before.
S   Yes, and that would be something we could do, not just once but a kind of campaign over a period of time.
C   Yes, build it up.
P   Yep, teaser campaign, OK.

🎧 2.2 (P = Paul, S = Stephanie, C = Courtney)
S   And then, again going back to cheaper solutions, we could use the contact base we've got, the market research we've been doing for this new website. We've got some very good contacts where I think we could … erm … send out glossy brochures, maybe a CD demonstration, CD ROM demonstration, of the site to human resource managers, training managers …
C   Yes, that's a good idea.
P   Right.
S   As we've already got contacts with lots of those and I'm sure we should …
C   … exploit them.
S   Yeah, we could build that up.
P   Yeah.
S   And direct mail them.
P   With information packs or …?
S   Yeah, we could do a big either CD ROM walk-through as part of a glossy brochure pack, that might be one way and erm …, or information brochure if we didn't have so much money.
C   Yeah, would it be worth it sponsoring some kind of event, I don't know?
S   Oh yeah.
C   You know, inviting the real movers and shakers of our, you know, our target customers, the ones we can count.
S   It would be great to do a presentation maybe on a boat going up the river or something. That would be …
P   Yeah.
S   Get the press in.
C   Yes.
P   That's a good idea Courtney, excellent. OK. What other areas of press advertising could we do, do you think? You know, we've done billboard advertising before but …
S   Mmm. Billboards, what about that?
C   I don't know.
S   I hadn't thought of that for this but …
C   I don't know what the costs are related to that. I think we would have to look at that. Underground, airports, maybe some of that.
P   Yep, OK, well, I'm going to wrap the meeting up now. We've come up with some really good ideas, we've got TV, radio advertising, obviously that's going to be dependent on the budget we're actually set at the end of the day. On-line

promotion, which is cheaper, but obviously we've got to certainly have some degree of on-line promotion. Press advertising, business journals, billboards, maybe? Depending on the budget again. The contacts with the human resources departments, definitely, I mean that's an area that we've really got to explore and certainly a sponsorship of a major event to tie into the launch would be a great idea.
C   OK, so when will we meet next?
P   I think we're scheduled for three weeks' time.
S   Yes, that's right.
P   By which time we'll have more of an idea of the sort of budget that we're working with.
S   Shall we cost some of these things and see … So that we can …?
C   I've got some research I can look at.
S   OK, then we'll bring that to the next meeting.
P   Great.
S   Great.
C   OK.
S   OK, thanks.

3 Building relationships

🎧 3.1 (I = Interviewer, WL = Ward Lincoln)
I   Ward, what are the key factors in building good business relationships?
WL I believe that relationships, business or otherwise, are about trust. And, in order to gain trust, you must be honest, you must be transparent, clear. Don't promise what you can't deliver. There is nothing worse in a relationship than being let down. It is also about being clear, being explicit. People present their products in brochures, pamphlets, flyers, e-mail, videos. All of those media, they're all very effective, but it must be clear. The customer must understand very quickly, what you are selling, what price you're selling at. The speed of that information, the speed of the response – it must consistently be fast. The restless customer of the 21st century does not have time on his or her hands, and there are a million other providers, all ready and eager to sell to that customer. In order to continue that relationship, maintaining the relationship, consistently answer their queries, respond quickly in a simple format.

🎧 3.2 (I = Interviewer, MA = Miguel Adao, TY = Tong Yan)
I   Miguel, what are the best ways of building good business relationships?
MA The first thing is that Latin people are very warm by nature so you have to have that personal contact. And personal contact really sometimes even means actually touching somebody and shaking their hand and a hug and a long lunch meeting or a long dinner meeting. It's not as common, for instance, to have power lunches where in 15 minutes you just go through your agenda and hash it out and come to a – an agreement and just part ways. Usually these are more long, drawn out happy hour cocktails leading into a three-hour dinner or luncheon where you really get to know the person before you make a professional or a business commitment. So that, in Latin America, in Brazil particularly, the personal side to business relationships is very, very important and it's something that needs to be emphasised.
Erm … the best way, really, to build a business relationship is through networking. If you get to somebody by a third – by a third party, by somebody that you trust, by a mutual friend or acquaintance or business partner, it just opens so many doors and it makes it so much easier for you to actually get in and make your proposition.
I   And Tong Yan, what advice would you give to people wishing to do business in China?
TY Well the first thing is that Chinese business culture is very different from Western business culture. For example, Chinese people tend to work with their friends or relatives. This is because of their traditional social system. So it's very important for people wanting to do business in China to find an intermediary before they actually go into the Chinese market. The intermediary knows both sides – your company

and the local people and organisations – and can help to establish good working relationships. Chinese business people trust those who are loyal to them and who show respect to them. So it's very important for foreign business people to really develop local business relationships, to spend time getting to know people and establishing mutual trust and respect.

🎧 3.3 (I = Interviewer, TY = Tong Yan)

I   What typical mistakes do foreigners make when trying to do business in China?

TY One of the commonest mistakes is to misunderstand how business decisions are usually made. Foreign business people may feel frustrated that, after two or three meetings, they don't seem to be getting to the point, to making the real business deal. There may be a lot of social meetings – tea and dinner and so on – but there's no sign of a decision. It may not be at all clear to foreigners how or when the really important decisions are made, and by who. It's all about reaching a point where the local company feels comfortable with you, trusts you, and is ready to say yes. And that might happen at the dining table as often as at the negotiating table.

🎧 3.4

A   How's it going in France, Gina? We didn't do too well there last year.

B   Yes, my job was on the line. Our results were terrible. We tried to build up market share but it just didn't happen. We just managed to hold on to what we had.

A   What exactly was the problem?

B   Unfortunately, our agent let us down. We thought we could count on him to boost sales but he had no commitment, no motivation.

A   Well, I suppose you terminated his contract then.

B   Yes, there was no way we could renew it. We sounded out a few possible replacements and found someone else. We get on really well.

A   Good. Let's hope he'll be better than the last one.

B   He should be. He's got a very good track record. We'd set up a meeting on Friday, but he had to call it off – something came up.

A   Well, I hope you get a result. I must be going. I've got to draw up an agency agreement myself, I've put it off far too long already.

B   All the best. Speak to you soon.

🎧 3.5

Conversation 1

A   Haven't we met somewhere before?

B   Really?

A   Yes. Wasn't it last year at the conference in St Petersburg?

B   You mean the one on database management?

A   That's it! We both went to that presentation on the first day and we were talking afterwards.

B   Oh, yes …

A   I'm Jill Davis from Trustwood Marketing.

B   Yes, of course. Harry Kaufman. Good to see you again.

Conversation 2

A   So, you work for Delta Systems. Do you know Henry Willis? I've been trying to get hold of him.

B   No, I don't think I do.

A   He's a designer with you.

B   Where's he based?

A   Well he was in Seattle the last time we were in touch …

B   Oh, that division's been restructured. Maybe he moved on. You could try to track him down through our New York office.

A   OK, thanks. I'll do that.

Conversation 3

A   Excuse me. Are you Gabriella Dietz?

B   Yes, I am.

A   I'm Tim Ross. I was given your name by Jon Stuart.

B   Oh, right.

A   He said you'd be a good person to talk to about Italy. We're trying to find an agent there.

B   Well, yes, I should be able to help. Look, I have to go right now. But here's my card though. Why don't you give me a call at the office next week. And say hello to Jon for me!

Conversation 4

A   I see you're with UGC …

B   That's right.

A   Are you on the sales or product development side of things?

B   Sales. I'm responsible for our new range of kitchen systems.

A   Oh, really? How's the response been to your new publicity campaign?

B   Pretty good. It generated a lot of interest and orders are starting to come in.

A   Do you do much business outside Europe?

B   It's early days but we're beginning to get enquiries from Latin America and Asia.

A   We've been working with some very good people in Singapore. Maybe we could help you out there.

B   Ah, now that's a market we're definitely interested in.

🎧 3.6

A   Hello, my name's Valentin Perez, I'm a friend of Silvana Belmonte.

B   Oh yes?

A   I hope you don't mind me phoning. Silvana said it would probably be OK. Is it a convenient time to ring or could I call you back at a better time?

B   No, it's OK. I'm not busy at the moment. How can I help?

A   Silvana mentioned that you might be able to advise me on franchising contracts. We're thinking of setting up a franchising network here.

B   Mmm, I don't know. I could maybe give you a little help, but I know someone who's an expert in that area. Her name's Stephanie Grant.

A   She sounds interesting. You haven't got her phone number by any chance?

B   Certainly, hold on a moment. I'll look it up in my book. I'm sure she won't mind if you call her. Just a minute, now…

A   Can I mention your name when I call her?

B   By all means. She's a close friend as well as a colleague.

4 Success

🎧 4.1 (I = Interviewer, SM = Sally Muggeridge)

I   How would you define a successful business person?

SM Well a successful business person is somebody who certainly knows their job very thoroughly; who's good at what they do and also has experience and capability of making sure that the people that they manage also do their job well. As an individual, they probably need to have a very good vision, a thought about what their business should be and do in the future; they should certainly be very capable in making a profit and in earning money for the business; they should be a very good team player – that means they should be working with others successfully for both themselves and for those people that they're working with – and they should be very good at managing relationships, understanding people and taking care of them in terms of the best performance from people comes from those who feel that they're comfortable in the company that they're working in. Generally, a successful person is very ambitious, er … and wants to succeed and wants their people to succeed as well. And I think you would find that most successful business people feel that they have not done it on their own. They need a good er … collection of other people to help them do it. So you may need a finance person, a marketing person, a sales manager, people that will help you be successful so that you all share in the success of the business.

I   And do you think there are other ingredients for personal success?

SM I think as an individual you need to manage the time you spend at work and the time you don't spend at work, we call that work / life balance, and it is very hard in many businesses today to manage to do that. You need to have other interests, a family, interests and hobbies; you should be able to relax; you should be able to take yourself away from work and not think about work for periods. I think personal success is very much based on an individual managing themselves and their life, as well as managing their business.

4.2 (I = Interviewer, SM = Sally Muggeridge)

I   What makes a successful company?

SM Well this is quite a difficult question because a successful company could mean a lot of different things to different people. Many successful companies have names that you would be very familiar with. We call those 'brands', for example, Coca-Cola or Disney or Microsoft, and they're often regarded as examples of successful companies. Successful companies are generally very good places to work. They're places where everyone wants to be, and everyone likes working for success. A successful company is generally a business that has been in existence for quite some time and that's why their brand and their name is known. And, of course, one of the most important features of a successful company is a very good, strong management team. And we have our share price and there are other different measures that different companies have to judge their success, but generally, of course, we're looking for financial success.

I   Do you think that more of today's businesses are learning how to become successful than in the past?

SM Well, I think a lot of today's businesses are learning from those businesses that have not been successful. There are a lot of new companies, companies that did not exist ten years ago and, equally, there are many companies who have been around, been in existence for a great … er … great many years. I think there is always a learning process. Businesses that are successful learn from those that have not been successful; businesses that have not been successful are often taken and made successful by people other than those that started them.

4.3

1   Could you go over that again please? Why can't you deliver by the end of May?
2   Let me make a suggestion. Why don't you hire an outside haulage firm to deliver the cars to us?
3   We want all the vehicles to be painted in our company colours – green and black.
4   I'm not sure I follow you. Do you mean that the discount is reduced if we want them all green and black?
5   I've got a question for you now. Are you willing to consider payment by instalments?
6   OK, we agree then. The colours will be green and black but the discount will only be 10%. However, you'll let us pay in two instalments.
7   Could you clarify one point for me? It's about the length of the warranty.
8   We'll give you a five-year warranty if you want, but you'll have to pay a little extra for that, I'm afraid.

5 Job satisfaction

5.1 (I = Interviewer, AO = Andrew Oswald)

I   Professor Oswald, you've carried out a lot of research into what makes people happy at work. Which groups of workers have you found to be the most satisfied and why?

AO Women are quite a lot more satisfied with their jobs than men in most of the western countries. Just as you would expect, a high level of pay goes with a large amount of satisfaction with your work. People seem to enjoy promotion opportunities a lot, in other words, they need a hierarchy that they feel they can move up through their life. They don't like working long hours. They don't like large workplaces. A good example of that is that among the most satisfied people in countries like Britain or the rest of Europe, are the self-employed. They enjoy the independence of running their own business. And finally, a very large effect comes from insecurity at work. If you think you're about to lose your job, then you, in our kinds of surveys, report much lower job satisfaction.

I   And who were the least satisfied, and were there particular nations that showed up in your surveys?

AO A typically very dissatisfied worker would be a man, on low pay, in a large office or factory, who has to, for example, commute a long way to work, and who fears that he is close to being sacked, close to losing his job. If we look across nations, we find that small European countries tend to be at the top of the job satisfaction league table, so Denmark and Ireland, Switzerland, the Netherlands, for example, they do very well. American workers also have high levels of job satisfaction. And down the bottom we have particularly Eastern Europe, Poland, the old parts of the Soviet Union and so on, Japan and France too, are relatively low down the job satisfaction league table.

I   And what are the strongest motivating factors in people's working lives?

AO If you take large random samples of people, so we look across say hundreds of thousands of individuals in the major industrial countries, you see things that make a lot of sense. High pay, that motivates people. Job security and insecurity, that matters a lot to human beings, and promotion opportunities, the chance of moving up, of becoming a boss – that certainly seems to motivate people.

I   And how do you see the changing patterns of work affecting people's satisfaction in the future?

AO It is often thought that job insecurity is rising, that the notion of a job for life has somehow disappeared. That's not true. When you look at the data, the common journalist's idea appears to be wrong. The average length of a job is very little different from what it was 10 or 20 years ago, so in that sense, insecurity doesn't seem to have worsened. Commuting times are going up all the … all the time in the western countries, and that's a big blow to many workers, that pulls down their satisfaction with work.

5.2

Conversation 1

A   Good morning, John Slater.
B   Hi, John. I'm just calling to confirm the arrangements for your trip. We've organised a really full programme. Everyone's looking forward to meeting you.
A   Luis, I was about to call you. I'm really sorry. We're going to have to reschedule things. Anne's just resigned and I've got to cover for her until …

Conversation 2

A   … and then I said we can't possibly have it ready by then. I mean the deadline's only three weeks away after all …
B   Look – sorry but could we talk about this later? It's just that I'm already late for a meeting.

Conversation 3

A   He just doesn't listen to a word I say. It goes in one ear and straight out of the other.
B   Yeah, I know what you mean. You're not the only one who feels like that.

Conversation 4

A   I'm up to my eyes at the moment. Would you be able to give me a hand with these progress reports for tomorrow's meeting?
B   I'm sorry, I really can't. I'm busy with next year's budget. Maybe Janice can help.

5.3 (KJ = Karl Jansen, CN = Claudia Northcott)

KJ Well Claudia, thank you very much for coming to see me. Erm, what exactly is the problem in the General Office?
CN Well, it's a bit difficult to say …, to explain …, but one of the problems …, the main problem seems to be that Derek is …, we think …, I'm speaking on behalf of the part-timers …
KJ Uh huh.
CN Well, we think Derek is giving too many hours to Petra.
KJ I see.
CN And, well, this makes the rest of us, the rest of the part-timers feel, well, between irritated and angry really.
KJ Right.
CN And it's now become very obvious, I have to say.
KJ And is it affecting the work of the department, would you say?

CN Oh, well I don't know about that, but it does mean that, you know, if she has so many hours, one wonders how well she can do the work on a part-time basis. But also it means that there are one or two of us who would quite like the extra hours, and don't get a chance, or haven't been given a chance.

KJ Uh huh, well, that's obviously unfair.

CN Although it's work we could do equally well, we're sure. It's nothing personal, nothing against either Derek or Petra, but we would like a bit more openness, a bit more transparency about what's going on.

KJ Right. So this is obviously a situation that we'll have to deal with.

6 Risk

6.1 (I = Interviewer, AS = Allan Smith)

I What types of risks do companies face?

AS I'd like to start with just four types of risk and that would be, firstly the risk of simply doing nothing. Another type of risk is what's called credit or guarantee risk. There's also political risk and a final example I'd like to give is the risk of catastrophe or other disruption happening to a business.

6.2 (I = Interviewer, AS = Allan Smith)

I So, can you tell me more about risk and the four types you mentioned?

AS I'd say in its very traditional sense, risk is the chance of harm, injury or loss – and I call these all threats. But in business taking a risk can also mean the chance of change in direction and growing and making profits and, at the end of the day, businesses are into making profits and I'd call those all opportunities. Business is all about striking the right balance at the end of the day between risk and reward and, to help you with this I'll give you some examples, to illustrate this. The first is the risk of doing nothing and, strange as that may seem, many businesses flounder on that simple concept. This could be the company that tries to preserve the exact position that's always served it well in the past, and here the risk is the company will end up with an obsolete product in an obsolete market and will end up going out of business. Now you might say to me that there's many companies in the world that have done very well on the back of a very simple product and that's absolutely true. But if you look really closely at what they're doing, you'll find that they're constantly reviewing their price, they're constantly reviewing their marketing position and they'll also invest really heavily into investing and protecting their brand. So the message here is never do nothing.

The second risk relates to companies that give credit or take and rely on guarantees from others. Both of these will reduce profits if they go wrong. Let me start by explaining the credit side of things. If you want to increase sales, you need new customers and this may mean selling on credit. So you ship out a consignment of stock and you sit back and you wait for the customer to repay you.

Unfortunately, sometimes the customer doesn't repay you. They may have gone out of business or simply they may have 'gone away'. This will leave you with a problem.

On the guarantee side of things, you're relying on the guarantee of a person or a company to do X, Y or Z. Quite often, though, the guarantee is only as good as the person giving that guarantee.

A third risk that I'd like to give you is to always be aware of the political agenda. You need to know what's on the government's current agenda. Is that likely to change, and if so, how will that affect my business?

The fourth and final example of risk I can give you is a company being caught up in some sort of catastrophe or other disruption, such as fraud or criminal damage, that causes interruption to trading. The key question here is, does the business have the people and the plans to cope with that sort of disruption and catastrophe? 'Cos believe me here, many major disruptions have been the end to many a good business in the past. That's particularly so if the business is located in a single location.

6.3 (I = Interviewer, AS = Allan Smith)

I So what problems do companies have when managing risk?

AS Risk is all about threats and opportunities and one of the biggest problems that companies face is the quality and the timing of the information that is available on the risks they face. So I always say that good information gives you power and, if you have current, relevant and reliable information at your finger tips, then you've got a much better chance of managing risk. The management of the risk is absolutely key here and you need to have a reliable management team that can, in turn, act on that risk and I just have to give emphasis to that, 'cos that's the second problem that companies face. Because once you've identified a threat, or indeed an opportunity, you need to have really good communication lines between the key players in that company.

This'll basically let you quickly harness support, so that you can then take appropriate and swift action on those risks or those opportunities.

6.4 (I = Interviewer, AS = Allan Smith)

I Can you give us some examples of risk management?

AS Well I certainly know that doing nothing, which I mentioned earlier, became a major factor that caused many firms to go bust in the past. I remember when I was working in the insolvency department of a big accountancy firm and visiting an old family firm which had the most wonderful 1930s printing presses and a very loyal and skilled workforce. It was a real shame because the market had moved on and their printing presses were simply obsolete. So the firm wasn't able to compete with other companies that had invested in new printing techniques and eventually the firm had to close down. Sadly it ended with the company's equipment being sold off at auction.

I've also encountered many examples of selling stock on credit to new customers who initially seemed impressive but had no real proven track record. These situations often ended with the company simply never receiving payment.

6.5 (P = Paul, S = Stephanie, C = Courtney)

P Right, if you remember from the last meeting we came up with a list of ideas where we wanted to spend this budget we've just been set for the launch of the website. We came up with TV, radio advertising, on-line promotion, press advertising and a launch event of some kind. We've got the costs in, you can all see them. We've got this budget. We've got to decide where we're going to spend it. Does anybody have any strong feelings about any particular areas that we came up with?

S Well, unfortunately, I think we'll probably have to abandon plans for an event and probably TV advertising 'cos this is so expensive.

C Well hold on, I'm not sure if I agree with that. I mean do we have to? I think that those are both really valuable ideas and that there's a lot of potential in them if we target on the network television that reaches our customers.

S Well, if we had to choose one that was targeted I think the event's arguably more targeted than the TV advertising.

P I think I'd agree with you there, Stephanie.

S But they're just both so expensive if we look at the cost.

P Yes, I don't think ....

C Is this the final budget?

P It is the final budget. I don't think we can get any more money allocated to this budget, but I certainly think that there's not enough money there to do both – the TV advertising and the sponsorship, the launch event.

S Well, I would say I don't even think there's enough money to do effective TV advertising. I mean, we don't really have any positive experience, or much experience with television advertising ourselves, although other companies have done it effectively, so I would say it's really risky to put so much money into that one ...

P But then all our competitors do that, they have a fairly high profile.

C Yes, were going to miss out on a whole lot.

S All our competitors? We're one of the first to come out with an on-line training set of solutions. I don't agree because we actually are one of the first to have an on-line business solutions website.

P But they're advertising their traditional training provision.

S OK

C All right. Well, if our budget doesn't stretch for TV, what about if we focus it on business magazines.

S Yes, I would agree with that.

C Traditional press, newspapers, journals.

S Yes, we've been really successful with that so we know the readership.

P Yes, we've had some good responses to those adverts.

C And we can reach a really wide audience, and erm … whilst still making sure that it's our target audience.

P Yeah, I think that's important. We've got to make sure it's focussed.

S Yes, I would say it's that as well as some much more targeted initiatives. I said last time, and I keep on going on about this, but it's very important that we use the contacts we've already got and build on the market research we've done with big companies' human resource training managers and use that as pre-sales. They're ready to buy this product.

P Yeah, and it wouldn't be that expensive really.

S Not really. I mean, a CD ROM, that would be the biggest as you see from the costs, the biggest, the biggest, err …, contributory cost but …, and the brochure, but it's not bad really. Could we combine the two maybe?

C Well, yes. As long as we allocate enough to the press advertising, I just think we have a customer base and find we can exploit that, but we also need to build our base and by reaching a wider audience that's how we're going to do it.

S But, if we cut the event and we don't do the TV, we are going to have enough money to balance the two and do some on-line stuff, because that's under £500 what we're proposing, it's nothing.

P Yeah.

C OK.

P I mean the risk is, if it's unfocused and we lose a lot of impact, we're not targeting the right people. But as long it is focussed …

S And then the word-of-mouth. If we hit the right ones and they talk about us, that's going to be as effective as anything else.

P OK. Well, can I just clarify that I think we've all agreed that the sponsorship event and the TV advertising is too expensive and we're going to blow the budget if we go along, go down that route. So, on-line promotion, as we said but also focussed advertising in business journals, and we've got the list in front of us.

S I'd agree.

P And the approved journals.

C And newspapers and magazines.

P And newspapers and magazines, absolutely. OK. But also this, building on the established contacts we've already got with HR departments as well which is …

C OK.

P … which is a fairly cheap option.

7 e-commerce

7.1 (AR = Adam Rhodes, I = Interviewer)

AR Well, EFDEX stands for the Electronic Food and Drink Exchange and essentially, the service we provide to our customers is to enable them to trade electronically, through the Internet. So if you're a buyer you can source goods through a much, much wider universe of potential suppliers and if you're a supplier, you suddenly have access to a much, much wider community of customers; and for, again relatively small organisations with limited resources and small sales teams, then that is a tremendous community to be a part of.

I And what are the key success factors in e-commerce?

AR I think there are probably three and … er, I guess the first is that you really need to have a strong business proposition; a strong idea, putting it simplistically, that, that you have to have a way of bringing to the market place. And in EFDEX's case, EFDEX was found by … er, a guy called Tim Callam-

Brown, who was actually the purchasing and logistics director for … er, a company that bought all of the food and drink products which were to go on P&O cruise ships. When, when a cruise was departing from Southampton to go for 20 nights in the Caribbean, Tim's job was to buy all of the … er, everything from the shellfish to the champagne that will be required for that journey, and he found that the fluctuation in pricing was so significant that he had to actually, had to actually recruit an army of researchers who'd be out there checking who the suppliers were, what the prices were, whether the fact that the price of coffee had just declined because of some drought in South America was actually true or just another reason for hiking prices and, and I think this is a business idea that we are then using technology to bring to the market place. So I think that's the first thing – have a good business idea.

Secondly, I think you need a management team that has experience of the market place, er, that you're seeking to penetrate and in our case we're in the food and drink market and we have, again, a management team from the Chief Executive downwards, all of whom have had considerable industry experience in that market place, so I think that's the second factor.

And the third thing is, you need resources. In blunt terms, even the best ideas executed by the best management teams won't be successful unless you've actually got the resources and the finance to actually bring it to a reality. So I think many start-up companies in e-commerce will fail because frankly they run out of cash. But if you have those three things: a good business idea – not just a technology, er, idea that is looking for a business home, but a business idea that uses technology – a good management team and the resources – then those will be the three most important ingredients.

I And are there any downsides to e-commerce in your view?

AR I think it's fair to say that the e-commerce revolution will probably be as significant as the industrial revolution, er, or perhaps even more so in terms of the changes it will effect on society. I think we're only really waking up to the wider implications of what some of those things are. I mean some of the things we'll all read about is that as people spend more time, erm, finding solutions that are Internet-based, it perhaps can at times be at the expense of other social pastimes which is, is not a business issue, but I guess is a broader issue for society.

7.2

OK, let's get started. Good morning everyone and thanks for coming. For those of you who don't know me, my name's Roger Marris and I'm the Head of Business Development at Smarterwork.

Perhaps I should start off by asking how many people here have heard about Smarterwork. Can you just raise your hands? OK, and of you people who have heard of it, how many of you have used the site? … Thank you.

This morning, I'm going to talk to you about Smarterwork. I'm going to begin by giving you an overview of Smarterwork, then I'll go on to tell you about our two types of users and finally I'll explain how it all works. Feel free to ask any questions you like as we go along.

OK, what is Smarterwork? Well, I think *Internet* magazine were able to sum up what we do very well. They said, 'Smarterwork does an excellent job of matching freelance professionals to organisations looking for particular skills.' For example, finding someone who can translate your instruction manuals into a foreign language. We've been around for 14 months. We have 60,000 users of the site, which means that we have people who have come to the site, have registered and are using the site, er, on what we call a regular basis. There are 90 people in our company and I think that's interesting because I think people have an impression of on-line companies that it's just a site and there's no one behind it. Smarterwork is very much the leader within the UK, and now Europe, in providing business services on-line. We've built a platform that will allow small companies to come on to the Internet, post their requirements and then meet an approved supplier to do that work in a sort of quality-controlled environment.

OK. I'll now move on to tell you about our two types of users. We have clients on one side and suppliers on the other. Our clients are typically small businesses like yourselves. Our suppliers have all been pre-screened. What that means is that if they want to work through the Smarterwork platform, they have to prove their ability. All our suppliers have quality ratings, which have been given to them by other clients – again, like yourselves. Now these suppliers could be in any part of the world, so it means that businesses like yourselves in the South of London can work with suppliers in India, based on a quality rating. The great thing about the Internet is that it is a community bringing together clients and suppliers from all over the world.

7.3

Right. The next thing I'd like to do is explain how it all works. Let's look at the chart. As you can see, it outlines the steps involved. Firstly, the client posts a project, and we can help you with this. You post this project in an area in Smarterwork called 'My office'.

Then the suppliers visit the site and make bids and include their CV or company résumé detailing the type of work they've done before. After that the client evaluates the bids. I'd just like to highlight one of Smarterwork's USPs here. We provide account managers free of charge; a free service to help the client choose the supplier.

At the next stage, the client assigns the project to a supplier and then the client transfers the agreed fee to a secure holding account.

The client and supplier then develop the project. The work gets completed. The client is happy. Finally, the client signs off the work and the money is paid to the supplier – and that's where Smarterwork makes their money. We take a commission.

7.4 (MJ = Michael Johnson, HD = Hanna Driessen)

MJ Frankly, Hanna, I'm really worried about the way things are going. It's pretty obvious we have serious problems. And I think we need, you know, a really radical solution. We've got to get out of high-street retailing altogether. Now's the time to do it. If we wait around, hoping for things to get better …

HD Hold on. What do you mean? In what way should we change, Mike?

MJ Go completely on-line. Sell all the stores, every one of them. It wouldn't be too difficult to do that. Then use the money to set up an e-commerce operation. A 100% on-line operation. Think of the saving in costs, lower overheads, wage bills. Surely the market's telling us this is the way to go?

HD Oh, come on, it's not as simple as that. We've got no experience in that area whatsoever. And look at what's happening in dot com businesses. They're going bust every day. I think they're just a fad and people will soon come to their senses. They're not the answer, believe me.

MJ OK, so what is the answer? We've got to do something, that's for sure.

HD I'm not against on-line selling, Mike. But it won't solve our problems. We've got good products and a loyal customer base. Where are we going wrong? Well, I think we're not promoting our goods properly. We've been doing all our marketing in-house – it's a mistake. We should be outsourcing our advertising and promotion. We need to get a really creative ad agency who'll work on our image and rebrand us.

MJ That's it? That's your solution?

HD Not just that. I think we ought to pay more attention to the findings of the study done by the Marketing Department. Another thing – why not get a consultant to look at our product range? Have we got it right? Do we need new products and services? Do we need to target different segments of the market? But, we must stay in the high street – that's the business we know.

MJ I can't agree. Our profits are falling, costs are increasing. Most of our customers are over 40, we're not bringing in the younger ones at all. We can't stay as we are. It's just not an option. Look at our share price – it's half what it was a few years ago …

8 Team building

8.1 (I = Interviewer, DC = Doug Cole)

I What are the key elements in team building?

DC I think, rather than look at the key elements in team building, what you're looking at is the key elements of a team. So to build a team you need to know what your strengths and weaknesses are – of course weakness isn't the right word – but areas where you need added input, and so the key thing about a team is to establish, if you like the baseline, where you are, in terms of your skills, in terms of your activities, in terms of your experience. From … from … and you have to relate that to the task in hand. So you can't have the generic 'Right, this is a good team' for any task it's set. It is a task-specific team in a sense. So you identify what the project is or the task is. Look at your strengths and weaknesses and then you start looking at building a team around what you need to complete the task.

8.2 (I = Interviewer, DC = Doug Cole)

I Does the team have to have a leader?

DC The fundamental answer to that question is no. Erm, but having said that, again we come back to what I was saying earlier in terms of this task-specific thing. There are certain situations where a team will most definitely need someone to take the lead, erm but you can't say as a general rule, every team must have a leader. What I've found over the years, working with managers in this area is that, generally speaking, the larger the group and the more complex the task, there is a need for someone to co-ordinate. Now that's not necessarily a leading role, as you're probably identifying it. It's more of a co-ordination thing – again, in pulling people together, checking progress against the targets and deciding what the next course of action is. Having said that, there are distinct times when, especially when time is pressed, erm, there's a strict time scale on, that you will need to have someone to drive the situation.

9 Raising finance

9.1 (I = Interviewer, RL = Rosemary Leith)

I Which are the commonest ways in which businesses can raise money?

RL Business can raise money either through debt or equity. If business is raising debt they go to the bank, get a bank loan; it could be secured or unsecured, er, in its simplest form. If a business is raising money, er through equity they can go to private investors, venture capitalists or through a public offering on the stock market.

9.2 (I = Interviewer, RL = Rosemary Leith)

I And are some of these ways preferable to others?

RL The means that you use to raise the money depends very much on the type of business, the business stage that your business is at, and the revenue flows that come from a business. Now, you need to match them up to the type of instrument that you are using to raise the money. Erm, if you're in a start-up situation, er, it's very unlikely that you go and get a bank loan. You would definitely, er, go more to private investors and equity. Erm, if you're in a growth business with strong cash flow, you would probably use debt, although it can be more expensive than equity because of the interest that you need to pay to the bank or to whoever is lending you the money. Erm, in our experience – we're a small start-up company – er, we went to … for equity and to private investors.

I And how difficult has it been to raise money for business in your experience?

RL In our experience and in our type of industry, which was, er, Internet-related, although not completely focussed on Internet, it was quite difficult in the beginning to raise money. Er, it … Again raising money depends on the economy, it depends on the concept of your business at the start-up stage, and it also depends on having the right people in your business and having contacts with investors outside in the market. Erm, for us, er, we went to the private investor route, but in other larger businesses, er, that are more established, I would say you could easily go to a venture capitalist or to other, erm, investors to subscribe to the equity in the company.

I   Raising money can mean becoming very dependent on lenders. Has this posed any problems in your experience?

RL In our experience, we wanted to maintain control of the company. That meant that we chose equity as the vehicle to raise money and, er, with my business partner, we are the controlling shareholders, so our investors then, erm, are able to give us input and support, but in the decision-making, because we own the majority of the shares of the company, we are able to control the company.

10 Customer service

🎧 10.1 (I = Interviewer, CS = Chris Storey)

I   How would you define good customer service?

CS Good customer service is doing two things. Firstly, doing the right thing. This is basically doing what we promised to do as a service organisation erm, making sure mistakes do not happen, satisfying customers, being reliable, being courteous. If things go wrong, then dealing with complaints quickly. The second element is very much about delighting customers, doing something over and above what we … customers expected. I, for example, mean a company like Amazon.co.uk. Er, you order a book there, five o'clock in the evening, it turns up at nine o'clock the next morning. The first time that happens, people think 'wow', and it's very much about putting this 'wow' into the service. Once you do that, then these customers are likely to come back to you time and time again. But most companies still fail, fail on the first thing, about doing it correctly, making mistakes, etc.

I   Are companies paying enough attention to their customer service operations?

CS Some are. I mean, I mentioned the example of Amazon.co.uk, obviously very good at customer service; other companies are very good as well. Others aren't. Others have been moving into e-commerce and areas like that, setting up websites, then if you perhaps, erm, have a query, you e-mail them, because most websites have an e-mail contact address. The e-mail contact address often is the Computer Services Department. They've got nothing to do with customer service, erm, but as a customer you don't know that. That's the equivalent of the phone number that they've given out for you to get in touch with them, but the person on the end of that phone number doesn't care about customer service. They just want to have queries about the websites and not queries about the service or the products that you're offering and a lot of companies are failing to answer these, erm, these e-mail messages. That's just an example of the fact that companies can go into an area and they can forget about the customer service aspects.

🎧 10.2 (I = Interviewer, CS = Chris Storey)

I   And is new technology, for example call centres, improving customer service?

CS Yes and no. On the downside, call centres are often replacing personal service. So, for example for the banks, er, you used to have a personal relationship with a bank manager, now you have an anonymous, er, call centre. Basically, though you can use the technology to enhance this customer service. Erm, any time you ring up a call centre the person on the end of the phone should be able to dial up your details and speak to you as though they've dealt with you three or four times before: they know your history from the call centre, erm, computer systems. However, a lot of call centres, the people are managed in the way that they have to answer so many calls per hour. This means they have to get off the phone with each individual customer as quickly as possible. That's going against the ethics of good customer service where, basically, you are supposed to be dealing with customers as individuals, staying on the phone until you've answered that problem or those queries to the satisfaction of the customers, and that sort of, erm, goes against the way that the call centres' performances are evaluated.

I   Are people prepared to pay more for good customer service?

CS Yes and no. You can actually use customer service as a form of segmentation, i.e. breaking your market, your customers, into different groups of people. Some people will be prepared to pay more money for customer service because these people perhaps want more advice or more help in their purchase process. For example if somebody wants to buy a mortgage, people may have not bought a mortgage before, they may be unfamiliar with financial products, erm, they don't understand about interest rates, endowment policies, repayment plans, all the things that go with the mortgage, and they want advice, they want to be sat down, taken through the process. From a financial services institution point of view, you want to be able to charge for that and they, obviously the people who want advice, will be willing to pay that. Other people, sophisti… more sophisticated consumers don't need that advice. They want it, erm, without the frills and they'll just order a mortgage, sign it on the piece of paper because they know what they want. Equally, erm, you've got some people, very sophisticated consumers, aren't bothered about price. They want the delivery, they want it now. They don't want to wait two days for delivery, they want it delivered when they want it. They want it delivered nine o'clock in the evening because that's when they're going to be in at home. So, they're willing to pay for a service as well. So, it's all about breaking up your market into different segments, different groups of customers who you're basically putting together a package that will satisfy that particular group of customers.

🎧 10.3

Conversation 1

A It was just before Christmas …

B OK.

A I went into this wine store and bought two bottles of red wine. I bought them because they were promoted as 'wine of the month', so I thought, well, they must be good. When I tried one of them, I found the wine was much too sweet, like fruit juice almost.

B Fruit juice?

A Yes, Really! I offered a glass to my neighbour, who was our guest. She took one sip and asked me if I had anything else!

B So, what did you do?

A Well, I took the bottles back to the store and complained about the wine. The salesman didn't argue. He took the bottles back and told me to choose another two bottles. 'I'll look for something at the same price,' I said. 'Don't do that,' he said, 'choose any two bottles you like.' I chose two which were quite a bit more expensive and thanked him. I always go to that store for my wine now because I like the way they treat their customers.

Conversation 2

A I flew to Spain recently with my family and I was really impressed with the level of customer service we received. We were flying with a relatively cheap, no frills airline and they didn't promise much – no meals for example – but what they did promise, they delivered.

B Really?

A Yes. The service was excellent and friendly; it was service with a smile. They were particularly friendly and helpful to people with small children. We took off on time and arrived on time. We'll definitely use them again.

Conversation 3

A Something so irritating happened recently with a delivery that I'd ordered. I certainly won't be using the supplier again.

B Oh, what happened?

A Well, I work from home as a translator for a leading bank. My printer had broken and I needed a new one urgently. The person who took my order was extremely friendly and promised it would be there the next day.

B OK.

A It didn't arrive and I had waited in all day to receive it! When I phoned the supplier I got the same friendly, helpful treatment again – they were very sorry, it would definitely be there the following day. But they let me down again. This went on for the rest of the week.

B How awful!

A I was very put out indeed. It was all talk and no action.

🎧 10.4 (C = Customer, E = Employee)

Complaint 6

C I'm calling because I went into one of your shops this morning to look at some phones. I really have to complain about one of your sales staff.

E Oh dear, what happened?

C They were on me as soon as I got into the shop. I don't know if they're on commission or not but they really pounced on me.

E Oh?

C And didn't listen to me at all. They seemed to be pushing a particular package which was far too expensive and not suitable at all. I'm a pensioner, I have to be really careful with my money.

E I quite understand. Sorry you felt you were being hassled. Which branch was it?

C Your main branch.

E So do you remember who served you?

C Yes, but I don't want to say.

E Well, if you want me to take this seriously, we need to know who was at fault.

C It wasn't just one person. They were all bothering me. In my opinion, you ought to look into your training methods. It's just not good enough.

Complaint 7

This is Ingrid Williams calling. I'd just like to thank you for your excellent service. A saleswoman has just come round with a replacement phone, and this one works perfectly. I'm really impressed with the way you treat your customers. I'll certainly recommend your company to my friends. A final point. What happened to the new catalogue you promised me? I still haven't got it. In case you've lost my address, it's Flat 2a, 10 High Street, London, W1 5AP.

11 Crisis management

🎧 11.1 (I = Interviewer, JW = Jan Walsh)

I What are some of the commonest crises which companies face today?

JW The main crises facing companies today is that of loss of reputation. Damage to reputation. Which damages the share price and it damages public confidence. You can think of a number of companies who've suffered damage to their reputation. Shell for instance, the Brent Spar incident, their, er, problems in Nigeria; Nike with problems with their suppliers – their ... their supply chain; and BP in Colombia. Reputation is like money in the bank. You can invest in your reputation and you can make planned withdrawals. But what you can't afford is seepage – that means to let it just drain away slowly. Because, as those companies have found out, it costs a huge amount of money to regain the reputation that you've lost.

I How can companies prepare themselves for managing crises?

JW The main thing is to understand what's going on around you, to continue dialogue with your stakeholders. Stakeholders are your employees, your customers, your shareholders, your suppliers – people who have contact with your business. To understand what they expect of you so that you can anticipate what may become a reputation risk.

🎧 11.2 (I = Interviewer, JW = Jan Walsh)

I And what steps should companies take in dealing with a crisis?

JW Oh, be quick. Deal speedily with ... with a crisis. If it's your fault, sometimes you know we make mistakes ... admit it. Admit it quickly, tell the public, tell your stakeholders what went wrong, tell them what you're doing about it and keep communicating. The important thing is to keep communicating. If you don't, then that loss of public confidence, the damage to your share price will follow. So you need to keep telling the public what is happening.

I Can you think of some examples where companies have dealt with a crisis well?

JW Well, the famous one is Johnson & Johnson, the American company who erm, who had a major crisis with one of their headache pills, which was called Tynenol. This happened a long time ago, but it's still given as an example of a brilliant way to handle a crisis. They had noticed that there was poison in one or two of their ... some of their erm ... Tynenol tablets and without question they withdrew every single one. They took adverts in the newspapers. They took adverts on the television. They told their ... they told their public that there might be a problem. They weren't sure, there might be. But, for the sake of their confidence in their product, they withdrew it – and their reputation never suffered; their share price didn't suffer. And Johnson & Johnson is a company which guards its reputation as its most important asset and it paid off.

I And can you give us some examples of poorly-handled crises?

JW Without being sued you mean? Well clearly the ... the ones that I mentioned earlier in the interview, the Shell issue with ... with Brent Spar and ... and Nigeria. You know, had they listened to their stakeholders earlier they ... they might have averted that ... that ... that crisis. But there has ... there have been some notable problems with drinks companies, with some of the oil companies again, who haven't acted quickly. They've been like ostriches – they've hidden their heads in the sand; they've pretended it's not happening and they've underestimated the intelligence of the public. And so – damage to their reputation, damage to their share price – and it's cost them a huge amount of money to recover their reputation.

🎧 11.3

1 Could you answer my question?

2 Would you mind answering my question? What is your policy about gifts to customers?

3 Could you please tell me how many sales staff you employ?

4 Could you tell me how many sales staff you employ?

5 Do you deny that bribery is a common sales strategy of your company?

6 Could I ask why you're replacing your Sales Director?

7 Do you mind if I ask how many letters of complaint you've had from doctors?

8 I'm interested in knowing whether you consider yourself an ethical company.

9 Isn't it true that you don't care how your staff behave as long as they meet their sales targets?

10 May I ask why you didn't investigate the allegations more quickly?

11 Surely you're not saying that no payments were made?

12 Could you clarify what gifts can be offered to customers?

🎧 11.4 (CD = Carla Davis, HS = Hugo Stern)

CD Let me tell you a bit about what's happened. You've read the article in *Euronews*, so you know the basic facts. Our CEO was interviewed and denied everything. We're now investigating the matter, of course, and we're not happy with what we've found out.

HS Oh, is there any truth in the accusation?

CD Well, yes, there is unfortunately. Someone in the buying department ordered the games from a supplier in Hong Kong. We contacted him, the supplier I mean and, after a lot of persuasion, he admitted the games were from an unusual source and could be illegal copies. He said he'd bought them from a firm who'd gone bankrupt. He bought them in good faith, he said, and wouldn't accept any responsibility for them.

HS Mmm, why didn't you buy the games from the manufacturer?

CD Well, we did when they first came out, but it seems this supplier made us an offer we couldn't refuse – 30% off the usual price – so, we snapped them up. There's a lot of competition in computer games, you've got to take your opportunities when they arise.

HS What are your relations like normally with the game's manufacturer?

CD Well, they're pretty good actually. We supported them in the early days when they started up. We bought several of their products when no one else seemed very interested in them. We got them going really. But, you know, like all manufacturers, they don't like to hear that their games are being pirated.

HS What about your stocks of 'Race against Time'? Have you sold most of them.

CD We've sold most of the original consignment. But we bought another 50,000 last month, and they're lying around in our distribution centre. Heaven knows what we'll do with them!

HS There are a lot of questions I'd like to ask you. I don't need to tell you, this is a serious situation, and we need to work out how you'll handle it. One of the first things you must do is form a crisis management team and bring in an expert from outside the company to advise you.

CD Right.

HS I can help and suggest someone suitable for the job.

12 Management styles

12.1 (I = Interviewer, SC = Stuart Crainer)

I Is there such a person as an ideal manager, and if so what essential qualities should they have?

SC I don't think there's such a thing as an ideal manager in the same way as there's no such thing as an ideal chair or an ideal piece of furniture. Er, it's an impossible aim. The qualities er, managers need are increasingly complex and many in number. First of all they've got to be able to manage their time successfully, because they're inevitably juggling lots of activities and projects. Secondly, they need to be able to deal with complexity. Increasingly the management task is not about simple budgeting but is about far more complex issues. Er, thirdly, they have to be able to deal with uncertainty. In the past, management was about creating certainty. Now managers have to live with uncertainty. Er, the uncert... uncertainty of not knowing what will happen in the future, how secure their jobs will be, what their organisation will look like in the future, what their organisation will do in the future. The fourth aspect of management is being able to deal with people. Er, managers, for all the training they've received, are notoriously poor at managing people and relating to people. Added to that are other ingredients such as flexibility. Managers have to be able to change their ... their styles to fit the circumstances and they have to be sensitive to these circumstances. They have to recognise when things are different and they have to behave in different ways. They have to change their styles to fit the moment. So, if you put all these er, skills and competencies together then you would have an ideal manager. But in the real world, there aren't any ideal managers out there.

12.2 (I = Interviewer, SC = Stuart Crainer)

I And which management styles have particularly impressed you and why?

SC Er, well there are an array of management styles, er... the trick is to be able to produce the right style at the right time. Perhaps the person who has done this best is er, Jack Welch the Chief Executive of General Electric, who, over the last ten years, has re-energised er ... the company and created one of the biggest companies in the world, and certainly the best-managed company in the world. He has done that by an ability to change and keep changing constantly. So he's changed the company and he's changed his management style. Initially he was referred to as Neutra... Neutron Jack because of his capacity to er, decimate areas of the company. But since ... since then, he has reinvented himself as a person who is very tuned in to people and a person totally committed to training people for the future; and also a person totally committed to communica... communication. So I think Jack Welch stands apart as a ... a manager who really has mastered the art. Er, other ones I would pick out are people who are driven by er, values, such as er, Richard Branson of Virgin and Anita Roddick of Body Shop, who, whatever the fortunes of their companies, have proved that er, management can be led by values and organisations can be created around sound values. Talking of companies, I would select er, Scandinavian compi... companies such as IKEA and the Finnish company, Nokia, er, as exemplars of what good management can do. IKEA is a brilliantly-managed, networked organisation and Nokia is an incredibly innovative and imaginative organisation which has turned itself from a er, wood products maker in Finland into the er, leading maker ... leading maker of mobile phones worldwide. So those are the people and the companies I would say who have management styles that are worth emulating.

12.3 (I = Interviewer, SC = Stuart Crainer)

I Now business is becoming more and more international, how would you advise managers to prepare themselves for dealing with cultural difference abroad?

SC Yes, management is becoming more international and truly global, er, and the companies that appreciate that will be the ones that succeed in the future. Seems to me that the key to working globally and managing globally is the ability to reconcile difference. If you can reconcile differences between cultures and between peoples, you will be well-set to succeed as a global manager. Interestingly that's something that women are traditionally better at than men. However there aren't many er, women at the higher-most echelons of er, international corporations. So I think if you can prepare yourself and sensitise yourself and be able to reconcile differences then you will succeed globally.

12.4

A My manager never lets me know if I'm doing well. I have no idea what he thinks of me. I don't get any feedback, positive or negative.

B I was asked to review customers' attitudes towards our delivery service but I wasn't told how to do it, or how big the study should be. I was given no guidelines, no parameters.

C My boss lets me work on my own initiative too much. I don't meet the other team members enough, so I can't share my ideas with them. I never get any direction.

D I have no idea of the project team's objectives. No one has ever told me anything. I'm completely in the dark.

E I'm really enjoying working on this project. I'm given a lot of responsibility and am able to organise my time any way I want. I think I'm getting good results and making a real contribution to the company. My manager thinks so too.

F There's not enough preparation and thinking before important decisions are made. When we produced a set of guidelines for customer care, they were criticised by everyone. So my boss and a few of his colleagues got together at the weekend. Hey presto! They produced a completely new set of guidelines. They were no better than the other ones.

G Let's say I have to analyse telephone response times at our subsidiaries. My manager doesn't tell me how I should present the findings. If I do a report, he wants a memo, and if I do a memo, he'll ask for a report. I never know where I am with him.

H She doesn't like delegating work to me. If she does, it's some Mickey Mouse task which a child of five could do. She never gives me anything challenging where I have to use my brain, my analytical skills. Maybe it's because I'm a woman. The men seem to like her.

I Our manager wanted to amend the billing system which head office had agreed to. He had innumerable meetings and consulted everyone. The result? We still haven't got everyone's support yet and the deadline for introducing the system has passed. I wonder what head office will say about that. It's typical of the way people manage around here.

J He never encourages me when I do something right. I never feel that I am performing to a high enough standard.

K I never get enough resources to complete a task. For example, I had to hold meetings with the managers of all the factories and distribution depots. But I wasn't given enough time to do the task and I had no assistant to deal with my workload while I was away from the office.

13 Takeovers and mergers

🎧 13.1 (I = Interviewer, NP = Nigel Portwood)

I   You were involved in a very large acquisition recently. What are the essential preparatory steps for a successful acquisition?

NP The first step is to ensure that you have a strategy, a very clear strategy. You need to know where you want to compete, which markets; how you want to compete; and how you will get competitor advantage over the other players in the market. From that strategy you should understand which other companies in the market will help you achieve your objectives. Your other alternative, of course, is not to buy another company, but just to try and build a successful position on your own, through investment. But, assuming that you can find a candidate that you would like to acquire, the next essential step is to analyse that company – to understand its products, where it get its sales from, who its customers are, and what its cost structure is. You then need to think how, if you own that company, you would invest in it, and what the financial consequences of that would be. Because the third step is to essentially work out how much this company is worth, and you need to worry about two prices there. The first is what is it worth to the current owners, and the second is what is it worth to you? And the difference should be driven by the synergy that you see, that is, the benefits that you can bring to the company through your ownership. And er, we all spend lots of time analysing the projections for the company to try and arrive at a valuation. And the final step, of course, is just working out your tactics as to how you are going to buy this company – whether it be your pricing tactics or the way in which you approach the current owners.

🎧 13.2 (I = Interviewer, NP = Nigel Portwood)

I   And once the acquisition has happened. What needs to be done to ensure the successful integration of the new business?

NP The first thing you should do, even before you take ownership, is to plan what you do when you … when you take ownership of the company. And that means working out exactly how you are going to combine that company with your own. So, through every single function, you need to have a plan as to what you do with the people, what you do with the facilities, what you do with the assets, er, how you handle the customers and, it can't be said too much, that you must pay absolute attention to the detail in that process. The second thing that you should do is worry about the people. So, who are the most important managers and staff that you need to keep on-side during this process, because this will be a time of uncertainty for them and you do not want to lose them. And the third er, step towards a successful integration is to make sure that you move quickly. Too many companies take too long to plan and to implement and, once you lose momentum, er, the uncertainty around this process can cause you problems.

🎧 13.3 (I = Interviewer, NP = Nigel Portwood)

I   And how do you know whether an acquisition has been a success or not?

NP Well it hopefully will be driven from my answers to the first two questions. If you … if you've chosen your company correctly, if you've analysed the company correctly and if you've planned your integration properly, then you should have a basis upon which to measure the success of your acquisition, so you should be able to see whether it's met your strategic objectives. Did what you expected to happen actually play out? Do you have a stronger competitive position as a result of this acquisition? Did you get the cost savings out that you expected? Did the sales of the company continue as you had projected? And, therefore, was the price a sensible price to pay?

🎧 13.4

… So as you were saying a few minutes ago, Dave, there are so many pitfalls in takeovers and mergers that you really have to plan carefully, be rigorous in your analysis and be flexible about the way you approach things at the same time. And your experts will help you with that – your mergers and acquisition experts. But what are the sort of things that the experts forget generally?

There are three things in my mind and the first thing is, you've got to recognise the constraints that your organisation is under with regards to communication – legal and confidential documents that you tie yourself up in through a merger and acquisition. At the time when you most need it, i.e. when your people are most uncertain, that's when suddenly you're hamstrung in your communications and the only answer to this is to be absolutely honest with everybody about what you're doing and about the process you're going through and be clear with them where you cannot communicate with them and why. You've got to create that trust as the basis of managing the change moving forward. The second thing for me is about being … beware of the sycophants in your organisation. Remember, with a merger or a takeover, you're bringing two organisations together, two management teams – all of their roles probably duplicated – and in that process, you're going to get a whole lot of people vying for the same jobs. Of course they're going to be saying Yes! Yes! Yes! But actually, often they won't believe in that and when they go out and engage the business in taking it forward, what they will do is they will fail to collaborate. They will be nervous of collaboration with the employees, because they don't really believe in what they're doing, and so the only answer to that is to create that space with them beforehand, where they can genuinely express their concerns – draw them out as valid concerns, such that you can get a really good understanding of what they believe in, so they can take it forward.

And lastly, everybody works for an organisation with a core meaning to their work and a good example of this is the National Health Service, where people are very much focussed on, for example, caring as their primary task. They don't care about cost savings and they don't care about efficiencies. And the whole resistance to change in the National Health Service is based on that. When you bring your two organisations together, people are going to have this core purpose, whatever it might be for each of the organisations, the reason why they joined that organisation in the first place. Spend some time understanding that and helping them to re-establish one with the new organisation.

Before I finish I'd just like to run round the room, just would be ever so grateful if you would tell me – What's missing? What haven't I explained properly?

14 The future of business

🎧 14.1 (I = Interviewer, MP = Martin Phelps)

I   Will customer needs be different from now, looking ahead to the future?

MP The only constant in the world is change and that change will happen across all fields, in all environments. There are a number of very significant drivers of change that we're seeing at the moment in the world of consumers. These probably fall into three camps. The first is change in social environment; the second is the impact of technology and third is a subject I'll come on to – about time. Time becomes a very important commodity in our lives and will be more so in the future. First of all, looking at the social needs and the social changes that are taking place. We've seen a very big shift – and you'll have come across this in many news environments – towards more single households, single-person households where they've moved out of the classic family unit. If you look now at what we would take as the classic family unit – mum and dad and some kids in a household – they only constitute about a quarter of the population in the UK. The rest of it is this mish-mash of other people, often in single … single-parent households, single-adult households, joint… adults sharing a house but not really co-habiting. All sorts of circumstances which mean that they're adopting a much more individualistic lifestyle.

A second change that's happening is the whole issue of what's arising out of technology. Now, everybody has a telephone and, if you go back to last Christmas, something like 20% of children got mobile telephones as a Christmas present. Within two years you will find more than half of all households being able to interconnect with the Web.

Come on to my third driver – time – which is, erm, I think the most fascinating subject. Of why we're going to see substantial change in the way that business now begins to interact with those more individualistic consumers who have new ways of being able to interact with them because of technology. Henley Centre have been tracking time availability for the last 15 years or so and every year, year on year, you have seen a consistent rise in people saying 'I just don't have enough time to do all the things that I absolutely have to do. I've got real pressure on it'. Value for money was the main parameter in decision-making about what you … where you spent your money. Now there's a new parameter and the Henley Centre call it 'value for time'. Is this where I'm going to save time by short-cutting and get a streamlined service? Or am I going to invest time? Am I going to treat this buying experience as a pleasure, as a piece of leisure activity? And if you look – an archetypical example of the pleasure side of shopping would be women on a Saturday afternoon going shopping for clothes. This is a trip out, which used to be confined to women and increasingly we're now finding that men are doing it.

At the other end of the spectrum from trying to find this more elaborate experience is trying to save time. The Internet technology enables you to do lots of things that save time. So things like Amazon.com would be there as a means of saving time and money through being able to get you your books more easily, more cheaply by just going on to the Web. The opposite end of the same spectrum within the same product field would be somewhere like Waterstones who are now trying to create a much richer experience of going to a bookshop so that once you've gone in, you don't want to come out of there for five hours. You've got a coffee shop. You've got a restaurant. You've got an environment where you would like to spend time and really enjoy yourself and instead of coming back with the one paperback that you went in there to buy, you come out with a carrier bag full of books.

🎧 14.2

Dialogue 1 (CM = Carla Martinez, KT = Ken Tang, S = Switchboard, DC = Dan Chen)

CM Hello, Carla Martinez speaking. Could I speak to Mr Li Wang please?

KT Sorry, you seem to have got the wrong extension. This is Ken Tang here. Accounts Department.

CM Oh I see. Well, could you put me back to the switchboard please.

KT Certainly. Hold on a minute.

S Hello. How can I help?

CM Erm, I wanted to speak to Mr Li Wang, but you put me through to the wrong extension. I got the Accounts Department.

S Oh I'm so sorry. I thought you said Mr Tang. I'll put you through to Mr Wang right away.

DC Hello, Dan Chen speaking.

CM Hello, Carla Martinez here. I'd like to speak to Mr Li Wang please.

DC I'm afraid he's out of the office this week. Can I help you at all?

CM Oh really, I didn't know that. Actually, I need some information about one of your products. Your hairdryers – the Fairfax range.

DC Of course, but first of all, could I ask you, have you got our brochure and price list?

CM Yes, I have thanks, but I need to know a bit more about the product. For example, about colours, designs, speed settings, and so on.

DC OK, shall we have a look at the colours first?

Dialogue 2 (C = Customer, S = Supplier)

C Hello, Michael Bishop here. I'm calling about the cash machines we ordered. I'm really very unhappy. I want some action on this. They're now more than two weeks overdue. Our customer wants them urgently. What on earth's going on?

S Hold on, Mr Bishop. Could you give me a few details please?

C Details? What do you want to know? Surely you've got everything on file.

S Yes, but let me just check. When exactly did you place the order?

C What, you want to know the precise date?

S Er, yes, if you don't mind.

C Erm, wait a minute, let me get it up on the screen, er right, it was the … it was November the fourth.

S Thank you. And what was the model you ordered?

C Oh it was the TX40, your latest model, the one you've just brought out.

S Right. Could you tell me one more thing? What's the order number please, the order form number?

C Oh, it's erm, let me see, it's C, er, 270. And we ordered 50 registers.

S OK. I'll check it out right away and find out what's gone wrong. I'm sorry to hear about this problem. I'll call you back as soon as I can

C Well, thank you. Goodbye.

Dialogue 3 (C = Customer, S = Supplier)

S Can we go through it again please. You want 80 items, reference number JG 905.

C I'm sorry, I didn't catch that. What did you say the reference number was?

S JG 905

C OK. I've got that, I think. JE 95.

S No, that's not right. I said JG – J for Juliet, G for Golf – nine, O, five. OK?

C Fine. Shall I just read that back to you? JG nine, O, five.

S That's it. And you want delivery by June the 30th, Right?

C No, not June the 30th – June the 13th – at the latest.

S OK, Sorry. I've noted that. June the thirteenth. It shouldn't be a problem.

Dialogue 4 (C = Customer, S = Supplier)

C I'm calling about the sales invoice I've just received from you – for 50 car CD players.

S OK, what's the problem?

C Well, there seems to have been a misunderstanding. I haven't actually placed an order for them.

S Sorry, I don't follow you.

C Well, when I called your office last week, I was just making enquiries about the players – prices, availability …

S Are you saying you don't want them? My assistant told me you needed them urgently. We've packed them and we're just about to send them off to you.

C I'm sorry. To be honest, I was getting quotes from several suppliers. If I'd wanted to place a firm order, I'd have given you written confirmation. Your assistant was a bit too hasty, I'm afraid.

S OK, well, I suppose we'd better cancel the order then. I take it you don't want the CD players.

C I'm afraid not. We've ordered them from another source this time. I'm sorry if this has caused you any inconvenience.

S Don't worry. I'll have a word with my assistant, I don't want him to make the same mistake again.

C Yes, I think you should do that. Well, goodbye for now.

Glossary of business terms

Adjective *(adj)* Headwords for adjectives followed by information in square brackets [only before a noun] and [not before a noun] show any restrictions on where they can be used.

Noun *(n)* The codes [C] and [U] show whether a noun, or a particular sense of a noun, is countable (an agenda, two agendas) or uncountable (AOB, awareness).

Verbs *(v)* The forms of irregular verbs are given after the headword. The codes [I] (intransitive) and [T] (transitive) show whether a verb, or a particular sense of a verb, has or does not have an object. Phrasal verbs *(phr v)* are shown after the verb they are related to.

Some entries show information on words that are related to the headword. Adverbs *(adv)* are often shown in this way after adjectives.

Region labels The codes *AmE* and *BrE* show whether a word or sense of a word is used only in American or British English.

acquire *v* [T] if one company acquires another, it buys it

acquisition *n* [C] when one company buys another or part of another company, or the company or part of a company that is bought

advertising campaign *n* [C] an organization's programme of advertising activities over a particular period with specific aims, for example an increase in sales or awareness of a product

agenda *n* [C] 1 a list of the subjects to be discussed at a meeting
2 the things that someone considers important or that they are planning to do something about

aggressive *adj* 1 an aggressive plan or action is intended to achieve its result by using direct and forceful methods
2 an aggressive person or organization is very determined to achieve what they want

alliance *n* [C] an agreement between two or more organizations to work together

amend *v* [T] to make small changes or improvements to a law or a document

AOB *n* [U] any other business; the time during a meeting when items not on the agenda can be discussed

application *n* [C] 1 a formal, usually written, request for something or for permission to do something
2 a formal request for work
3 a practical use for something
4 a piece of software for a particular use or job

apply *v* 1 [I] to make a formal, usually written request for something, especially a job, a place at university, or permission to do something
2 [T] to use something such as a law or an idea in a particular situation, activity, or process
3 [I,T] to have an effect on someone or something, or to concern a person, group, or situation

approximate *adj* an approximate amount, number etc is a little more or a little less than the exact amount, number etc
—**approximately** *adv*

asset *n* [C] something belonging to an individual or a business that has value or the power to earn money

assign *v* [T] to give someone a particular job or task, or to send them to work in a particular place

attend *v* [I,T] to go to an event such as a meeting

attribute *n* [C] a characteristic, feature, or quality

awareness *n* [U] knowledge or understanding of a particular subject, situation, or thing

background *n* [C] someone's past, for example their education, qualifications, and the jobs they have had

balance sheet *n* [C] a document showing a company's financial position and wealth at a particular time. The balance sheet is often described as a 'photograph' of a company's financial situation at a particular moment

bankrupt¹ *n* [C] someone judged to be unable to pay their debts by a court of law, and whose financial affairs are handled by a court official until the debts are settled

bankrupt² *adj* not having enough money to pay your debts

bankrupt³ *v* [T] to make a person, business, or country go bankrupt

bankruptcy *n plural* **bankruptcies** [C,U] when someone is judged to be unable to pay their debts by a court of law, and their assets are shared among their creditors (=those that they owe money to), or a case of this happening

bank statement *n* [C] information sent regularly by a bank to a customer, showing the money that has gone into and out of their account over a particular period

barrier to trade also **trade barrier** *n plural* **barriers to trade** [C] something that makes trade between two countries more difficult or expensive, for example a tax on imports

benefits package *n* [C] the total amount of pay and all the other advantages that an employee may receive such as bonuses, health insurance, a company car etc

bid¹ *n* [C] 1 an offer to buy something, for example a company in a takeover, or the price offered
2 an offer to do work or provide services for a fixed price, in competition with other offers

bid² *v past tense and past participle* **bid** *present participle* **bidding** 1 [I,T] to offer to pay a particular price for something, for example a company in a takeover
2 [I] to offer to do work or provide services for a fixed price, in competition with others
—**bidding** *n* [U]

billboard *n* [C] *AmE* a large sign used for advertising. Billboards are usually called hoardings in British English

blueprint *n* [C] a plan for achieving or improving something

board also **board of directors** *n* [C usually singular] the group of people who have been elected by shareholders to manage a company

bonus *n* [C] an extra amount of money added to an employee's wages, usually as a reward for doing difficult work or for doing their work well

boom¹ *n* [C,U] 1 a time when business activity increases rapidly, so that the demand for goods increases, prices and wages go up, and unemployment falls
2 a time when activity on the stockmarket reaches a high level and share prices are very high

boom² *v* [I] if business, trade, or the economy is booming, it is very successful and growing

boost v [T] to increase something such as sales, production or prices

bottom line n [C] the figure that shows a company's total profit or loss

brainstorm v [I,T] to develop new ideas and solve problems by having a meeting where everyone makes suggestions and these are discussed

brand[1] n [C] a name given to a product or group of products by a company for easy recognition

brand[2] v [T] to give a name to a product or group of products

branded adj branded goods or products have brand names

branding n [U] the activity of giving brand names to products, developing people's awareness of them etc

brand leader n [C] the brand with the most sales in a particular market

bribe[1] n [C] money that is paid secretly and dishonestly to obtain someone's help

bribe[2] v [T] to dishonestly give money to someone to persuade them to do something that will help you

bribery n [U] dishonestly giving money to someone to persuade them to do something to help you

broker n [C] a person or organization whose job is to buy and sell shares, currencies, property, insurance etc for others

bureaucracy n plural **bureaucracies** 1 [C] a system of governing that has a large number of departments and officials
2 [U] disapproving all the complicated rules and processes of an official system, especially when they are confusing or responsible for causing a delay

bust adj [informal] if a company goes bust, it cannot continue to operate because it does not have enough money to pay its debts

buyout also **buy-out** n [C] 1 the act of buying a business
2 the act of buying all the shares in a company of a particular shareholder

canvass v [T] to try to get information or support from people

capitalization also **-isation** BrE n [U] 1 the total value of a company's shares
2 the total value of all the shares on a stockmarket at a particular time

cash cow n [C] a very profitable business or part of a business

cash flow also **cashflow** n 1 [U] the amounts of money coming into and going out of a company, and the timing of these
2 [C,U] profit for a particular period, defined in different ways by different businesses

cash generation n [U] money that a company gets from sales after costs are taken away. Cash generation is often used in talking about the degree to which the company is able to do this

chair n [singular] 1 the position of being the chairman of a company or organization or the person who is chairman
2 the position of being in charge of a meeting or the person who is in charge of it
—**chair** v [T]

challenge n [C] something difficult that you feel determined to solve or achieve

Chief Executive Officer (CEO) n [C usually singular] the manager with the most authority in the day to day management of a company, especially in the US. The job of CEO is sometimes combined with others, such as that of president

clock v
clock in/on phr v [I] to record on a special card or computer the time you arrive at or begin work
clock off/out phr v [I] to record on a special card or computer the time you stop or leave work

collapse v [I] if a company, organization, or system collapses, it suddenly fails or becomes too weak to continue —**collapse** n [C,U]

commission n [C,U] an amount of money paid to someone according to the value of goods, services, investments etc they have sold

commitment n [C,U] a promise to do something or to behave in a particular way

compatible adj 1 [technical] compatible machines, methods, ideas etc can exist together or be used together without causing problems
2 two people that are compatible are able to have a good relationship

compensate v [I,T] to pay someone money because they have suffered injury, loss, or damage

compensation n [U] 1 an amount paid to someone because they have been hurt or harmed in some way
2 the total of pay and benefits for an employee, especially a high-level manager

competitive advantage n [C] something that helps you to be better or more successful than others

complementary adj sold or used together with other products

concept n [C] an idea for a product, business etc

consortium n plural **consortiums** or **consortia** [C] a combination of several companies working together for a particular purpose, for example in order to buy something or build something

consumer behaviour BrE **consumer behavior** AmE n [U] how, why, where, and when consumers buy things, and the study of this

consumption n [U] the amount of goods, services, energy, or natural materials used in a particular period of time

contingency n [C] an event or situation that might happen in the future, especially one that might cause problems

controlling interest n [C,U] the situation where one shareholder owns enough shares to control a company

controlling shareholder also **majority shareholder** n [C] someone who owns more than half the shares in a company

core adj **core business/activity/product** the business, activity etc that makes most money for a company and that is considered to be its most important and central one

corrupt[1] adj using power in a dishonest or illegal way in order to get money or an advantage of some kind

corrupt[2] v [T] to encourage someone to behave in an immoral or dishonest way —**corrupted** adj, **corruptible** adj, **corruptibility** n [U]

corruption n [U] 1 the crime of giving or receiving money, gifts, a better job etc in exchange for doing something dishonest or illegal that helps another person or company
2 when someone who has power or authority uses it in a dishonest or illegal way to get money or an advantage

counterfeit[1] adj made to look exactly like something else, usually illegally

counterfeit[2] v [T] to copy something so that it looks like something else, usually illegally —**counterfeiter** n [C]

crash[1] n [C] 1 a time when many investments lose their value very quickly, usually when investors lose confidence in the market and sell
2 an occasion when a computer or computer software suddenly and unexpectedly stops working or fails to work properly

crash[2] v 1 [I] if stockmarkets, shares etc crash, they suddenly lose a lot of value
2 [I,T] if a computer crashes, or if you crash a computer, it suddenly and unexpectedly stops working

crisis *n plural* **crises** [C,U] 1 a period or moment of great difficulty, danger, or uncertainty, especially in politics or economics
2 a time when a personal problem or situation has reached its worst point

culture *n* [C,U] 1 the ideas, beliefs, and customs that are shared and accepted by people in a society
2 the attitudes or beliefs that are shared by a particular group of people or in a particular organization

customize also **-ise** *BrE v* [T] if something is customized, it is designed or built especially for a customer, making it different from other things of its kind

customs *n* [U] the government department responsible for collecting the tax on goods that have been brought into the country and making sure that illegal goods are not imported or exported

deceit *n* [C,U] when someone tries to gain an advantage for themselves by tricking someone, for example by making a false statement

deceive *v* [T] to make someone believe something that is not true in order to get what you want

decline *v* [I] 1 if an industry or country declines, it becomes less profitable, productive, wealthy etc
2 if sales, output, production etc decline, they become less —**decline** *n* [C,U]

defect *n* [C] a fault or the lack of something that means that a product etc is not perfect —**defective** *adj*, **defectively** *adv*

delegate *v* [I,T] to give part of your work or power to someone else, usually someone in a lower position than you

demand *n* [U] 1 spending on goods and services by companies and people in a particular economy
2 the total amount of a type of goods or services that people or companies buy in a particular period
3 the total amount of a type of goods or services that people or companies would buy if they were available

demerge *v* [I,T] if a company or unit demerges from a group, or if it is demerged, it becomes a separate company —**demerger** *n* [C]

deregulate *v* [T] if a government deregulates a particular business activity, it allows companies to operate more freely so as to increase competition —**deregulation** *n* [U]

devious *adj* using dishonest tricks and deceiving people to get what you want —**deviously** *adv*, **deviousness** *n* [U]

differentiation *n* [U] when a company shows how its products are different from each other and from competing products, for example in its advertising —**differentiate** *v* [T]

disclosure *n* 1 [C,U] the duty of someone in a professional position to inform customers, shareholders etc about facts that will influence their decisions
2 [U] the act of giving information about someone by an organization or person who would normally have to keep that information secret, for example when a bank gives information about a customer's accounts to the police
3 [C] a fact which is made known after being kept secret

dismissal *n* [C,U] when someone is removed from their job by their employer

dispense *v* [I,T] if a machine dispenses something, it gives it to someone when they put in money, a code number etc

disposal *n* 1 [U] the act of getting rid of something
2 [C] an asset that is sold, and the act of selling it

dispose *v* [T] 1 if you dispose of something, you get rid of it
2 *formal* if a company disposes of a particular asset, activity etc, it sells it

distribution channel also **distribution chain** *n* [C] the way a product is made available and sold, the organizations involved etc

diversify *v* [I] 1 if a company or economy diversifies, it increases the range of goods or services it produces
2 to start to put your money into different types of investments in addition to the investments you already have —**diversification** *n* [U]

downmarket[1] also **downscale** *AmE adj* involving goods and services that are cheap and perhaps not of very good quality compared to others of the same type, or the people that buy them

downmarket[2] also **downscale** *AmE adv* **go/move downmarket/downscale** to start buying or selling cheaper goods or services

dress code *n* [C] the way that you are expected to dress in a particular situation, as an employee of a particular company etc

drive *n* 1 [U] someone's energy, motivation, and ability to work hard
2 [C usually singular] an effort to improve or increase the level of something

drop[1] *v* 1 [I] to fall to a lower level or amount
2 [T] to stop doing or planning something
drop away/off *phr v* [I] to become lower in level or amount

drop[2] *n* [C usually singular] if there is a drop in the amount, level, or number of something, it goes down or becomes less

dumping *n* [U] the activity of selling products in an export market cheaper than in the home market, or cheaper than they cost to make, usually in order to increase market share

durable *adj* if something is durable, it lasts a long time — **durability** *n* [U]

economies of scale *n plural* the advantages that a bigger factory, shop etc has over a smaller one because it can spread its fixed costs over a larger number of units and thus produce or sell things more cheaply

economy drive *n* [C] a planned effort by an organization to reduce costs

efficient *adj* 1 producing goods using as little time, money etc as possible
2 doing a job quickly and well

endorse *v* [T] if someone, usually famous, endorses a product, they say how good it is in advertisements. People will buy the product because they like or trust the person — **endorsement** *n* [C,U]

enhance *v* [T] to improve the quality or value of something

ethical *adj* 1 connected with principles of what is right and wrong
2 morally good or correct —**ethically** *adv*

ethics *n* [plural] moral rules or principles of behaviour that should guide members of a profession or organization and make them deal honestly and fairly with each other and with their customers

etiquette *n* [U] the formal rules for polite behaviour

evade *v* [T] to not do something you should do according to the law, for example to not pay tax

expand *v* 1 [I,T] to become larger in size, amount, or number, or to make something larger in size, amount, or number
2 [I] if a company expands, it increases its sales, areas of activity etc —**expansion** *n* [U]

exploit *v* [T] 1 to use something fully and effectively in order to gain a profit or advantage
2 to treat someone unfairly in order to make money or gain an advantage for yourself

extort *v* [T] to illegally force someone to give you money by threatening them —**extortion** *n* [U]

facility *n plural* **facilities** 1 [C] a place or large building which is used to make or provide a particular product or service
2 **facilities** [plural] special buildings or equipment that have been provided for a particular use, such as sports activities, shopping or travelling

fake¹ *adj* made to look like something valuable or genuine in order to deceive people

fake² *n* [C] a copy of an original document, valuable object etc that is intended to deceive people into believing it is the real document, object etc

fall¹ *v past tense* **fell** *past participle* **fallen** *v* [I] to go down to a lower price, level, amount etc

fall² *n* [C] 1 a reduction in the amount, level, price etc of something
2 when a person or organization loses their position of power or becomes unsuccessful

fiddle *n* [C] *BrE informal* 1 a dishonest way of getting money or not paying money
2 **be on the fiddle** to be getting money dishonestly or illegally

flaw *n* [C] 1 a mistake or weakness in a machine, system etc that prevents it from working correctly
2 a mistake in an argument, plan, or set of ideas

flexible *adj* 1 a person, plan etc that is flexible can change or be changed easily to suit any new situation
2 if arrangements for work are flexible, employers can ask workers to do different jobs, work part-time rather than full-time, give them contracts for short periods etc. Flexible working also includes job-sharing and working from home —**flexibility** *n* [U]

flexitime *BrE* also **flextime** *AmE n* [U] a system in which people who work in a company do a fixed number of hours each week, but can choose what time they start or finish work within certain limits

flood *v* [T] to send a large number of things such as letters to an organization

fluctuate *v* [I] if prices, income, rates etc fluctuate, they change, increasing or falling often or regularly **fluctuating** *adj*

fluctuation *n* [C,U] the movement of prices, income, rates etc as they increase and fall

focus *n* [U] when a company serves particular groups of customers in a market with particular needs, rather than serving the whole market

focus group *n* [C] a group of people brought together to discuss their feelings and opinions about a particular subject. In market research, focus groups discuss their opinions of products, advertisements, companies etc

franchise¹ *n* [C] 1 an arrangement in which a company gives a business the right to sell its goods or services in return for payment or a share of the profits
2 a particular shop, restaurant etc that is run under a franchise, or a company that owns a number of these

franchise² *v* [I,T] to sell franchises to people —**franchising** *n* [U]

franchisee *n* [C] someone who is sold a franchise and operates it

fraud *n* [C,U] a method of illegally getting money from a person or organization, often using clever and complicated methods

free port *n* [C] a port where import duty does not have to be paid on imports that are to be sent to another country to be sold, or used to manufacture goods that will be sold abroad

fringe benefit *n* [C] an additional advantage or service given with a job besides wages, for example a car

gambling *n* [U] the practice of risking money or possessions on the result of something uncertain, for example a card game or a sporting event such as a horse race

gauge *v* [T] to measure how people feel about something

global *adj* 1 affecting or involving the whole world
2 including and considering all the parts of a situation together, rather than the individual parts separately —**globally** *adv*

global economy *n* [singular] the economy of the world seen as a whole

globalization also **-isation** *BrE n* [U] the tendency for the world economy to work as one unit, led by large international companies doing business all over the world

globalize also **-ise** *BrE v* [I,T] if a company, an industry, or an economy globalizes or is globalized, it no longer depends on conditions in one country, but on conditions in the world as whole

goodwill payment *n* [C] a payment made by a supplier to a customer because of a problem the customer has had, for example with quality or late delivery of goods

gross domestic product (GDP) *n* [singular] the total value of goods and services produced in a country's economy, not including income from abroad

gross domestic product per capita *n* [singular] the total value of goods and services produced in a country divided by the number of people living there

grow *v past tense* **grew** *past participle* **grown** 1 [I] to increase in amount, size, or degree
2 [T] if you grow a business activity, you make it bigger

growth *n* [U] an increase in size, amount, or degree

haulage *n* [U] *BrE* the business of carrying goods by road or rail

headquarters *n* [plural] the head office or main building of an organization —**headquartered** *adj*

hoarding *n* [C] a large sign used for advertising. Hoardings are called billboards in American English

hostile *adj* a hostile bid or takeover is one in which a company tries to buy another company whose shareholders do not want to sell

impose *v* [T] to officially order that something should be forbidden or taxed

incentive *n* [C] something which is used to encourage people, especially to make them work harder, produce more or spend more money

income statement *n* [C] *AmE* a financial document showing the amount of money earned and spent in a particular period of time by a company. This is usually called the profit and loss account in British English

incompetence *n* [U] not having the ability to do a job properly

incremental *adj* 1 an incremental process is one where things happens in small steps
2 an incremental amount, sum etc is small when considered by itself

indictment *n* [U] the act of charging somebody with a criminal offence

industrial espionage *n* [U] the activity of secretly finding out a company's plans, details of its products etc

infrastructure *n* [C,U] 1 the basic systems and structures that a country needs to make economic activity possible, for example transport, communications, and power supplies
2 the basic systems and equipment needed for an industry or business to operate successfully or for an activity to happen

inhibit *v* [T] to prevent something from growing or developing in the way it could, or to prevent it from being as good as it should be

innovate *v* [I] to design and develop new and better products —**innovator** *n* [C]

innovation *n* 1 [C] a new idea, method, or invention
2 [U] the introduction of new ideas or methods

innovative *adj* 1 an innovative product, method, process etc is new, different, and better than those that existed before
2 using clever new ideas and methods —**innovatively** *adv*

insider trading *n* [U] when someone uses knowledge of a particular company, situation etc that is not available to other people in order to buy or sell shares. Insider trading is illegal

integration *n* [U] when two or more units, organizations etc combine so that they work more effectively

integrity *n* [U] 1 the state of being united or kept together as one whole, and therefore strong, unit
2 complete honesty

interest *n* 1 [U] an amount paid by a borrower to a lender, for example to a bank by someone borrowing money for a loan, or by a bank to a depositor (=someone keeping money in an account there)
2 [U] the interest rate at which a particular sum of money is borrowed and lent
3 [U] the part of a company that someone owns
4 [C] the possession of rights, especially to land, property etc

interpreter *n* [C] someone who translates what someone says from one language into another, especially as their job

inventory *n plural* **inventories** [C,U] *AmE* 1 a supply of raw materials or parts before they are used in production, or a supply of finished goods. Inventories of raw materials or parts are usually called stocks in British English
2 a supply of goods, kept for sale by a shop or other retailer. Inventories of goods are usually called stocks in British English

inventory control *n* [U] *AmE* making sure that supplies of raw materials, work in progress, and finished goods are managed correctly. Inventory control is called stock control in British English

isolate *v* [T] to separate something so that it can be dealt with by itself

jeopardize also **-ise** *BrE v* [T] to risk losing or harming something

jet lag *n* [U] the tired and confused feeling you can get after flying a very long distance

joint venture *n* [C] a business activity in which two or more companies have invested together

junk *adj* [informal] **junk mail/email/fax** is mail etc sent to someone who has not requested it, usually to advertise something

knowledge worker *n* [C] someone whose job involves dealing with information, rather than making things

labor union *n* [C] *AmE* an organization representing people working in a particular industry or profession, especially in meetings with their employers. Labor unions are called trade unions in British English

laisser-faire also **laissez-faire** *n* [U] the idea that governments should do as little to the economy as possible and allow private business to develop without the state controlling or influencing them

launch¹ *v* [T] 1 to show or make a new product available for sale for the first time
2 to start a new company
3 to start a new activity, usually after planning it carefully

launch² *n* [C] 1 an occasion at which a new product is shown or made available for sale or use for the first time
2 the start of a new activity or plan

leading edge *n singular* the area of activity where the most modern and advanced equipment and methods are used

let *v* [T] *BrE* to allow someone to use a room or a building in return for rent

letter of credit (l/c) *n plural* **letters of credit** [C] in foreign trade, a written promise by an importer's bank to pay the exporter's bank on a particular date or after a particular event, for example when the goods are sent by the exporter

level¹ *n* [C] 1 the measured amount of something that exists at a particular time or in a particular place
2 all the people or jobs within an organization, industry etc that have similar importance and responsibility

level² *v past tense and past participle* **levelled** *BrE* also **leveled** *AmE present participle* **levelling** *BrE* also **leveling** *AmE*

level off/out *phr v* [I] to stop climbing or growing and become steady or continue at a fixed level

liability *n* 1 [singular] an amount of money owed by a business to a supplier, lender, or other creditor
2 **liabilities** [plural] the amounts of money owed by a business considered together, as shown in its balance sheet
3 [U] a person's or organization's responsibility for loss, damage, or injury caused to others or their property, or for payment of debts

liberalize also **-ise** *BrE v* [T] to make a system, laws, or moral attitudes less strict —**liberalization** *n* [U]

limited company also **limited liability company** *n* [C] a company where individual shareholders lose only the cost of their shares if the company goes bankrupt, and not other property they own

loan *n* [C] money borrowed from a bank or a person on which interest is usually paid to the lender until the loan is repaid

logo *n plural* **logos** [C] a design or way of writing its name that a company or organization uses as its official sign on its products, advertising etc

loophole *n* [C] a small mistake in a law that makes it possible to do something the law is supposed to prevent you from doing, or to avoid doing something that the law is supposed to make you do

lose *v past tense and past participle* **lost** *present participle* **losing** [T] 1 to stop having something any more, or to have less of it
2 to have less money than you had before or to spend more money than you are receiving
3 to fall to a lower figure or price
4 **lose something (to sb/sth)** to have something such as a contract or customers taken away by someone or something
5 **lose ground** to become less in value or to lose an advantage

loss *n* 1 [C,U] the fact of no longer having something that you used to have
2 [C] when a business or part of a business spends more money in costs than it gets in sales in a particular period, or loses money on a particular deal, problem etc

loyal *adj* if customers are loyal to a particular product, they continue to buy it and do not change to other products — **loyalty** *n* [U]

lucrative *adj* an activity that is lucrative makes a lot of money

mailshot *n* [C] *BrE* when information or advertising material is sent through the mail to a large number of people at the same time

malpractice *n* [C,U] when someone breaks the law in order to gain some advantage for themselves

margin also **profit margin** *n* [C,U] the difference between the price of a product or service and the cost of producing it, or between the cost of producing all of a company's products or services and the total sum they are sold for

market challenger *n* [C] an organization or product that may take the place of the organization or product that has the highest sales in its market or industry

marketing mix *n* [C usually singular] the combination of marketing actions often referred to as product, price, place, and promotion: selling the right product, through appropriate distribution channels, at the right price in relation to other products and for the profitability of the company, with the correct support in terms of advertising, sales force etc

market leader *n* [C] an organization or product that has the highest sales, or one of the highest sales, in its market or industry

market nicher *n* [C] a product or service sold in a niche market (=a market for a product or service, perhaps an expensive or unusual one, that does not have many buyers) or the company that sells it

market share *n* [C,U] the percentage of sales in a market that a company or product has

merchandise *n* [U] goods that are produced in order to be sold, especially goods that are sold in a store

merge *v* [I,T] if two or more companies, organizations etc merge, or if they are merged, they join together

merger *n* [C] an occasion when two or more companies, organizations etc join together to form a larger company etc

middleman *n plural* **middlemen** [C] a person, business, organization etc that buys things in order to sell them to someone else, or that helps to arrange business deals for other people

mission statement *n* [C] a short written statement made by an organization, intended to communicate its aims to customers, employees, shareholders etc

model *n* [C] 1 a particular type or design of a vehicle or machine
2 a simple description or structure that is used to help people understand similar systems or structures
3 the way in which something is done by a particular country, person etc that can be copied by others who want similar results

morale *n* [U] the level of confidence and positive feelings among a group of people who work together

mortgage *n* [C] a legal arrangement where you borrow money from a financial institution in order to buy land or a house, and you pay back the money over a period of years

motivate *v* [T] 1 to encourage someone and make them want to achieve something and be willing to work hard in order to do it
2 to provide the reason why someone does something —**motivating** *adj*

motivated *adj* very keen to do something or achieve something, especially because you find it interesting or exciting

motivation *n* 1 [U] eagerness and willingness to do something without needing to be told or forced to do it
2 [C] the reason why you want to do something

nepotism *n* [U] the practice of giving jobs to members of your family when you are in a position of power

niche market *n* [C] a market for a product or service, perhaps an expensive or unusual one that does not have many buyers but that may be profitable for companies who sell it

offset *v* [T] if one cost offsets another it has the effect of reducing or balancing it, so that the financial situation remains the same

open-plan office *n* [C] open-plan offices do not have walls dividing them into separate rooms

optimize also **-ise** *BrE v* [T] to make the best possible use of something or to do something in the best possible way

outsource *v* [T] if a company outsources its work, it employs another company to do it

overtime *n* [U] 1 time that you spend working in your job in addition to your normal working hours
2 time that a factory, office etc is operating in addition to its normal hours
3 the money that you are paid for working more hours than usual

panacea *n* [C] something that people think will help make everything better

partner *n* [C] 1 a company that works with another company in a particular activity, or invests in the same activity
2 someone who starts a new business with someone else by investing in it
3 a member of certain types of business or professional groups, for example partnerships of lawyers, architects etc
4 also **economic partner** a country that invests in another or is invested in by another, or that trades with another
5 also **trade partner, trading partner** one country that trades with another

partnership *n* 1 [C] a relationship between two people, organizations, or countries that work together
2 [U] the situation of working together in business
3 [C] a business organization made up of a group of accountants, lawyers etc who work together, or of a group of investors

patent¹ *n* [C] an legal document giving a person or company the right to make or sell a new invention, product, or method of doing something and stating that no other person or company is allowed to do this

patent² *v* [T] to obtain a patent, protecting the rights to make or sell a new invention, product, or method of doing something **patented** *adj* [only before a noun]

peak¹ *n* [C] the time when prices, shares etc have reached their highest point or level

peak² *adj* 1 **peak level/price/rate etc** the highest level, etc something reaches
2 **peak time/period/hours/season** the time etc when the greatest number of people are doing the same thing, using the same service etc

peak³ *v* [I] to reach the highest point or level

penny-pinching *adj* not liking to spend money

perk *n* [C] something in addition to money that you get for doing your job, for example a car

phone rage *n* [U] angry behaviour on the telephone by people who are not satisfied with the service they are receiving etc

pioneer *n* [C] the first person or organization to do something that other people and organizations will later develop or continue to do —**pioneer** *v* [T], **pioneering** *adj*

plummet *v* [I,T] to suddenly and quickly go down in value or amount —**plummet** *n* [C]

point-of-sale advertising *n* [U] advertising for a product in places where it is sold

portal *n* [C] a system for connecting a computer to another network, especially the Internet

positioning *n* [U] the way that people think about a product in relation to the company's other products or to competing products

predator *n* [C] a company that takes advantage of another company weaker than itself, for example by trying to buy it

premium *n* [C] if you have to pay a premium, you have to pay more than normal for something

prevail *v* [I] if someone or their arguments, views etc prevail, they finally win an argument, usually after a long period of time

prime time *n* [U] the time in the evening when most people are watching television, and the cost of advertising is at its most expensive

product portfolio *n* [C] all of a company's products considered as a group

profile *v* [T] to give a short description of someone or something in a newspaper or television programme

profit and loss account *n* [C] *BrE* a financial document showing the amount of money earned and spent in a particular period of time by a company. This is usually called the income statement in American English

promotion *n* 1 [C,U] a move to a more important job or rank in a company or organization
2 [C] also **sales promotion** an activity such as special advertisements or free gifts intended to sell a product or service

prospect *n* [C] someone who is not a customer yet, but may become one in the future

protectionism *n* [U] the idea that a government should try to help an industry in its country by taxing foreign goods that compete with it, limiting the number that can be imported etc, and the actions that it takes to do this —**protectionist** *adj*, **protectionist** *n* [C]

prototype n [C] the first form that a new design of a car, machine etc has

public limited company (PLC) n [C] a limited company whose shares are freely sold and traded, in Britain public limited companies have the letters PLC after their name

purchase v [T] to buy something

qualification n 1 [C usually plural] an examination that you have passed at school, university, or in your profession
2 [C] a skill, personal quality, or type of experience that makes you suitable for a particular job

quota n [C] an official limit on the number or amount of something that is allowed in a particular period

R and D n [U] research and development; the part of a business concerned with studying new ideas and developing new products

rationalize also **-ise** BrE v [I,T] to make a business or organization more effective by getting rid of unnecessary staff, equipment etc, or reorganizing its structure — **rationalization** n [C,U]

real estate n AmE [U] land or buildings and the business of buying and selling them

recall v [T] 1 if a company recalls one of its products, it asks customers to return it because there may be something wrong with it —**recall** n [C]
2 to remember something that you have seen or heard, such as an advertisement —**recall** n [U]

receipt n 1 [U] the act of receiving something
2 [C] a document given by someone, showing that they have received money, goods, or services
3 **receipts** [plural] money that has been received

recession n [C,U] a period of time when an economy or industry is doing badly, and business activity and employment decrease. Many economists consider that there is a recession when industrial production falls for six months in a row

reciprocal adj a reciprocal arrangement is when two people, countries, or companies do or give the same things to each other so that each is helped

recover v 1 [I] to increase or improve after falling in value or getting worse
2 [T] to get back money that you have spent or lost
3 [T] to get back something that was stolen, lost, or almost destroyed

recovery n plural **recoveries** 1 [C,U] when prices increase, or when the economy grows again after a period of difficulty
2 [U] the act of getting something back, such as money that you are owed

recruit[1] v [I,T] to find new people to work for an organization, do a job etc

recruit[2] n [C] someone who has recently joined a company or organization

recruitment n 1 [U] the process or the business of recruiting new people
2 [C] an occasion when someone is recruited

redundancy n plural **redundancies** especially BrE 1 [U] when someone loses their job in a company because the job is no longer needed
2 [C usually plural] a person who has lost their job in a company because the job is no longer needed

redundant adj especially BrE if you are redundant or made redundant, your employer no longer has a job for you

reference n [C] 1 a letter written by someone who knows you well, usually to a new employer, giving information about your character, abilities, or qualifications
2 a person who provides information about your character, abilities, or qualifications when you are trying to get a job

refund n [C] a sum of money that is given back to you

reliable adj someone or something that is reliable can be trusted or depended on —**reliability** n [U]

relocate v [I,T] if a company or workers relocate or are relocated, they move to a different place —**relocation** n [C,U]

resign v [I,T] to officially leave a job, position etc usually through your own choice, rather than being told to leave — **resignation** n [C]

resource n 1 [C usually plural] also **natural resource** something such as oil, land, or natural energy that exists in a country and can be used to increase its wealth
2 **resources** [plural] all the money, property, skill, labour etc that a company has available

restriction n [C] an official rule that limits or controls what people can do or what is allowed to happen

retailer n [C] 1 a business that sells goods to members of the public, rather than to shops etc
2 someone who owns or runs a shop selling goods to members of the public

retail outlet n [C] a shop through which products are sold to the public

retain v [T] to keep something or to continue to have it

rise[1] v past tense **rose** past participle **risen** [I] to increase in number, amount, or value

rise[2] n 1 [C] an increase in number, amount, or value
2 [C] BrE an increase in salary or wages. A rise is called a raise in American English
3 [singular] the process of becoming more important, successful, or powerful

rival n [C] a person, group, or organization that you compete with

rocket also **rocket up** v [I] if a price or amount rockets or rockets up, it increases quickly and suddenly

sample[1] n [C] 1 a group of people who have been chosen to give opinions or information about something
2 a small amount of a product that people can try in order to find out what it is like

sample[2] v [T] 1 to ask questions to a group of people chosen from a larger group, in order to get information or opinions from them, so as to better understand the larger group
2 to try a small amount of a product in order to find out what it is like

sanction n [C] an official order or law stopping trade or communication with another country in order to force political change in that country

scarce adj if something is scarce, there is not enough of it available

security n plural **securities** 1 [U] actions to keep someone or something safe from being damaged, stolen etc
2 [U] a feeling of being safe and free from worry about what might happen
3 [U] property or other assets that you promise to give someone if you cannot pay back the money that you owe them
4 [C] a financial investment such as a bond or share, or the related certificate showing who owns it

segment[1] n [C] 1 a part of the economy of a country or a company's work
2 also **market segment** a group of customers that share similar characteristics, such as age, income, interests, social class etc
3 also **market segment** the products in a particular part of the market

segment[2] v [T] to divide a large group of people into smaller groups of people of a similar age or with similar incomes, interests etc. Companies segment markets so as to be able to sell to each group the products that are most suitable for it — **segmentation** n [U]

sell-off n [C] when a business, company etc, or part of one, is sold to another company

share n [C] one of the parts into which ownership of a company is divided

share capital *n* [U] capital in the form of shares, rather than in the form of loans

shareholder *n* [C] someone who owns shares in a company

share option *n* [C] the right given by a company to its workers to buy shares at a fixed price.

skill *n* [C,U] an ability to do something well, especially because you have learned and practised it

sleeping partner *n* [C] a partner who invests in a business but does not take an active part in managing it

slip[1] *v* past tense and past participle **slipped** present participle **slipping** [I] to become worse or less or fall to a lower amount, standard etc than before

slip[2] *n* [singular] an occasion when something becomes worse or becomes less or lower

slogan *n* [C] a short phrase that is easy to remember and is used by by an advertiser, organization, or other group

slot *n* [C] a particular time when a television programme or advertisement is shown

soar *v* [I] to increase quickly to a high level

sole trader *n* [C] a legal form of company in some countries for someone who has their own business, with no other shareholders

speculate *v* 1 [I] to buy goods, shares, property etc in the hope that their value will increase so that you can sell them at a higher price and make a profit, often quickly
2 [I,T] to think or talk about the possible causes or effects of something without knowing all the facts or details
speculation *n* [U]

speculative *adj* 1 bought or done in the hope of making a profit
2 based on guessing, not on information or facts

sponsorship *n* [U] financial support to pay for a sports or arts event or training, in exchange for advertising or to get public attention

stabilize also **-ise** *BrE v* [I,T] to become firm, steady, or unchanging, or to make something do this

stake *n* [C usually singular] money risked or invested in a business

stakeholder *n* [C] a person who is considered an important part of an organization or of society because they have responsibility within it and receive advantages from it

stand *v* past tense and past participle **stood**
stand at *phr v* [I] to be at a particular level or amount

start-up *n* [C] a new company

status symbol *n* [C] something you own that you think is a sign of high social status

stock *n* [C,U] 1 *especially AmE* one of the shares into which ownership of a company is divided, or these shares considered together
2 also stocks a supply of a commodity (=oil, metal, farm product etc) that has been produced and is kept to be used when needed
3 *especially BrE* a supply of raw materials or parts before they are used in production, or a supply of finished goods. Stocks of raw materials or parts are usually called inventories in American English
4 a supply of goods, kept for sale by a shop or other retailer. Stocks of goods are usually called inventories in American English

stock control *n* [U] *BrE* making sure that supplies of raw materials, work in progress, and finished goods are managed correctly. Stock control is called inventory control in American English

straight *adj* **be/play straight with sb** to be honest and truthful with someone

strategic *adj* done as part of a plan to gain an advantage or achieve a particular purpose —**strategically** *adv*

strategy *n plural* **strategies** 1 [C] a plan or series of plans for achieving an aim, especially relating to the best way for an organization to develop
2 [U] the process of skilful planning in general

stress *n* [U] continuous feelings of worry about your work or personal life, that prevent you from relaxing —**stressful** *adj*

stressed also **stressed out** *adj* if someone is stressed or stressed out, they are so worried and tired that they cannot relax

strike *v* [I] to deliberately stop work for a while because of a disagreement about pay, working conditions etc

submit *v* [T] to give a plan or piece of writing to someone in authority for them to consider or approve

subsidiary also **subsidiary company** *n plural* **subsidaries** [C] a company that is at least half-owned by another company

subsidize also **-ise** *BrE v* [T] if a government or organization subsidizes a company, activity etc, it pays part of the cost —**subsidized** *adj*

subsidy *n plural* **subsidies** [C] money that is paid by a government or organization to make something cheaper to buy, use, or produce

surge *v* [I] to increase suddenly

sweetener *n* [C] 1 something used to make an offer, suggestion etc more attractive
2 a bribe (=illegal or unfair payment made to someone to persuade them to do something)

synergy *n* [C,U] additional advantages or profits that are produced by two people or organizations combining their ideas and resources

tactic *n* [C usually plural] a method that you use to achieve something

tactical *adj* done in order to achieve what you want at a later time, especially in a large plan

tailor *v* [T] to make something or put something together so that it is exactly right for someone's needs —**tailored** *adj*

take *v* past tense **took** past participle **taken**
take over *phr v* [I,T] 1 to take control of something
2 to take control of a company by buying more than half of its shares

takeover *n* [C] the act of getting control of a company by buying more than half of its shares

takeover target *n* [C] a company that may be bought or that is being bought by another company

target[1] *n* [C] 1 an organization, industry, country etc that is deliberately chosen to have something done to it
2 a result such as a total, an amount, or a time which you aim to achieve

target[2] *v* [T] 1 to make something have an effect on a particular limited group or area
2 to choose someone or something as your target —**targeted** *adj*

tariff *n* [C usually plural] a tax on goods coming into a country or going out of it

teaser *n* [C] an advertisement intended to get people's attention for advertisments that will come later or products that will be available later

teller *n* [C] especially *AmE* someone whose job is to receive and pay out money in a bank.

terminate *v* 1 [I,T] if something terminates, or if you terminate it, it ends
2 [T] to remove someone from their job

thrive *v* [I] if a company, market, or place is thriving, it is very successful

top-of-the-range *adj* used to describe the most expensive products in a range of products or a market

track record *n* [C usually singular] all the things that a person or organization has done in the past, which shows how good they are

trade union also **trades union** *n* [C] *BrE* an organization representing people working in a particular industry or profession, especially in meetings with their employers. Trade unions are called labor unions in American English —**trade unionist** *n* [C]

transaction *n* [C] 1 a business deal, especially one involving the exchange of money
2 the act of paying or receiving money

transition *n* [C,U] *formal* the act or process of changing from one state or form to another

trend *n* [C] the general way in which a particular situation is changing or developing

trial *n* 1 [C] a legal process in which a court of law examines a case to decide whether someone is guilty of a crime
2 [C usually plural] a process of testing a product to see whether it is safe, effective etc **trial** *v* [T], **trialling** *n* [U]

triple¹ *adj* [only before a noun] having three parts or members

triple² *v* [I,T] to become three times as much or as many, or to make something do this

turnaround also **turnround** *BrE* *n* [C usually singular] 1 the time between receiving an order for goods, dealing with it, and sending the goods to the customer
2 a complete change from a bad situation to a good one
3 a complete change in someone's opinion or ideas

turnover *n* [singular] 1 *BrE* the amount of business done in a particular period, measured by the amount of money obtained from customers for goods or services that have been sold
2 the rate at which workers leave an organization and are replaced by others
3 the rate at which goods are sold

underperform *v* [I,T] if a company or investment underperforms, it is not as profitable as it should be

unique selling proposition also **unique selling point** (USP) *n* [C usually singular] the thing that makes a particular product different from all other similar products

unscrupulous *adj* behaving in an unfair or dishonest way — **unscrupulously** *adv*, **unscrupulousness** *n* [U]

upgrade¹ *v* [I,T] 1 to make a computer, machine etc better and able to do more things
2 to buy a new computer, machine etc that is better and able to do more things than your old one
3 to get a better seat on a plane, a better rented car etc than the one you paid for, or give someone a better seat etc than the one they paid for

upgrade² *n* [C] 1 the act of improving a product or service, or one that has been improved
2 new computer software that replaces previous software of the same type
3 an occasion when someone is given a better seat on a plane, a better rented car etc, than the one they paid for

upmarket¹ also **upscale** *AmE* *adj* involving goods and services that are expensive when compared to others of the same type, or the people that buy them

upmarket² also **upscale** *AmE* *adv* **go/move upmarket/upscale** to start buying or selling more expensive goods or services

voice mail *n* [U] a system for leaving messages for people by telephone, or the messages themselves

volatile *adj* a volatile market or situation is changing quickly and suddenly, for example rising and falling without much warning

volume *n* [C,U] 1 the amount of space that a substance or object contains or fills
2 the total amount of something

warranty *n* plural **warranties** [C,U] a written promise that a company gives to a customer, stating that it will repair or replace a product they have bought if it breaks during a certain period of time. Warranty is another word for guarantee

welfare *n* [U] help that is given by government to people with social or financial problems because they are unemployed, ill etc

whistleblower *n* [C] someone working for an organization who tells the authorities that people in the organization are doing something illegal, dishonest, or wrong

whizz-kid *n* [C] a young person who is very skilled at a particular activity or is very successful in a particular area of work

wholesaler *n* [C] a person or company that sells goods in large quanitities to other businesses, who may then sell them to the general public

windfall *n* [C] an amount of money that a person or business gets unexpectedly

withdraw *v past tense* **withdrew** *past participle* **withdrawn** [T] 1 to take money out of a bank account
2 to remove something or take it back, often because of an official decision
3 if a company withdraws a product or service, it stops making it available, either for a period or permanently

withdrawal *n* 1 [C,U] the act of taking money out of a bank account, or the amount you take out
2 [U] the removal or stopping of something such as support, an offer, or a service
3 [C,U] also **product withdrawal** the act of no longer making a product available, either for a period or permanently
4 [U] the act of no longer taking part in an activity or being a member of an organization

workforce *n* [C] all the people who work in a particular country, area, industry, company, or place of work